Also available in the series:

Hospitality Operations

A *Systems Approach*

Peter Jones, Stephen Ball, David Kirk
and Andrew Lockwood

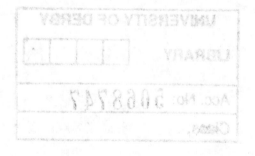

continuum
LONDON • NEW YORK

Continuum

The Tower Building
11 York Road
London SE1 7NX

370 Lexington Avenue
New York
NY 10017-6503

www.continuumbooks.com

First published 2003

British Library Cataloguing-in-Publication Data
A catalogue record for this book is available from the British Library.

ISBN: 0-8264-5761-4 (hardback) 0-8264-4826-7 (paperback)

Typeset by YHT Ltd, London
Printed and bound in Great Britain by Bookcraft (Bath) Ltd, Midsomer Norton, Bath

CONTENTS

PREFACE

This book is aimed at those studying the hospitality industry for the first time, whether at diploma, undergraduate or postgraduate level, and forms part of a series that develops a comprehensive understanding of hospitality operations management. The focus of this book is hospitality 'systems' – the technology and processes that enable goods and services to be delivered to the customer. A companion introductory text – *Introduction to Hospitality Operations* – looks at the hospitality industry, its various sectors and different types of operation, such as hotels, restaurants, and so on. Building on these two is a further text, *The Management of Hospitality Operations* (previously published as two separate texts, *The Management of Hotel Operations* and *The Management of Foodservice Operations*). A fourth book, currently in the planning stage, will be called *Strategic Management of Hospitality Operations*.

In one particular respect, this book differs from other studies of how hospitality businesses operate, in that it takes a 'systems perspective'. While systems theory and systems analysis have been used for the teaching of hospitality operations for many years (indeed, in 1974, a book was published that applied systems thinking to foodservice), in our view they have never been fully developed.

So what is systems theory and why should it be applied to hospitality? A full explanation of systems theory is given in Chapter 1. But, in short, systems theory is all about applying a consistent set of ideas and concepts to the analysis of real-world situations and problems. These ideas and concepts provide a *structure* that allow us to make comparisons, understand relationships and diagnose how things really work. With this theory, it is possible not only to describe operations but also to analyse them.

Furthermore, the hospitality business is a huge global industry. It is highly complex, made up of many different types of operation, managed by many different firms and serving many different groups of customers. Systems theory provides a way of making sense of this complexity. In Chapter 2, we highlight the three basic types of operation, each of which has systems specifically designed to function within it. In addition, there are 'hybrid' systems that span more than one operational type, and hence involve unique combinations of systems.

Our systems analysis of the hospitality industry has led us to identify four key operational systems that are common to all operations: procurement and control (Chapter 3), stores (Chapter 4), maintenance (Chapter 5) and environmental and waste (Chapter 6). In addition, the accommodation sector of the industry has two key systems, namely front office (Chapter 7) and housekeeping (Chapter 8). Foodservice (or catering) relies on five interconnected systems: food preparation and production (Chapter 9), holding, transportation and regeneration (Chapter 10), dining (Chapter 11), clearing and dishwash (Chapter 12) and bars (Chapter 13).

Each of these chapters contains a consistent and clear analysis based on the concepts and principles explained in Chapter 1. This demonstrates that whatever the type of operation, there is a specific and insightful way of analysing what is going on. Using this approach should enable you to identify problem areas more easily and suggest ways of resolving them more quickly and effectively. As Kirk (1995) explains, 'the earliest use of the term "systems" in its modern sense resulted from the realisation that scientific/analytic methodologies sometimes failed because they did not take into account the interactions which take place and which were frequently missed when following scientific/analytic methodologies'. So systems theory and systems thinking was developed and used by engineers working in computers, biologists and others interested in 'ecology', and scientists seeking to explore space.

When Kirk refers to 'scientific' he means 'science' in a specific sense – a particular way of viewing the world (or 'paradigm'). This view – the analytical view – is based on methods developed over many years in the natural sciences for investigating physical phenomena. The analytic researcher first comprehends the individual parts of what is being studied and then adds these together to create an understanding of the whole. Hence the phrase, 'the whole is the sum of the parts'. But the systems researcher bases their study on a different assumption, namely that the whole differs from the sum of the parts. This is due to the concept of 'synergy', which is created when individual parts are put together. A typical example often cited, is the picking of a soccer team. The analytical team selector would simply pick the 'best' player in each position in order to create the 'best' team; whereas the systems thinker would select players who would play well together, irrespective of whether they were individually the 'best'.

At this stage, you do not need to worry too much about synergy or paradigms. These are philosophical issues that relate to the essence of science and how we should think about the world. But we also want to make it quite clear that we are trying to change the way you think. Throughout most of our modern schooling we are all trained to think analytically. While this is fine for many situations – especially mathematics and the natural sciences – when it comes to understanding socio-technical phenomena, we believe systems thinking is a much better approach. All the authors of this text have taught hospitality operations for many years and it is how we think about the world. Until now, no book existed that explained this concept properly.

Bibliography

Kirk, D. (1995) 'Hard and soft systems: a common paradigm for operations management?' *International Journal of Contemporary Hospitality Management*, 7(5), 13–16.

PART A

SYSTEMS THINKING

One aim of this book is to show you how understanding systems will enable you to become a better manager. In his book *The Spirit to Serve*,[1] J. W. Marriott Jnr, Chief Executive of one of the world's largest and most successful hospitality companies, has written a chapter called 'The devil is in the details, success is in the systems'. In this chapter he writes, 'systems help bring order to the natural messiness of human enterprise. ... Efficient systems and clear rules help everyone to deliver a consistent product and service.' He goes on to say, 'Systems have been deeply ingrained for so long in our corporate culture that I'm always a little surprised when I come across companies that aren't as devoted to them as we are.'

The two chapters in this part of the book introduce you to the idea of systems and show how systems thinking can be applied to all parts of the hospitality industry. They are relatively 'theoretical', but do not let that put you off! The rest of the book goes on to explain many times over how this theory is applied in practice.

---

1. Marriott, J. W. and Brown K. A. (1997) *The Spirit to Serve*. New York: Harper Business Press.

CHAPTER 1

Understanding systems theory and principles[1]

After completing this chapter you will be able to:

- *define systems and systems thinking*
- *identify and explain inputs, transformational inputs, process, outputs and feedback*
- *explain five key features of systems theory*
- *explain seven key systems principles*
- *apply systems analysis to any hospitality operation.*

INTRODUCTION

In the hospitality industry, the terminology and jargon of systems is everywhere. Managers commonly talk about their management information system, property management system, central reservation system or food production system. These are all examples of so-called 'hard' systems, based on technology. Just as important are other non-technological systems, sometimes called 'soft' systems, such as marketing planning, total quality management, budgeting or employee recruitment and selection policies and procedures. This book focuses on one particular type of system – the socio-technical system, comprising both the physical infrastructure (hard systems) and processes (soft systems), that enables a hospitality operation to deliver goods and services to customers.

There is an important difference between hard and soft systems. As the former comprise physical artifacts (i.e. equipment, machinery, technology), they behave in predictable ways according to scientific laws. Hence a hard system can be modelled as having precise outcomes which can be quantified precisely and analysed mathematically. It is what is called 'deterministic'. For instance, it is possible to calculate

1. Parts of this chapter are based on an unpublished article by Professor Peter Jones, which was subsequently adapted into three short articles, in collaboration with Dr Nick Johns, for publication in *The Hospitality Review*.

3

exactly how long it will take for a deep-fat fryer to cook different portion sizes of French fries. Soft systems, on the other hand, usually involve humans and technology – a 'human activity system'. And human beings do not conform to scientific laws in terms of their behaviour. Hence it is not so easy to calculate precisely how long it will take different workers to prepare a portion of French fries – it will depend on their ability, their skill, their motivation and the particular context.

This book looks at these socio-technical hospitality systems *systematically* (i.e. in a planned, structured and relevant way), developing an understanding of systems, so that it becomes *systemic* (that is, part of the way you see the world and do things). Although the term 'system' is used widely in everyday speech and in the hospitality industry, it is also misused and hence misunderstood. It is often used to 'describe an assembly of parts ... [or] package of components which can be purchased "off-the-shelf" with little thought of the way in which they are going to be used' (Kirk, 1995). Such 'systems' come as ready-made solutions to problems, which often fail in practice because they are not properly designed for the environment in which they are installed. In the hospitality industry there are examples of IT systems and catering systems, such as cook-chill or cook-freeze, which have 'failed' because they were inappropriate for the operation in which they were placed. Hence the right way to think of a system is as a set of components and the relations between them, usually configured to produce a desired set of outputs, operating in the context of its environment.

In each of the chapters in this book, devoted to a specific socio-technical system, we shall identify the components of the system and the relations between them. We will then show how different contexts – i.e. types of hospitality operation – configure these to achieve the specific objectives of that operation. For instance, when we look at storage systems, we identify that operations may or may not have a loading bay, depending on their size and frequency of delivery; that the size and type of refrigeration will vary from one type of outlet to another; and we suggest that stocktaking and inventory control measures will vary in complexity to reflect the kind of stock held and its value, along with other factors.

KEY ASPECTS OF SYSTEMS

This chapter identifies five key aspects of systems:

- the general systems view
- systems hierarchy
- systems interaction
- simultaneous multiple containment
- cohesion and dispersion.

One or two of these ideas will already be familiar to you (although you may not call them this), but you are likely to be unfamiliar with them all, as well as the implications they have for effective management.

The chapter then goes on to discuss seven principles of the so-called 'unified systems hypothesis', each of which is illustrated and explained by examples drawn from the hospitality industry. Understanding systems theory and these seven principles enables managers to be more effective as managers and to better manage their business's performance. This is because systems theory helps to identify and understand complex relationships, while the principles explain how these relationships change over time and how the interactive forces create change. In this way each activity can be understood as part of a business operating in a complex environment. Too often managers fail to see or understand this big picture and become victims of the changes around them, as opposed to proactive visionaries who use these forces to restructure activity and reshape operations in response to external pressures.

General systems view

The standard systems model shows the relationship between inputs, transformational inputs, processes, outputs and feedback (see Figure 1.1). Inputs, or resources, are typically divided into materials, energy and information; while outputs are the same, although often described, especially in man-made systems, as product (inputs transformed in the desired way), waste (inputs transformed as a by-product) and residue (unused inputs). The conversion of inputs into outputs is achieved by a transformation process that typically requires a physical infrastructure, order, structure and capacity that we call the 'transformational inputs'. These largely remain unchanged by the process, although over time machinery wears out, buildings need refurbishment, and so on. In order to ensure output conforms to established requirements, it has to be monitored. If there is a deviation from expectation, there is a feedback loop in place so that the inputs or processes may be adjusted. Finally, this input–process–output activity is situated in a systems environment (i.e. all those things with which the system interacts). This introduces the idea of a systems 'boundary'. The boundary delineates what is 'in' the system

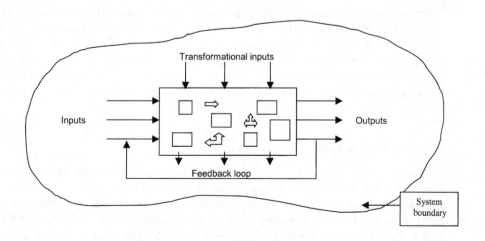

Figure 1.1 *The systems model*

and what is 'outside'. Sometimes this is quite clear, but at other times can be quite difficult to determine.

Systems hierarchy

A system may be very small, such as an administrator's work station, or very large, such as Disneyworld. This great diversity of scale illustrates the idea that many systems are interrelated. They are made up of subsystems and are themselves subsystems of a larger system. This concept of hierarchy is commonly applied in the hospitality industry to the way in which operations are organized. For example, a hotel chain (the principal system) is usually made up of a head office, regional offices and individual hotels (the first-level subsystem). Each hotel is organized into departments such as food and beverage, engineering and sales (second-level subsystem), which in turn are divided into sections or operating units such as bar, kitchen, coffee shop and so on (third-level subsystem).

This hierarchical systematization of organizational processes has major implications. Significantly, boundaries between systems are created. It is common for physical boundaries between systems to exist already, such as the distance between the hotels in a chain or the wall between the kitchen and the restaurant. But hierarchy may also create non-physical boundaries that prevent the effective flow of information and disrupt the order and structure of the system. Historically the industry has been quite good at recognizing the problems of physical boundaries and has removed them. One of the unique (at the time) and innovative aspects of McDonald's was the removal of the traditional barrier between the kitchen and the restaurant. On the other hand, in an effort to exert control over operations, non-physical barriers have been created such as job descriptions, standard operating procedures and performance measurements. These serve to reinforce systems boundaries and to isolate managers from each other. This helps to explain why there has often been resistance to innovations that cross traditional boundaries, such as business process engineering or total quality management.

This book focuses on the key transformational processes within operations, for each of which a system has been (or systems have been) created. When the Ritz Carlton hotel company developed its total quality management strategy, they identified 18 processes. In this book we identify 11 systems, each of which relates to a part of a hotel or foodservice operation, and each of which has a chapter devoted to it. Four of these are operations-wide (procurement, stores, maintenance and environmental systems), two are accommodation systems (housekeeping and front office) and five are catering systems (production, holding, dining, bars and clearing systems).

Systems interaction

This concept of a hierarchy implicitly means that systems must interact with each other. The outputs of one system form all or part of the inputs of another system. In this book some processes combine to deliver an accommodation experience to a hotel guest, while others combine to create the foodservice experience for the diner in a restaurant. All of these are supported by other systems operation-wide with which they interact. You should be aware that separating the systems out in this way, and devoting a chapter to each one, is necessary but dangerous! Remember that systems thinking incorporates the notion of *synergy*. This idea suggests that the whole is greater then the sum of its parts. A well-designed hospitality operation has to select the most appropriate forms of these socio-technical systems and fit them together to achieve its desired outcomes. As long ago as 1958, Fred Turner devised a 75-page operations and training manual specifying how almost everything in a McDonald's should be done (Schlosser, 2001). But successful management is all about managing the whole, as well as managing each of the parts.

Simultaneous multiple containment

Simultaneous multiple containment (SMC) is the idea that systems may exist as subsystems of more than just one system. Thus, a hotel may be part of a hotel chain, but is also part of the local or regional economy, an employer in the local labour market and a processor of resources in its immediate environment.

The implications of SMC are twofold. First, it adds considerably to the complexity of the system, so that understanding system behaviour and managing its performance becomes more difficult. Second, there can be tension between the outputs desired by the different systems. There are many examples of this. For instance, a hotel chain in the UK was keen to know why some hotels were more able to implement its new 'green' policy than others. It found that successful hotels were located in cities where local councils with green policies had already established separate waste collections and educated the public and hence the local workforce in best practice. As Chapter 6 on environmental systems illustrates, it is no longer acceptable for residue and waste outputs from an operation to be dumped into the environment. Care needs to be taken to ensure their impact on other systems, both natural and human, is minimized.

Cohesion and dispersion

The final aspect of systems is concerned with the idea that there must be forces that bind subsystems together, balanced by forces that prevent them from merging into one. Franchising is a good example of this. Hotels and restaurants are 'bound together' by franchising agreements to create chains of independently owned but mutually operated businesses (cohesion). The characteristics of this relationship are a partnership-based long-term perspective, personal contact and joint planning. However, there are many instances of franchisees falling out with the franchisor, leading to litigation between the two (dispersion). In some cases, franchisee independence has led to some benefits for everyone. For instance, the Big Mac was not devised by the McDonald's head office but by a franchisee in Chicago. This also illustrates that many socio-technical systems are not permanent, but can change and adapt if new ways of processing are developed. This book contains many examples of alternative ways of doing something, or alternative processes leading to similar outputs. The selection of a particular process is based on matching the right system to the right environment.

SYSTEMS PRINCIPLES

Having identified the key features of systems, we shall now look at seven principles which govern the behaviour of systems. Each of these will be explained and then illustrated with hospitality examples. If systems are to be managed effectively, these seven principles must be clearly understood.

The principle of reactions

In the physical sciences it is generally accepted that in 1888 Le Chatellier was right to say that 'if a set of forces [i.e. a system] is in equilibrium and a new force is introduced then, in so far as they are able, the existing forces will rearrange themselves so as to oppose the new force'. It is less generally understood or accepted that the same is true of *all* systems – commercial, economic, political or social. Change is generally resisted.

This principle is most commonly observed when a new hospitality business opens in a locality. Existing operators may independently take a series of actions that are remarkably similar to each other. They may introduce loyalty bonuses or raise wages to retain their employees, they may increase advertising spend, they may organize promotions or special events to coincide with the new opening, and they may discount heavily to deny the new business the customer volume it needs to maintain cash flow.

Reaction is also typically seen in response to the introduction of a new technology or new processes. For many years, work study experts and method study analysts identified that employees working in pairs could clean a hotel bedroom more productively than working individually. At various times, in a range of different properties, firms experimented with this approach. Indeed, when Ritz Carlton analysed this process they found this to be the case. But for many other firms, this 'new' approach did not appear to work, due essentially to the reaction principle. The people in this human activity system did not 'allow' it to operate effectively. The room attendants failed to work co-operatively, engaged in disputes with each other or did not follow the new procedures. Supervisors failed to resolve disputes and train staff effectively in the new methods. And when the standards and speed of cleaning did not improve, managers reverted to the old way rather than resolving the problems with the new way.

It should be noted that the nature of this reaction might take a variety of forms. It may be slow or fast, it may be chaotic and even catastrophic. Ultimately the existing system may be unable to resist the change. For instance, traditional British fish and chip shops have been unable to resist the introduction of burger and chicken outlets. Between 1975 and 1985 their numbers had reduced from 10,000 down to 5,000. Likewise, as corporations downsize, industrial contract foodservice provision is matching the decline. In response, contract caterers have moved into new markets such as schools, hospitals and the armed services.

The principle of systems cohesion

Every system has 'dispersive' elements that seek to break it up, perhaps because they are also part of other 'stronger' systems due to multiple system containment.

For instance, a hospitality outlet may have very high levels of staff turnover due to low unemployment rates in the locality or other employers who pay higher wages. At the same time there will be 'cohesive' elements that keep the system together. To maintain any system in its current form, cohesive and dispersive elements must be balanced. In social systems, this is usually achieved dynamically. This principle applies not only to a system but also to a set of interacting systems.

In turning around the American fast-food chain Taco Bell, John Martin recognized that the Mexican concept would not survive in its former configuration. The dispersive elements far exceeded the cohesive elements. Too much resource went into preparing food on site and not enough into serving customers. Too much space in the unit was given over to the kitchen and not enough to the revenue-generating dining area. Too much effort was focused on food quality, while too little effort was made to deliver a speedy service. Hence sales and profits were too low to sustain the chain. The redesign of Taco Bell's food production system, information systems and market positioning created a much more cohesive operation.

Managers can spend a lot of time engaged in activities designed to create cohesion, largely because there are so many dispersive forces. Thus, managers draw up plans, budgets and schedules so that colleagues work together towards the same goals; they hold meetings to ensure team members share information; they manage by walking around to observe behaviour and correct any deviance; and they interact with key opinion-makers to influence their behaviour in support of the business.

The principle of adaptation

Since a system exists within an environment, cohesion can only be achieved if the rate of change in both the system and the environment are matched. The history of American cuisine is an example of this kind of adaptation. New foodstuffs discovered by the colonists were quickly integrated into their European diet to become traditional American dishes; classic French cuisine was adapted and developed by ambitious restaurateurs to create new dishes such as Lobster Newburg and Eggs Benedict; the same is true of Italian dishes, so that by the 1950s an Italian perusing a menu in an Italian restaurant in Chicago would be unable to decipher a single item (Bryson, 1994)

The hospitality industry is full of examples of this principle in action. Over the years the industry has adapted to meet the changing demographics and lifestyles of the population. The hotel industry has seen the development of the motel to match the growth in car ownership, the resort property to reflect the increase in disposable income, and more recently the all-suite concept to reflect the increase in job mobility and family get-togethers. One of the most common examples of adaptation is the way the market and competitors react to price rises or price cuts by the market leader. Muller (1997) analysed the decision by McDonald's to discount its signature item, the Big Mac. He writes, 'the change in philosophy for "quick service restaurant" (QSR) market leader McDonald's … may signal the company's recognition of a substantial change in the QSR environment'.

The principle of connected variety

As we identified earlier, one of the five key features of systems is that they interact with each other. This principle states that the interaction between systems is more stable the greater the variety and amount of interconnection between them. The main reason that we can identify the existence of the socio-technical systems discussed in this book is a result of the interconnectivity between the parts of the system and the processes they engage in.

It is frequently the case that in local markets, hotel management teams from different properties routinely keep in touch with each other and share information. They do so out of a desire to maintain stability in their competitive environment. Thus, a variety of contacts are established that are frequent and routinized. For instance, managers attend local commercial or industry events and discuss business; the Front Office Manager daily phones colleagues in other properties to check on occupancy; managers meet informally and socially, and so on.

Recently a number of management ideas have been proposed that build on this principle. For instance, total quality management requires a high degree of teamwork. 'Quality teams are often interdepartmental, and a quality assurance *system* [my emphasis] makes it difficult for divisions to see themselves as independent operators' (Breiter and Bloomquist, 1998). Thus TQM recognizes and values variety, but sets out deliberately to create connections that ensure stability and guarantee the delivery of established standards.

The principle of limited variety

This principle states that the variety of systems is limited by the available space and level of differentiation possible. Hence, while new systems will be created to fill any gaps or niches in the systems environment, there is ultimately a limit to how many new systems can be established.

For example, a restaurant's menu is constrained by the available technology, expertise and physical space in the kitchen. The operational implications for McDonald's of a number of innovative menu items, such as meatballs, salad, chicken, vegetarian burgers or fish, neatly illustrate this principle. One of the reasons for not serving breakfast all day is that processes and the technology were not designed to serve items from the breakfast menu and main menu simultaneously.

The principle of preferred patterns

This principle highlights the idea that interacting systems will adopt configurations that are locally stable, especially if there is systems variety and a high level of connectivity.

Chain operators have direct experience of this principle in negotiating management contracts, in either the lodging or foodservice sector. In contract foodservice there are a wide range of alternative contractual forms. In different countries, however, different forms have tended to predominate. In the UK, until recently most have been cost-plus contracts; while in France contracts were typically required to operate on a profit and loss basis.

The principle of preferred patterns applies especially to managers' attempts to control processes. One of the key elements of total quality management is the identification and standardization of processes. Horst Schulze, in describing Ritz Carlton's experience, explains how key processes were selected for analysis and how each process was analysed over an 18-month period in order to systematize them. Prior to this study, these processes were all more or less effectively managed, but in slightly different ways by each hotel, influenced, as they were, by employees' previous experience, working relationships, levels of skill and training, and so on. Each hotel had its own preferred pattern based on 'local stability'.

The principle of cyclic progression

This principle suggests that all interconnected systems go through a cyclic progression of five stages:

- system variety is generated

- dominance emerges

- variety is suppressed

- the dominant mode decays or collapses

- survivors emerge to regenerate variety.

The original response to the rapid growth of car ownership in the USA was not the motel but the tourist court or cabin camps. By 1925 there were 2,000 of these businesses (with names like U Like Um Cabins and Kozy Kourt), letting out wooden huts to travellers. The first motel was the Milestone Mo-tel, which opened in December 1925 on Route 101 in California. By 1948 tourist courts had all but disappeared (although the concept still exists in some places, such as Nova Scotia) and there were 26,000 motels. Most of these were small family operations until Kemmons Wilson, frustrated by the low quality and sleazy nature of most motels, developed the Holiday Inn concept in 1952 and Howard Johnson followed suit by adding lodging properties to their restaurant chain (Bryson, 1994).

Another example of cyclic progression is the way in which hotel management contracts have developed over the last twenty years. The nature of such contracts was relatively stable and conformed largely to an industry-wide norm (i.e. dominant form) throughout the 1980s. The economic crisis of the late 1980s created new circumstances that led to the revision of such contracts to accommodate the demands and increased power of the owners. By 1993, significant changes in contractual agreements were taking place and practice was more diverse. But by 1997, as James Eyster (1997) reports, 'these shifts have become well-established and standard in contract negotiation and practice'.

INTEGRATION OF PRINCIPLES

As well as their separate influence on systems, these seven principles may be integrated into a single 'unified systems' model, as illustrated in Figure 1.2. All managers should keep this model in mind when considering any problem, as it demonstrates that the world is both extremely complex and dynamic. While it may appear chaotic, the model identifies specific relationships that enforce a structure on this apparent chaos. Thus the model:

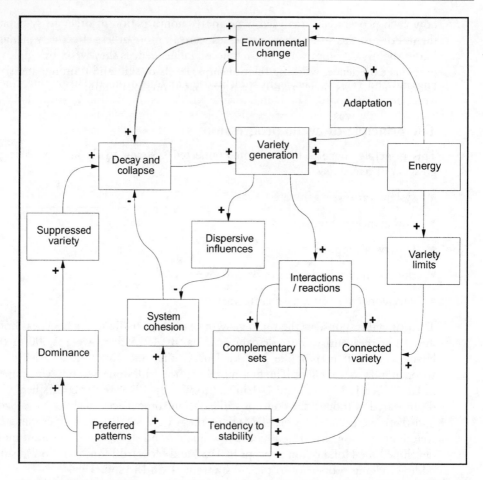

Figure 1.2 *The unified systems model* (adapted from Hitchins, D. K. (1992) *Putting Systems to Work*. Chichester: John Wiley & Sons)

- identifies the extent to which the system is stable or unstable
- helps to forecast likely events in the system environment
- suggests appropriate plans of action that will counteract negative influences and sustain the system
- emphasizes that change is inevitable.

To apply and use the model, you must remember the notion of hierarchy. Do not apply the model at more than one level in the hierarchy at once. Take a 'one level view', i.e. at an industry, firm, unit or socio-technical system level. Remember, though, that relationships clearly exist between each of these levels.

In this chapter we have cited many examples of the unified systems model at work – the emergence of motels in America, the development of McDonald's, changes in foodservice management contracts and hotel management contracts, the implementation of cook-chill technology, and so on. But in order to explain the model more fully let us look at the in-flight catering sector to see how it has changed over time.

CASE STUDY: THE DEVELOPMENT OF FLIGHT CATERING

In Europe the first regular airline passenger services started in 1919 between England and France. The flight took two hours and, from the beginning, 'meals' were served on board. The Dutch airline KLM was founded in October 1919 and four days later was serving pre-packed meals on its flights (Jones and Kipps, 1995). Although other airlines appeared throughout the 1920s and 1930s, they continued to serve sandwiches and hot beverages from thermos flasks, even when the first on-board galleys were introduced (*variety limits*). Each passenger's food and equipment were packed in individual bags, which the cabin crew would unpack and place on a tray (*complementary sets*). There were no tray tables on the back of seats, so passengers were provided with a pillow so that they could rest their meal tray on their knees. American Airlines new DC3 aircraft operated in this way from 1936 onwards but there was no electrical supply in the galley (McCool, 1995). Even when Boeing introduced the 307 Stratoliner, which was the first passenger aircraft with a pressurized cabin, in-flight catering remained unchanged (*tendency to stability*).

By 1934 global routes had developed. Imperial Airways (the forerunner of British Airways) and Qantas flew passengers from London to Brisbane in 13 days for less than £200. In the late 1930s Imperial Airlines set up the first dedicated food production unit or central kitchen, specifically for servicing their in-flight provision. In the USA, United Airlines also built flight catering kitchens – the first was opened in Oakland, California, in December 1934. It was so successful that the company quickly built a further 19 units throughout the USA and even began to cater for other airlines. American Airlines, on the other hand, continued to source its food provision from local suppliers, until in 1946 it decided to build restaurants in airport terminals that would also supply aircraft (*variety generation*). In 1941 the company set up Sky Chefs Inc., which today is one of the largest flight caterers in the world. Eventually Continental Airlines and TWA also built their own kitchens, but not until the 1950s (*dominance* and emergence of *preferred pattern*). On international routes, Pan American and other carriers established commissaries at key destinations, which were stocked by supplies provided from local hotels or restaurants.

The Second World War (*environmental change*) resulted in aircraft that had the capability to generate electrical power in flight. Consequently, after the war, galleys could be equipped with holding ovens to keep food hot (American Airlines), convection ovens to reheat frozen meals (Pan American in 1945) and automatic coffee brewers (American Airlines). American Airlines also pioneered the seat tray table and pre-laid tray carriers, which facilitated loading and storage on board (*variety generation*). In the 1960s air travel was further transformed by the introduction of jet aircraft. This significantly increased the speed of travel, reduced costs and led to an enormous growth in demand (*environmental change*). The increase in the size of aircraft required the development of new types of loading equipment based around the hi-lift truck and modular systems in use today (*connected variety*).

13

SYSTEMS ANALYSIS[2]

So far we have tended to focus on systems theory. But systems thinking is not very theoretical – it is highly applied. In particular it can be used for analysing operational activities. One relatively straightforward way of doing this is through process flow charting. Flow process charts are diagrams that use *codes* to show the features of the system. For instance, boxes show subsystems and lines between the boxes indicate relationships. Such diagrams can function as 'models' of processes but only if they are constructed clearly. Rigorous presentation is the essence of diagrammatic model-building. The prime directive is to show the system features in a readily visible form, like a map. And just as with a map, the code, the key to the symbols, is vital.

This is fairly straightforward if the intention is to represent a process as a 'black box', a system into which inputs go and from which outputs emerge, without apparent subsystems. But such 'models' are not helpful, because they give no idea of how the system *works*. One way to produce a rigorous diagram that achieves this goal is to use a tried-and-tested recipe, such as the detailed flow chart style diagrams favoured by engineers and other exponents of the 'hard' systems approach. Diagrams of this kind have been adapted for modelling 'classic' food-service systems, such as cook-freeze and cook-chill. An example developed by

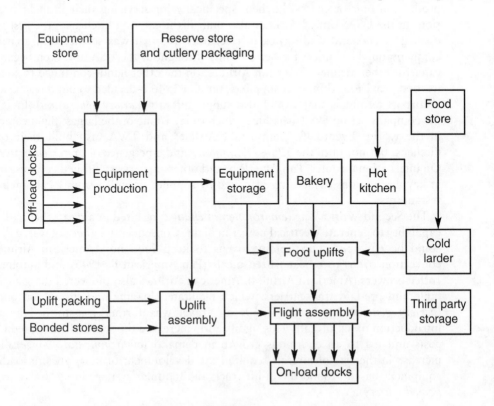

Figure 1.3 *A workflow chart of a typical kitchen* (*source*: British Airways)

2. This section is reproduced with permission from Johns and Jones (2000).

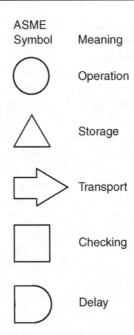

Figure 1.4 *ASME symbols*

Foskett (1995) of a flight kitchen[3] is shown in Figure 1.3 and demonstrates how versatile diagrams can be. You may be thinking that the process chart concentrates overmuch on one aspect, namely the flow of food materials through the operation. But that is exactly the point. Foskett wanted a way to identify what went into his system and the processes it went through to make it ready for loading onto aircraft. His diagram is powerful precisely because it is specialized. It shows that different items could follow very different routes through the system, due to their characteristics. This helps to identify any potential bottlenecks, caused by the overuse of one type of raw material. It also identifies activities that are carried out in parallel and how these need to be co-ordinated when they come together at the dispatch point.

Other types of 'off-the-peg' flow chart can also be used for modelling/mapping food production and service systems. They are mostly elaborations of the familiar box-and-arrow diagram. For instance, American Society of Mechanical Engineers (ASME) diagrams have, instead of boxes, symbols indicating different types of process stages (see Figure 1.4). 'Avery diagrams' (Milson and Kirk, 1979), named after an American researcher, use 'boxes' to represent the process stages, and arrows to show different types of inputs, intermediates and outputs: food, waste, dishes and so on. It is possible to refine this type of diagram by using coloured dotted and hatched lines to show not just 'food' but different stages or types of food progressing through the fine structure of the food production system. For instance, the different stages used by Foskett could be represented with coloured

3. Although developed for a flight kitchen, this flow process chart could be applied to any large cook-chill facility (except for the final stage, which shows the output being dispatched to aeroplanes via on-load docks!).

lines, or different classes of foodstuffs (meat, fish, vegetables) could be colour-coded to show hygiene hazards.

These diagram types are undoubtedly useful in certain situations, and they do demonstrate basic, simple systems principles. However, the problem with 'off-the-peg' solutions is that they may not apply to all the cases where systems thinking is useful. For instance, all of the examples presented here regard a process as the system, and its stages as subsystems. This is helpful if we want to understand, and perhaps change, the process, but what if we only want to understand the *structure* of the system? The basic principles still hold in this case: the diagram/model must show the outer boundary and subsystems and the relationships between the sub-systems. If understanding the process is not the aim, it is not absolutely necessary to show the inputs, intermediates and outputs. (However, interest in a system seldom stops with its structure, so it is often a good idea to think how inputs, outputs, etc. could be represented in the diagram when the inevitable 'how does it work?' questions start to crop up.) Relationships between subsystems do not have to be based on the flow of materials, and the lines linking them do not need to be linear. It may be perfectly acceptable to draw 'spider diagrams' in which a complex web of relationships radiates outwards, joining up the subsystems. However, all lines of a given type must represent a particular kind of relationship. If, for instance, green lines represent flow of information, different types or colours of line must be used to show the flow of materials, or paperwork, etc.

Successful systems thinking requires the manager to take two conflicting view-points. In order to gain the most comprehensive overview of any system, it is necessary to gather as much relevant data as possible. This not only means looking at a problem in fine detail, it also entails standing back and taking a wide overview of the situation, which may include the environment, the supersystem and other parallel or related systems. It is more or less always the case that no diagram can express all of this, so no diagram can provide the complete solution to a systems problem. The flow diagram shown above has proven useful in process design, but may fail to solve other issues, such as how staff react to the new process. A more widely drawn diagram might provide some insight into this, but it in turn may fail to solve even wider issues, such as the impact of waste upon the environment etc. Thus it is usually necessary to draw a *series* of different diagrams, and to tackle a problem piecemeal, rather than attempting a holistic solution in one go. Also, flow chart problems are comparatively simple, because subsystem, intermediates and processes can be defined completely. As diagrams are more widely drawn, they rapidly move into the realm of 'soft systems', where subsystems and the relation-ships between them are less clearly defined. Despite this, systems theory can still provide considerable insight into all levels of a problem, and it is always worth investigating as widely as the data allow.

SUMMARY

Systems exist all around us in the hospitality industry. Most are hard, or techno-logical, systems in combination with soft, or human activity, systems. Together they make what we call 'socio-technical systems'. The relationship between these systems is both complex and dynamic. But understanding the characteristics of systems and the ways in which they behave gives managers the opportunity to control resources (system inputs), operate processes both efficiently and effectively, and assure the required output.

You have been introduced to some very important ideas. First, there is the notion of synergy, i.e. what you get out can be *more* than what you put in! Second, there is the unpredictability of human activity systems. Third, there is the idea of systems inertia – things do not change unless they are made to change. Fourth, systems work better if there are lots of interactions between the parts of the system, just as different systems work better together if there are lots of interactions between them. Finally, adaptation and change are inevitable, due to changes in the environment, but there will always be resistance to such change.

As Johns and Jones (2000) state:

> At first sight, system behaviour may appear to be too complex to grasp and too chaotic to comprehend. But systems behave according to a set of seven principles that make it easier to understand this apparent chaos, and hence to manage it. These principles do not simply identify **what** is happening, they also explain **how** change is taking place and **why** it is occurring. Managers therefore have the means by which to turn from being passive reactors to circumstances into proactive visionaries.

CASE STUDY: 'BIGFOOT'

In his autobiography, Anthony Bourdain (a celebrated American chef) writes, 'I have met and worked for only one perfect animal in the restaurant jungle ...'. He calls this paragon of management 'Bigfoot'. Throughout this book, we shall refer to Bigfoot's approach to management, as reported by Bourdain, in a number of different chapters. Here we shall look at Bigfoot's 'system'.

As Bourdain explains, 'His greatest gift was the Bigfoot System, which I use still. My inventory sheets, for example, are set up like the master's: in clockwise, geographical order ... I know if an order has been called in, and if a particular item was, in fact, ordered – the telltale Bigfoot-style notations appear. Nothing is left to chance.' Not only does Bourdain use this man's system, he can even 'tell a Bigfoot restaurant from the street' by the way the staff are dressed, their standard of cleanliness and how they stick to clearly laid-down procedures. Bigfoot's operations run like clockwork because 'a lot of his time was spent figuring out ways to make the restaurant run more efficiently, more smoothly, faster and cheaper ... everything is always easy to clean and easy to store'. So attuned is Bourdain's hero to running a restaurant it is as if 'the entire restaurant were simply an extension of his central nervous system'. This man clearly understands systems and we shall hear more of him later!

Further study

Visit three different types of foodservice outlet (restaurants, fast food, pub, cafeteria). In what ways do the customer service processes vary?

Select a local hospitality business. How many different systems does this business interact with?

Draw a process chart for any hospitality operation you are familiar with (perhaps your college teaching restaurant), showing the flow of materials through the system.

The next chapter contains a case study about 'Sunnyside Up'. Use this case study as the basis for explaining the unified systems hypothesis.

Bibliography

Bourdain, A. (2001) *Kitchen Confidential: Adventures in the Culinary Underbelly*. London: Bloomsbury.

Breiter, D. and Bloomquist, P. (1998) 'TQM in American hotels', *Cornell Hotel and Restaurant Administration Quarterly*, February, 26–33.

Bryson, Bill (1994) *Made in America*. London: Minerva.

Eyster J, (1997), 'Hotel management contracts in the US: The revolution continues', *Cornell Hotel and Restaurant Administration Quarterly*, June, 14–20.

Foskett, D. (1995), in Jones, P. and Kipps, M. *Flight Catering*. Harlow: Addison Wesley Longman.

Johns, N. and Jones, P. (2000) 'Systems and management: understanding the real world', *The Hospitality Review*, January, 47–52.

Jones, P. and Kipps, M. (1995) *Flight Catering*. Harlow: Addison Wesley Longman.

Kirk, D. (1995) 'Hard and soft systems: a common paradigm for operations management?' *International Journal of Contemporary Hospital Management*, 7(5), 13–16.

McCool, A. (1995) *Inflight Catering Management*. New York: John Wiley & Sons.

Milson, A. and Kirk, D. (1979) 'The caterer as process engineer', in Glew, G. (ed.) *Advances in Catering Technology*. London: Applied Sciences Publishers, 157–72.

Muller, Christopher C. (1997) 'Redefining value: the hamburger price war', *Cornell Hotel and Restaurant Administration Quarterly*, June, 62–73.

Schlosser, E. (2001) *Fast Food Nation*. London: Penguin Press.

Recommended further reading

Jones, P. (1996) *Introduction to Hospitality Operations*. London: Cassell, chapters 1, 2 and 9.

Jones, P. and Kipps, M. (1995) *Flight Catering*. Harlow: Addison Wesley Longman, chapter 1.

CHAPTER 2

Systems in hospitality[1]

After completing this chapter you will be able to:

- *differentiate between materials processing, customer processing and information processing operations*

- *identify and describe three eras of operations development*

- *describe five main trends affecting process design in the hospitality industry*

- *identify and explain the three main process types in the hospitality industry*

- *identify the four main types of process configuration*

- *understand the impact process choice and process configuration have on operations design.*

INTRODUCTION

In Chapter 1 we identified that all operations can be modelled as a system. But we did not address the question as to whether or not all operations in the hospitality industry are the same or not. In the companion volume to this book – *Introduction to Hospitality Operations* – Jones (1996) clearly identifies six different types of accommodation operation (business hotel, resort hotel, budget hotel, guest house, hospital and residential care, and hostel). There were nine types of foodservice operation (restaurant, hotel foodservice, motorway and roadside, licensed trade, fast food, employee feeding, welfare catering, travel catering and outdoor catering). This suggests that differences exist between these types, but that these might be due to their location or market, or technological ('hard') or organizational ('soft') systems. In this chapter we look at how operations may vary from one another in order to understand how and why they adopt different systems.

In Chapter 1 we identified a number of features of operations – separation of back-of-house from front-of-house, differences between inputs and transformational inputs, and so on. One feature we did not identify was what specifically flows through the system or operations process. Johnston and Morris (1987) suggest there are basically three types:

---

1. The first part of this chapter is based on the inaugural lecture given by Professor Peter Jones at the University of Surrey on 8 November 2000.

19

- materials processing operation (MPO) – more commonly referred to as man-ufacturing

- customer processing operation (CPO) – typically described as a service

- information processing operation (IPO) – mostly considered as services.

In most cases, an operation is never exclusively an MPO, CPO or IPO. This is certainly true in most hospitality operations. For instance, during the so-called 'meal experience', materials are processed (food and drink prepared for con-sumption, transported to the customers), information is processed (customer selects from menu, order taken, bill prepared) and customer processing occurs (customers' requests are responded to, social interaction takes place). We also identified in Chapter 1 the idea of a systems hierarchy. While this book con-centrates on socio-technical systems designed for the processing of materials, customers and/or information through an operation, this chapter considers the *operations* themselves, i.e. one level up from the socio-technical systems.

TYPES OF OPERATION

Let us consider the development of operations management practice and thought over the last 150 years. In a recent book, Brown *et al.* (2000) propose an evolution through three eras of operations management:

- The craft era – the period when the artisan made customized goods, usually working in the context of their own small business.

- Mass production – the period of large-scale production of relatively standard outputs, accompanied by the growth of large firms and organizations.

- Mass customization – the present day, in which features of the craft era, notably customized goods, are incorporated into features of mass production, i.e. large-scale output.

This is not to suggest that there are simply three forms of operation. Within each of these eras, goods or services are produced either as one-off activities with a single unique output, or activities with multiple, replicable outputs. And within the category of multiple outputs, output is produced on an item-by-item or discrete basis, or on a flow process basis. Typically, process operations take a few raw materials and blend or split them into a range of product outputs (Cokins, 1988), whereas discrete manufacturing has relatively few 'end items [which] contain many different components' (Fransoo and Rutten, 1994). In all we can identify eight separate operational forms, three of which existed during the craft era and may continue today; four that emerged during the era of mass production, also in existence today; and one that reflects contemporary practice in some industries, namely mass customization (see Figure 2.1).

The three basic types of operation that existed during the craft era were as follows:

Simple project – a craftsman, group of artisans or skilled professional work to

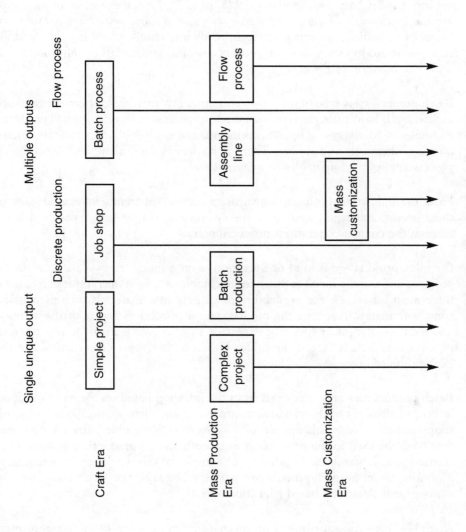

Figure 2.1 *Evolution of eight operational forms*

21

produce a unique output. Typical examples of this were, and remain, house construction, bridge-building, works of art such as Michelangelo's painting in the Sistine Chapel, writing a book, some management consulting, hairdressing. As these examples illustrate, simple projects may be materials, information or customer processing operations.

Job shop – this can be defined as 'the production of small batches of large numbers of different products, most of which require a different set or sequence of processing steps' (Chase and Aquilano, 1995, p. 127). Typical examples of job shops are the blacksmith's forge, auto repair shops, à la carte restaurants, traditional forms of education, general practice in medicine, jewellery-making, bus and air transportation. Job shops too can process customers, materials or information, or some combination of these.

Batch process – this type of operation combines raw materials, often natural (such as wood, oil, foodstuffs, etc.), on a continuous process basis into finished products. Examples of batch process operations include the areas of pharmaceuticals, microbrewing, chemicals and rubber. There is no service equivalent, and hence batch process applies predominantly to materials.

From the industrial revolution onwards, a number of trends influenced each of these operational types, leading to the emergence of four new types, which we place in the context of the mass production era:

Complex projects – this kind of operation is on a much larger scale than simple projects, and usually involves much more complexity. Such operations derive from three main influences: the availability of entirely new materials such as plastics, composite metals, concrete; the mechanization of some elements of the activity; and the development of specialist expertise, such as architects. Examples of complex projects include large-scale bridge-building, skyscraper construction and the exploration of outer space.

Batch production – this developed from the job shop based on the mechanization of certain elements of the production process, some division of labour and work simplification, along with the use of various interchangeable parts (components that could be used in the production of more than one product). It is sometimes referred to as a 'standardized job shop'. Examples of this type of operation include a printing shop, hospital outpatients, package holidays, fast-food restaurant and conventional classroom-based education.

Assembly line – this also relied on mechanization, division of labour and interchangeable parts, but with the addition of the moving production line or the substitution of the customer for the production worker in services (i.e. self-service). The phrase 'assembly line' was probably coined by Henry Ford, who applied it to car production in 1913, but vegetable canners, meat wholesalers and others were using 'flow production' methods many years earlier (Bryson, 1994). This approach to work and production thus subsequently became known as Fordism. The application of mass production processes to services was first identified by Levitt

(1976). Examples of this type of operation include white goods and computer manufacturing, supermarket retailing and automated banking services.

Flow process – Flow process operations involve the almost continuous production of commodity products. The most typical examples of this type of operation are paper, keg beer, oil and steel production. The process was derived from influences such as the development of new materials, scientific discoveries and mechanization.

All seven of these operational types exist today. But the last twenty years have seen the emergence of one new type of operation:

Mass customization – this refers to an operation in which the process is agile and the output flexible. The National Science Foundation defines agility as 'the ability to alter any aspect of the manufacturing enterprise in response to changing market demands'; while flexibility has been defined in the landmark report *Made in America* as the ability 'to deliver high quality products tailored to each customer at mass production prices'. Such agility and flexibility has largely come about through the introduction of IT into the design and production processes. Examples of this type of operation include a number of organizations engaged in automobile manufacture, banking, open/distance learning and book retailing.

A number of important points emerge from this analysis. First, there are some **industries** that have operated, or continue to operate, only in the context of one era, whereas others span two or all three eras. For instance, hairdressing and sculpture remain craft-oriented operations, likewise oil production is solely a flow process operation from the mass production era; building construction is both craft and mass production; and car-making may be craft, mass production or mass customization. Within industries that span more than one era, it follows that some **firms** will only focus on one type of production process. For instance, craft car manufacturers include Morgan, TVR and Lamborghini, mass produced cars were largely the product of American and European manufacturers, while mass customization originated in Japanese car manufacturing. It is also the case that within firms, some **operations** are craft based, industrialized or customized. For instance, the R&D function within firms may still be based around craft operational principles, while the employee wage payment system may be an industrialized process. We shall consider shortly where the hospitality industry and hospitality firms sit in relation to these types of operation.

TRENDS IN PROCESS DESIGN

There are clearly a number of general trends that lead an industry to shift from one process choice to another. In his consideration of the hospitality industry, Jones (1988) identified three main trends as 'production-lining', 'decoupling' and 'self-service'. The concept of the production-lining of service was first identified by Ted Levitt (1976). He recognized how different sectors of the service economy were using technology in similar ways to manufacturing firms, citing fast food as a good example of this. Decoupling is the notion of separating back-of-house (or back office) functions from front-of-house (front office). In services, front-of-house location is constrained by the need to be near the customer. This does not apply to back-of-house. Indeed, by locating these processes elsewhere they can be configured to take advantage of both economies of scale and production-lining. Self-service, in which the customer replaces the service employee, has also been identified in the literature (Bateson, 1985).

In a more recent article Jones (1999) identified two further trends – the move towards 'micro-footprint operations' and dual-use transformation inputs or infrastructure. The former has emerged in the face of market saturation and the unavailability of conventional sites for restaurants. Large chains have now developed scaled-down versions of their outlets so that they can fit into a small space, i.e. a 'micro-footprint'. Thus we see Au Bon Pain carts in shopping malls, Burger King (BK) in cinemas, and so on. The second trend is to use the physical infrastructure to deliver more than one brand. ACCOR have built a hotel in Paris that is divided between their Novotel and Orbis brands. Likewise the Marriott Hotel County Hall, London, has a Travel Inn on the non-river side of the building. Little Chef have also been systematically adapting their roadside offer to include a BK.

CASE STUDY: SUNNYSIDE UP[2]

Chris Cowls, a former senior manager with Burger King, and his colleagues asked themselves the question, 'How would you go about designing a new fast-food restaurant concept for the UK?' They were all experienced foodservice managers who had personal experience of downsizing and had decided to go it alone. They faced a tough challenge in a market that is dominated by major international brands, such as McDonald's and KFC. These brands enjoy high public recognition and a national network of outlets, usually in prime high street locations. Any new concept would have to overcome these barriers to entry, provide competitive advantage and appeal strongly to customers. Cowls' team believed that 'Sunnyside Up' could do just that.

Success in the fast-food business depends on a number of key factors. High-volume business is essential, so outlets need to be located where pedestrian and/or vehicle traffic is high. Most brands are in prime retail areas, which in Britain means the 'high street'. To increase sales opportunities in these high-rent locations, take-out as well as eat-in sales are essential. The meal product therefore must be designed to enable this, hence the success of the hamburger. To sustain high volume, meal prices have to be competitive, which requires low levels of waste and tight control over production. Fast-food operators achieve this by keeping to a minimum the product range (i.e. menu items), so that stock control is simplified. Each commodity may be used in a variety of ways. For instance, the bun can be used for the hamburger, the cheeseburger, the jumbo burger and so on. In some operations, food items are cooked to order, also avoiding waste; but in burger restaurants at peak times, burgers are pre-cooked and ready-wrapped for immediate sale – hence 'fast' food. To avoid waste here, operators depend on accurate forecasting of demand to ensure they produce the right quantity of each

2. A longer version of this case appears in Brown *et al.* (2000).

item. They also forecast demand to ensure they staff their operations as efficiently as possible, by rostering staff to work flexible shift patterns. Chris Cowls was aware of all this, having worked for major fast-food and roadside dining chains. The question was how could he and his colleagues capture a share of this growing and lucrative market?

They began with the product. Every major product segment had at least two major brands competing for business. What was needed was a menu concept for which there was high demand but no major competition. They selected the 'all-day breakfast in a bun' as their core product – hence the brand name 'Sunnyside Up'. Most of the big burger chains were diversifying their product in response to the changing tastes of customers, who were switching from beef to chicken, and from meat to fish. They were also offering fast-food breakfasts, i.e. in a bun, but all of them stopped serving it by 11.00 a.m. in order to switch production to their own core product. But experience showed, especially from roadside sales, that breakfast was popular all day, not just in the morning. Market research also showed that breakfast was an expanding segment of the market. The menu would therefore be based around combinations of egg, bacon and sausage served in a bun, along with savoury or sweet pancakes. This led to another feature, namely serving freshly ground coffee. Most fast-food chains did not serve this kind of coffee, although new speciality outlets such as Costa Coffee were starting to do so.

The next issue was location. All the best locations were occupied by existing fast-food outlets. Sunnyside Up needed different locational criteria to the typical restaurant. Cowls and the team decided that the concept should be aimed at 'host environments'. Rather than on the high street, their outlets would be located inside existing service businesses, such as supermarkets, cinemas, petrol filling stations, sports arena, workplaces and so on. This had a number of advantages. First, such locations afforded the high level of passing traffic or fixed capture/high usage patterns this operation required. Second, franchise contracts could be signed with major companies, thereby facilitating access to the finance needed to build each outlet. Third, the concept could be rolled out very quickly, thereby achieving the economies of scale needed to sustain marketing, IT and systems expenditures.

But location in a host environment creates one major problem – outlet size. While the supermarkets or cinemas want a fast-food service, they did not want to allocate it too much space. So Sunnyside Up is designed to have a micro-footprint; that is to say, it maximizes sales in the smallest space available. A range of layouts was developed. At its smallest, the total space required is 16 sq. m. This is the smallest footprint of any UK fast-food concept. To achieve this, the team researched the latest fast-food equipment to find deep-fat fryers, griddles, hot cupboards and coffee machines that were small, easy to use and efficient. This equipment also had to fit together to create the system the team had designed.

One consequence of the small scale is that staffing levels are low. One person can operate the food production area along with one or two on the service counter. The use of disposables means that wash-up is almost non-existent. Equipment maintenance and cleaning are carried out by these staff during slack periods. In most types of location, there is limited provision for eat-in customers, on stools at eating shelves. Whereas most customers are expected to take away (which makes sense in filling stations, sports arenas and cinemas), in workplaces it was recognized that most customers would eat in and that more seating would be required.

While the sales volumes of such small operations will not match those achieved by fast-food restaurants on the high street, Cowls and his team have rewritten the 'rules of the game'. Their concept can be built into a host environment for less than £50,000, and their operating costs are also low. The average projected sales volume of £3,000 to £5,000 per week is more than enough to give a good return on capital invested.

PROCESS CHOICE IN THE HOSPITALITY INDUSTRY

So what about types of operation in hospitality? The hospitality industry has tended to regard its processes and related technologies as unique. And in some senses they are. Few, if any, other industries prepare meals, service bedrooms, organize conferences and banquets, serve alcoholic beverages and provide leisure facilities. Likewise, while the paint industry only processes paint and the car industry only makes vehicles, they are seen as sharing some characteristics, along with many other types of manufacturing operation. For increasingly it is being recognized that concepts in relation to process choice, process configuration and process technology can be applied to *all* sectors, including the hospitality industry.

It is clear from the above that some of the eight processes discussed above cannot apply to the hospitality industry. Batch and flow processing are both industrial activities that solely process materials, not customers. As far as projects are concerned, there are specialist parts of the hospitality industry, such as management consultants, hotel developers and designers, kitchen designers and installers, that are engaged in projects.

Essentially, however, three process types are used to deliver services and products to hospitality customers:

* job shop, e.g. à la carte restaurants, most hotels

* batch production, e.g. cook-chill production, conference hotels, fast food

* mass production, e.g. in-flight catering.

We shall look at the implications this has for layout and technology in a moment.

One reason why process choice theory has never really been applied to the industry is the latter's great diversity, with its many different forms of operation across the lodging, food and beverage sectors. In particular, the physical plant of a typical hospitality operation may process both materials and customers. Hence it is possible for one part of the operation to have one process type, for instance food production back-of-house may be cook-chill (i.e. batch production process), while front-of-house may have different process type, such as table service restaurant (i.e. job shop). Jones and Lockwood (2000) have termed such operations 'hybrid operations'. Process choice theory, developed largely by researching manufacturing operations, suggests that such hybridization is undesirable on a small-scale basis since it is more difficult to manage, less efficient and creates short-term problems at the interface between the two types.

PROCESS CONFIGURATION OR LAYOUT

There are four basic layout types found in manufacturing and service settings (Brown *et al.*, 2000). These are:

- fixed position

- process layout

- product layout

- combination of product and process layout.

Fixed position – refers to a single, fixed position at which the product is assembled or service is processed by workers who move to that position in order to carry out their work. This layout is applied to products that are heavy, bulky or fragile, such as in ship-building, aerospace or dentistry.

Process layout – machines or activities are grouped together non-sequentially to allow a range of different products to be made. Products move to a particular location for processing according to need. Workers tend to operate within one area, but may be sufficiently multi-skilled to work across areas. This is the typical layout associated with job shop and some batch production. It allows for a wide variety of products to be made in relatively small volumes. The breakdown of one machine does not halt production. Examples of sectors that use this approach are jewellery-making, hairdressing and low-volume furniture manufacture.

Product layout – machinery is dedicated to a particular product, and is usually laid out in a sequence, with distinct stages in manufacture. Workers are typically required to perform relatively simple tasks at one particular stage in the process. Whenever possible such tasks have been automated. This is the layout associated with mass production. It is used in car manufacture, chocolate production and fast food.

Process/product layout – this combines elements of the process layout, such as clusters of machines, with product layout, with each cluster being organized sequentially. Hence each cluster or cell can produce in high volumes a variety of outputs based around a single product. In essence this is mass customization, and is adopted in high-tech manufacturing operations.

Until Jones (2000) no one had discussed the notion of process configuration as it applies to the hospitality industry. It seems that all four types of layout can be found in the industry. The provision of accommodation services (see Chapter 8), i.e. hotel bedrooms, is an example of a **fixed position** layout. Room attendants move from room to room in order to service them. This means that they have to take the technology they need to perform this task with them. The same is true of table service restaurants – staff go to each table to perform their duties and deliver service.

Most traditional food production kitchens have a **process layout**. The kitchen is organized into different sections – larder, sauce, vegetables, pastry, and so on – each of which can produce a wide variety of outputs (see Chapter 9). The technology in each section is carefully selected to support this activity. For instance, a large wooden chopping block in the larder, marble-topped tables in pastry, boiling pans in the vegetables section. The same is true when production is scaled up for cook-chill production, albeit the equipment is of considerably larger capacity.

One reasons why fast food was innovative was that it adopted a **product layout** in order to achieve high-volume, low-variety mass production style output. The technology of these operations is organized so that raw materials are processed in a highly sequential way by individual crew members. Each worker carries out one or two simple tasks, such as cooking the beef patty, toasting the bun, topping the patty with dressing, assembling and wrapping the finished product or serving the customer.

The **combined process/product layout** is probably only found in the flight catering sector. Large-scale food production facilities of this type may produce up to 20,000 in-flight 'meals' a day. They therefore have product layouts, particularly for the laying up of trays; while they have process layouts for the production of different types of meal items, such as starters, main meals, sandwiches, and so on.

ISSUES IN PROCESS CHOICE AND LAYOUT IN HOSPITALITY

This analysis of choice and layout identifies some interesting issues regarding the industry. In manufacturing there tends to be quite a close fit between process choice and layout (see Table 2.1). This derives from the fact that manufacturing is essentially a materials processing operation. Any 'service' elements of a product are usually decoupled from the actual manufacture of the product.

Industry example	Process choice	Process layout
Ship-building, construction	Project	Fixed position
Blacksmith's forge	Job shop	Process layout
Print shop, small engineering	Batch production	Process layout
Car assembly	Mass production	Product layout
High tech	Mass customization	Combined process/product

Table 2.1 *Fit between process choice and layout in manufacturing*

However, in many hospitality operations both manufacture and service happen simultaneously. Hence such operations are both hybrids of process choice and may have more than one process layout. Jones and Lockwood (2000) consider both process choice and process flow (MPO, CPO or IPO) to create an overview of operations in the industry, and classify them into distinct systems (see Table 2.2).

This highlights the fact that the industry is complex in a number of ways. Jones and Lockwood (2000) identify four key features:

- Hotels, because they incorporate both accommodation and foodservice, are the most complex form of hospitality operation.

	Customer processing operations	Combined CPO and MPO	Materials processing operations
Job shops	Full service hotel Mid-service hotel		
			Home delivery
Batch production	*Table service* Residential hostel	Restaurant	*A la carte kitchen*
			Hospital tray serve systems
Mass production	*Counter service* Budget hotel	Cafeteria	*Batch production kitchen*
			Cook-chill Flight kitchen
	Counter service	Fast food	*Assembly serve kitchen*

Table 2.2 *Classification of hospitality operations by process choice and process flows*

- Hybrid operations (both MPOs and CPOs) are more complex than non-hybrid types.

- Service or job shops tend to be CPOs, with very few examples of MPOs.

- Batch and mass production tends to have been applied to MPOs.

This explains why process choice and process configuration do not fit as well as they do in manufacturing (see Table 2.3). It looks at different departments in a hotel from a choice and layout perspective.

Fortunately (it could be argued) many of the processes in the industry are relatively simple and do not require sophisticated technology or highly skilled labour. Thus the lack of fit between the type of process and the process layout has not

Hotel department	Type of process	Process layout
Front office	Job shop	Process layout
Housekeeping	Mass production?	Fixed position
Bars	Job shop	Process layout
Kitchen	Job shop	Process layout
Restaurant	Job shop	Fixed position
Banqueting service	Batch production	Fixed position
Leisure facilities	Job shop	Process layout
Room service	Job shop	Fixed position

Table 2.3 *Process choice and layout in a hotel*

become an issue. Housekeeping is a good example. The processes or activities undertaken to clean a guest room are basically identical and would normally lend themselves to both production-lining and even automation. If it were physically possible, one could envisage a factory in which rooms moved slowly along a production line as a worker (or machine) polished the mirror, another vacuumed the floor and a third dusted the lampshades, and so on. Of course, this cannot happen due to the size of the room and its fixed position. Hence tasks which could (should?) be dealt with on a mass production basis are actually managed as a job shop.

The development of fast food is an example of how the traditional job shop restaurant with process layout has been turned into batch production with both product and process layout. By reducing the range of products, and thereby the range of ingredients, food production could be broken down into simple tasks, each of which is performed in a different part of the 'factory' (back-of-house area) by individual workers performing a separate task. The finished product is then stored on a shelf for immediate sale. It is removed from the shelf by workers who have a process layout that enables them to respond to the individual food and drink orders of each customer. The problem of having fixed position tables and chairs in the dining area is removed by getting customers to serve themselves. Thus, although this remains a fixed position layout, it is highly labour efficient.

SOCIO-TECHNICAL SYSTEMS IN HOSPITALITY OPERATIONS

This discussion of process choice and configuration, linked with the technique of flow process charting (discussed in Chapter 1), now enables us to identify the key socio-technical systems that exist in the hospitality sector. The theoretical framework of systems encourages the application of modelling to real-life situations in order to understand them as systems, identify hierarchies and analyse interactions. Such models are typical input–process–output models, or so-called 'operations flow charts'. Jones (1996) has considered both accommodation and foodservice, developing systems models for them both.

For accommodation, he argues that there is a core system comprising the four subsystems of reservations, reception, overnight stay (housekeeping) and payment (or billing) (see Figure 2.2). In addition and depending on the type of market being served, a number of ancillary systems may or may not be offered. These subsystems include laundry, restaurants, bars, business services and leisure services. Jones identifies that a hotel is largely a customer-processing operation, especially with regards to the core system. He does not suggest how many different types of hotel arise from the potential combinations of the core system with ancillary systems, but *de facto* such a typology would resemble quite closely the typical approach to hotel classification adopted by tourist boards and guidebooks.

Foodservice, on the other hand, is a materials processing operation and customer processing operation. Jones (1996) and Jones and Huelin (1990) have made a number of attempts to classify foodservice operations based on an analysis of their systems design, technology and configuration. They identify ten subsystems of foodservice, namely storage, preparation, cooking, holding, transport, regeneration, service, dining, clearing and dishwash.

For the purposes of this book, these analyses have led us to identify the socio-technical systems that are discussed in the next eleven chapters, as follows:

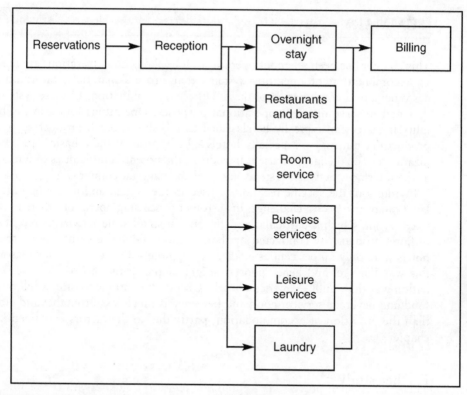

Figure 2.2 *A systems model of hotel operations* (Jones, 1996)

- Operational Systems (Operations-wide)
  Procurement and control
  Stores
  Maintenance and engineering
  Environment and waste

- Accommodation Services
  Front office
  Housekeeping

- Food Production Systems
  Food preparation and production
  Holding, transportation and regeneration

- Food and Drink Service Systems
  Foodservice and dining
  Clearing and dishwash
  Bars

SUMMARY

This chapter has been all about operations. It explains how operations are made up of a combination of operating systems that process materials, information or customers, or a combination of these. Different combinations of these systems are designed to serve different operational purposes. Operations found in the hospitality industry can typically be classified as job shops, batch production or mass production, but may – especially hotels – be hybrids of these basic types. Hybridization is a challenge, because it introduces the potential difficulties of integration at the interfaces between systems and adds managerial complexity.

In addition, the specific technology used in the system and its configuration or layout may also pose a challenge. In customer processing operations there is often a fixed layout, which is particularly inefficient for small-scale activity. A recent study of hotel productivity conducted by the McKinsey Global Institute found that UK hotels were only 50 per cent as efficient as US hotels. One of the major reasons for this was the age, and hence poorer design, of the British hotels. Another explanation was that, unlike American hotels, UK hotels continue to offer a full range of food and beverage service. Food and beverage is much less profitable and efficient than the provision of accommodation, partly due to the factors explained in this chapter.

Further study

Choose a hospitality operation that you are familiar with, and draw a flow process chart that clearly shows the relationship between customer processing, materials processing and information processing.

How might hospitality operators go about introducing mass customization?

Bibliography

Bateson, J. E. G. (1985) 'Self-service consumer: an exploratory study', *Journal of Retailing*, **61** (3), 47–76.

Brown, S., Lamming, R., Bessant, J. and Jones, P. (2000) *Strategic Operations Management*. Oxford: Butterworth-Heinemann.

Bryson, Bill (1994) *Made in America*. London: Minerva.

Chase, R. B. and Aquilano, N. J. (1995) *Production and Operations Management*. Chicago: Irwin.

Cokins, G. M. (1988) 'Control systems for process industries', *Manufacturing Systems*, 6(5), 79–83.

Fransoo, J. C. and Rutten W. G. M. M. (1994) 'Typology of production control situations in process industries', *International Journal of Operations & Production Management*, **14**(12), 47–57.

Johnston, R. and Morris, B. (1987) 'Dealing with inherent variability: the difference between manufacturing and service', *International Journal of Operations & Production Management*, 7(4).

Jones, P. (1988) 'The impact of trends in service operations on food service delivery systems', *International Journal of Operations & Production Management*, 8(7), 23–30.

Jones, P. (1996) *Introduction to Hospitality Operations*. London: Cassell.

Jones, P. (1999) 'Operational issues and trends in the hospitality industry', *International Journal of Hospitality Management*, **18**, 427–42.

Jones, P. (2000) Inaugural lecture, University of Surrey.

Jones, P. and Huelin, A. (1990) 'Thinking about catering systems', *International Journal of Operations & Production Management*, **10**(8), 42–51.

Jones, P. and Lockwood, A. (2000) 'Operating systems and products', in Brotherton, Bob (ed.) *An Introduction to the UK Hospitality Industry*. Oxford: Butterworth-Heinemann.

Levitt, T. (1976) 'The industrialisation of service', *Harvard Business Review*, November/December.

Recommended further reading

Brown, S., Lamming, R., Bessant, J. and Jones, P. (2000) *Strategic Operations Management*. Oxford: Butterworth-Heinemann, chapter 3, 67–96.

Jones, P. and Lockwood, A. (2000) 'Operating systems and products', in Brotherton, Bob (ed.) *An Introduction to the UK Hospitality Industry*. Oxford: Butterworth-Heinemann, 46–70.

PART B

OPERATIONAL SYSTEMS (OPERATIONS-WIDE)

The four chapters in this section examine the operating systems that are common to every type of operation. Each chapter is concerned with the flow of inputs into the operation and how these are properly processed so that the operation can be effectively managed and unwanted outputs, such as waste and residue, are minimized. This part focuses largely on materials processing and information processing. Chapters 3 and 4 are concerned with the supply of material inputs into the operation. Chapter 5 explores managing the transformation inputs (i.e. the physical infrastructure of the operation). Finally, Chapter 6 looks at the management of energy and other resources that may be needed to support the infrastructure or that are consumed as part of the operation's business activity.

Procurement and control[1]

After completing this chapter you will be able to:

- *identify the main purposes of the procurement system and the control system*
- *describe different procurement systems*
- *describe different approaches to control*
- *explain the key processes in procurement*
- *explain the key processes in control*
- *identify current trends in procurement and control systems.*

INTRODUCTION

Procurement and control are the two key information processing systems that underpin hospitality operations back-of-house. Hence in many operations the team that places the orders with and pays suppliers also oversees the control function within the operation. The procurement system ensures that all operational systems have the material inputs they require, while the control system ensures that processing departments have handled these materials in an effective and efficient way. Prior to the introduction of IT, these two systems tended to operate separately. This is because effective control tended to be post-operational, that is to say after the event, being based on weekly or monthly stocktakes to establish stock usage. With the advent of IT, it is now possible to link sales directly to inventory, especially where the unit of purchase is similar to the unit of sale, and hence directly link procurement and control.

PURPOSE OF SYSTEM

Food and beverage commodities constitute one of the largest single costs in a

---

1. This chapter has been adapted from parts of Chapters 7 and 15 in Jones, P. and Merricks, P. (1994) *The Management of Foodservice Operations*. London: Cassell.

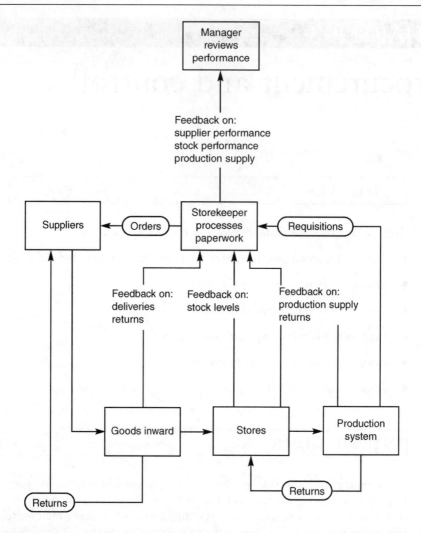

Figure 3.1 *Stock control system.* Source: Jones, P. and Merricks, P. (1994).

foodservice business. A variation of just 1 per cent in these material costs will have very significant effects on profit. Materials enter the establishment as purchases received, they are stored and issued from the store, from where they are processed and either sold or wasted. A foodservice manager who is planning a procurement system has to establish the nature of materials required, a process for obtaining supplies, define how and when purchases are to be made, keep accurate records of orders, and liaise with the stores system (see Chapter 4). The nature of the total control system is illustrated in Figure 3.1. Once materials are stored within the operation, control systems have to be set up to ensure their correct usage within production departments.

Even with an apparently simple purchasing decision a manager has to appreciate its implications for the business. First, the item will need to be paid for, which will affect the cash flow of the business. Second, the item will have to be stored, and storage costs can be considerable. Third, the item becomes an asset of the business, and management has a duty to protect and preserve these assets from deterioration, pilferage and misuse.

It is clear from this overview of the purpose of the system that successful procurement performance can be measured by:

- continuity of supply

- value of stock held

- quality of relationship with suppliers.

Successful control can be measured by:

- achievement of target profit performance

- low wastage of materials

- accurate and timely measurement of operating department performance.

GENERIC SYSTEM CHARACTERISTICS

The aim of a procurement system is to ensure that the right suppliers are used and that the procurement process is itself controlled. This means having in place policies for selecting suppliers and for controlling the purchase activity. Subsequently control must be exerted over the receipt, storage and issuing of materials (see Chapter 4). Finally, control systems have to be established to ensure that production departments utilize these materials effectively.

One example of the food purchasing process developed by the School Meal Service in the USA is illustrated in Figure 3.2. It shows that there are two types of relationship in the purchasing process, depending on the types of commodities required. The **formal method** is for major purchase items from large-scale suppliers. The **informal method** is for less significant or less frequently purchased items

---

Pre-purchase functions
1. Plan menus
2. Determine quality and quantity needed
3. Determine stock levels
4. Establish order sizes
5. Write purchase specifications

Formal method	*Informal method*
6. Develop purchase order	6. Develop purchase order
7. Establish bid schedule	7. Obtain price quotation
8. Issue invitation to bid	8. Select supplier
9. Evaluate bids (or tenders)	9. Place order
10. Award contract to supplier	10. Receive goods
11. Issue delivery order	11. Evaluate and follow up
12. Receive goods	12. Issue commodities for use
13. Evaluate and follow up	

Figure 3.2 *The food purchasing process* (Jones, 1996)

from local suppliers. Effective supply depends on managing each stage of this process, whatever the method, to ensure that the most satisfactory terms are agreed for both parties. Good relationships are possible only if both the supplier and the operator feel happy about the deal they have struck.

Selecting suppliers

There is a wide range of alternative sources of supply for every commodity a hospitality manager may wish to purchase, ranging from growers and manu-facturers, through wholesalers, cash and carries, to retail outlets. Higher fuel and labour costs and scale economies of distribution are making it less likely that single hospitality operations will be able to purchase directly from growers and manu-facturers in the future. Thus only very large chains are likely to purchase direct; other operations will use a middleman. Large chain operations have two main options with regard to supply. They can either own and operate their own dis-tribution system or they can contract a distributor to make deliveries from the manufacturers to their units on their behalf. Most fast-food chains negotiate a bulk price with the manufacturers and then make delivery arrangements with a dis-tributor. Such chains pay the manufacturer directly for the contracted goods. The distributor orders enough goods from the manufacturer to meet the supply requirements of local franchises and is invoiced by the chain at the rates charged to franchises less a fixed percentage as a distribution allowance. Finally, the fran-chisees pay the distributor. This has several advantages, in that the manufacturer only supplies a limited number of locations in bulk and chain franchisees are assured of weekly deliveries of all commodities in any order size.

For operators who are not part of a chain, commodities must be purchased either from wholesale markets, from wholesale suppliers, from cash-and-carry outlets or from retail outlets such as supermarkets. The tradition of chefs getting up at 5 a.m. to visit the local market to select fresh meat, fish, fruit and vegetables has become the exception rather than the rule. The growth in availability and use of frozen and irradiated food has resulted in less reliance on truly fresh commodities, and con-sequently the number, scale and frequency of markets are declining. As markets decline, changes in operations, such as the shift from skilled to semi-skilled per-sonnel, smaller production and stores areas and lower profit margins, have meant a consequent move towards what has been called 'one-stop shopping'. This refers to the use of total supply distributors who can provide the operators with all their commodity requirements, including foodstuffs, cleaning materials, disposables and alcoholic beverages. Total supply entails only one delivery, which cuts down on paperwork, opportunities for pilferage and time spent on receiving goods.

Increased distribution costs have led many suppliers to rethink their delivery policy and, especially where order quantities are small, operators often have to go to the warehouse or cash-and-carry themselves. The main advantage of cash-and-carry supply is that there is no minimum order size. There are, however, significant disadvantages, in particular the lack of credit facilities. Operators who use cash-and-carry outlets also have to pay for their own distribution costs, which are often comparatively higher than those of a wholesaler.

Whatever the form of supply, effective control requires that there is a systematic approach to placing orders. In most cases, this will be done through a purchase order book, which provides a standard form in duplicate or triplicate, thereby providing a copy for the supplier, purchaser and/or storekeeper. These should be completed even when orders are made by telephone to ensure that only goods ordered are actually delivered. Small operators who purchase direct from cash-and-carries could still use such a procedure in order to provide their 'shopping list', and thereby avoid purchasing items on impulse which they do not really need.

Procurement control

In deciding how to control purchases of materials stocks, three standards need to be established: quality, quantity and prices. Such decisions are usually influenced by the three Vs: volume, variety and value. Turner (1991) describes volume as 'the size of demand for each commodity', variety as 'the range of commodities on offer', and value as 'the relative aspect of the function of the commodity'. Quality standards derive largely from the decisions made about the concept and service or production standards. The concept determines the basic cost–price relationship, the technology to be used for production purposes and the customer expectations about quality. The most basic decision that will be made is whether to 'make or buy'; that is to say, to produce on the premises or buy in items prepared elsewhere (see also Chapter 9 with reference to kitchen design). Once this has been decided, there are still decisions to be made about grades, brands, degree of freshness, sizes and method of packaging. Many operations define each of these factors by preparing standard purchase specifications. The advantages of such specifications are that they eliminate confusion between suppliers and the operator; they make it easier for suppliers tendering to supply; they provide guidance for storekeepers when receiving goods inwards; and they help in planning menus or service standards by enabling variety reduction if necessary.

In addition, it is essential to establish the required quantities of items. The ideal stock level for a specific commodity depends on the nature of the business and the characteristics of the commodity, in particular the level of sales, the stability of demand, the terms of supply, the costs of stockholding, cash flow limitations, the shelf-life of the commodity, the storage space available and market trends in price and availability. Cash flow and storage costs are affected by the extent to which items are purchased in bulk. The advantages of buying in bulk are that items may be cheaper because of bulk discount; there may be protection against sudden increase in demand or sudden shortage in supply, and potentially protection against inflation. The disadvantages of buying in bulk include the fact that the cash flow position worsens; stockholding costs increase; deterioration or pilferage may occur; and future demand may decrease. As far as fresh food is concerned, the disadvantages obviously outweigh the advantages. With other products the reverse can hold true. With vintage wine, for example, the product may appreciate in value considerably during the storage period (it may also decrease in value).

In general, unless there is a sound reason to the contrary, stock levels should be kept as low as possible. However, with high-cost, high-usage items, it is often useful to plan the stock levels and reorder methods in more detail. The starting point for planning stock levels is an analysis of the usage rate. Where items are used infrequently (often the case with non-perishable commodities), the **periodic order method** can be used. Periodically, for instance once a week or once a month, items will be reordered on the basis of forecast need plus buffer stock to avoid stock-out, less stock in hand. A more sophisticated approach is based around the idea of

	Invoice cost	Administration cost	Storage costs
Many small orders	High	High	Low
Few large orders	Low	Low	High

Table 3.1 *Effect of purchase order size on purchase costs*

economic order quantity (EOQ). The total cost associated with a purchase is a combination of the invoice cost, plus the administration cost (postage, clerical time, etc.) plus the storage cost (running the freezer etc.). These costs will vary, as shown in Table 3.1. Somewhere between the extremes of one large order and very many small orders lies the point where the total cost will be lowest. The EOQs can be calculated using mathematical formulae or by preparing cost tables. Either method is laborious and time-consuming, and as such the useful application of EOQs is limited to very large-scale purchasing. It should be remembered, however, that there is such a thing as an ideal purchase quantity.

Careful planning and control of stock levels for individual commodities is not completely satisfactory as the only method of stock monitoring. It is useful to have an easily monitored measure of total stock value, and the use of *number of days' stock* is to be recommended as a system. It is calculated by dividing the value of current stock multiplied by 365 days by the total value of stock used. Trends in number of days' stock give useful control data on a four-weekly basis – but evaluation of the raw data is more difficult. The norm for restaurant operations is about 10 days' food stock, but this varies with the type of stocks held and volume of business. In addition to being useful for assessing total stock, this measure is helpful for highlighting slow-moving stock.

Production controls

The main area in which control is exercised is in operational departments such as the production kitchen or housekeeping. In the stores the goods may be broken down into smaller units, but essentially remain unchanged. In the production kitchen, however, the goods are transformed from raw materials into finished product, from food items into meals. Such transformation is achieved through employing a wide range of different techniques and cookery principles, during which there is always the chance that unnecessary waste will occur. At the same time, these goods are potentially subject to the risk of pilferage and damage.

Food production control is aimed at ensuring that dishes are prepared to conform to a portion size, quality standard and cost consistent with the menu concept. This can be achieved by implementing a system of standard portioning, standard recipes and standard costing. Standard portions are established by quantifying any item that is to be serviced by weight, by volume or by count. For instance, UK steakhouse chains have tended to use a 250 g steak as a standard size; in the licensed trade many items are required by law to be served in specific volumes, such as 125 cl for wine by the glass; and particularly for pre-portioned items, it is possible to specify portions by the number each customer should receive. In some cases implements are used to establish effective portioning, such as scoops for ice cream or french fries, ladles for soups and sauces, and slotted spoons for vegetables. Once the portion size is established it is possible to define the standard recipe. Such recipes should ensure consistency of appearance, taste and customer satisfaction. The combination of portion size and recipe, along with the known commodity costs, enables the manager to establish a standard portion cost for each item on the menu. The level of complexity of costing will vary widely. Some items may be sold in the same form in which they were purchased, for instance bread rolls or a glass of milk; in such cases the costing is simply the purchase price per unit divided by the number of portions per unit. In other cases, a dish may be very complex, involving the use of many different kinds of commodity, so that the standard recipe will require very careful costing.

Production control also requires that waste is accounted for. There are two possible methods of treating waste food: either an allowance for waste can be built into the overall potential food cost percentage, or waste can be included in the variance allowed on each dish item. Different approaches are taken in industry. If waste is a significant problem worthy of individual control, an alternative is to record waste written off, value this at portion cost and itemize the total as a separate variance. The principle is that measuring the nature and level of waste should reflect the current control problems.

SYSTEM PROCESSES

Having created a system for selecting suppliers, placing orders and controlling materials in production, the control system has to manage these processes.

Managing suppliers

Any budgetary variance (i.e. a difference between the budgeted spend and actual spend) related to the cost of supplies indicates a problem, and it will be necessary to work with suppliers in order to correct this. Such collaboration depends on having effective supplier relationships. The exact nature of purchasing will vary from one type of foodservice to another. For a franchise in a chain operation, supplier selection will not be an issue, as suppliers will be specified as part of the franchise agreement. For an independent restaurateur in a large city, a continual review of suppliers may be required, with some switching from one to another. Where an institutional operator employs long-term contracts with suppliers, supplier evaluation may take place only every one or two years. Finally, a small outlet, possibly some distance from urban areas, may have to rely on a single source of supply.

Reid and Reigel (1988) surveyed the selection criteria and relationships of large-scale foodservice organizations with their suppliers. Most of the 61 organizations surveyed were company-owned retail restaurant chains, hence 60 per cent of respondents operated more than 100 units. Others included institutional foodservice operators – both private and government – and hotel foodservice operators. Nearly three-quarters of the respondents reported average unit sales of over $500,000 per year. The research showed that about 40 per cent of the foodservice organizations used 100 or fewer suppliers, while 20 per cent used over 500 annually. It made no difference whether the organization was a retail, hotel or institutional foodservice operator. However, operators with larger annual sales had a larger number of suppliers. The operators were asked to specify the number of suppliers they used; how many new suppliers they had; how often they used international suppliers; and about aspects of supplier relation, such as how often the foodservice organization visited the supplier facilities. The study investigated the basis on which the foodservice organizations selected their suppliers. Respondents were given a list of 20 supplier characteristics and asked to rate their importance. The six most important characteristics, across all types of organization, were:

- accuracy of filling orders
- consistent quality level
- on-time delivery
- willingness to work together to resolve problems
- willingness to respond in a 'pinch'
- reasonable unit cost.

Institutional foodservice operators and the larger firms also were concerned about:

- reasonable minimum orders
- volume discounts
- frequency of delivery
- payment policies.

The least important characteristics tended to be tangential services provided by suppliers, such as:

- ability to sole-source
- training in product use
- willingness to break a case
- provision of recipe ideas.

Good supplier relations take some time to establish. The survey asked operators how many new suppliers they had added in the past year. All the organizations, especially government foodservice, reported an increase in the use of new suppliers. This is due to a wide range of factors, including the product range and geographical growth of the foodservice firms themselves. There was also growth in international suppliers, particularly among larger firms and hotel and retail foodservice organizations. Only the largest foodservice firms – about 10 per cent of the sample – actually visited more than three-quarters of their suppliers. This practice may not be necessary on an annual basis if firms have long-established relationships with their suppliers.

Supplier negotiation

When dealing with suppliers, foodservice managers must be good negotiators and know something of the law. The basis of satisfactory negotiation is that both parties feel happy about the deal they have struck. As Figure 3.2 illustrated, such negotiation can be formal, through a process of inviting tenders and reviewing bids, or informal, by simply asking a range of suppliers to quote prices. Although the goal of minimizing the cost of purchases is desirable, this should never be achieved by accepting a lower-quality product. Successful negotiation means getting a supplier to agree on a lower price for a specified quality. Most suppliers' methods of setting price allow some margin for negotiation, but there is always a price below which the supplier will not go. The foodservice manager needs to be aware of just how much latitude there is for cost reductions.

Suppliers are more likely to negotiate a price if they recognize that the foodservice manager is really price conscious. This price consciousness is most prevalent in industry sectors with very tight profit margins, such as institutional foodservice, or when purchasing expensive items like meat and fish. By 'shopping around' and learning the current range of market prices, foodservice managers can then demonstrate a price awareness to the suppliers. This supports their negotiating stance, helping them to obtain the best possible price. Even if suppliers cannot reduce prices further, foodservice managers may be able to negotiate more favourable credit terms or extend payment schedules. Alternatively, discounts may be agreed upon for bulk purchases or prompt payment.

In the Reid and Reigel study (1988), firms were asked how they managed good supplier relations and how they ensured accurate supply and on-time delivery. The most frequently employed practice was through prompt payment, reasonable requests and shared cost data. Also, firms were not reluctant to threaten to take their large amount of business elsewhere. Of relatively little use were long-term contracts with performance clauses or exclusivity contracts.

Managing supplier credit

When commodities or services are purchased, several different terms of supply can be negotiated. Payment may be made some time, often weeks, after the delivery has been made. It may be made at the time of the delivery, as in the case of cash-and-carry purchasing. Occasionally payment may be made before the delivery occurs or discount applied for payment within a certain time period. Within the limits imposed by the purchasing agreements, payment of accounts should be delayed as long as possible, as this represents an interest-free unsecured loan to the business. Managers in foodservice businesses must keep careful control over suppliers' credit. The most useful way of measuring this is by monitoring the **average credit taken on purchases** (ACTOP). This is established by dividing the average level of credit by the total annual purchases multiplied by 52 weeks to identify the granted, i.e. ACTOP. This is the equivalent of enough interest-free loans to pay for that number of weeks' purchases. By monitoring supplier credit, it is possible to identify when remedial action is necessary. If ACTOP dropped from three weeks to two weeks, the business might need to borrow from the bank. However, it might be possible to regain this credit by systematically reviewing each supplier account and establishing how long payment can be deferred. In many cases, regular payment is more important than payment on time.

SYSTEM ADOPTION

All operations will have procurement and control systems.

CASE STUDY: LITTLE CHEF, EAST SUSSEX

The Little Chef restaurant chain is now part of the Compass group. The chain has a central purchasing department that has negotiated a contract with 3663 to supply it with all food, drink and retail items. A separate supplier, King UK, delivers cleaning items. The Little Chef menu is based on popular British-style dishes, such as the all-day breakfast, burgers, fish and chips, and so on, along with popular dishes from other countries, such as lasagne and chicken tikka. There are a total of 65 dishes on the menu, of which 29 are main courses. The beverage menu has 30 items, including only four types of wine and three beers. This low proportion of alcoholic items reflects the restaurants' location – by the roadside serving motorists. The menu and beverage list requires an inventory of nearly 1,000 separate food commodities.

Little Chefs are open seven days a week from 7.00 a.m. to 10.00 p.m., every day of the year except Christmas Day. The A27 Little Chef has 80 covers and is staffed by a manager, two assistant managers, four part-time supervisors and eight team members. During a busy period, such as Sunday lunch time, there may be a maximum of 5 staff working on a shift. Weekly turnover is approximately £5,000. The manager checks stock and notes what is required on a standard order form. She then uses this listing to order supplies twice a week by telephone for delivery two or three days later.

All stores are delivered on a pallet, sealed with a polyurethane sheet, to the back door of the restaurant. Each item is checked and then taken directly to its appropriate storage area (see next chapter). The delivery is accompanied by a triplicate invoice. Any damaged items are returned immediately, and this is noted on the accompanying invoice. The top copy of the invoice is retained by the supplier, and the manager sends the other two copies to head office, having first entered all items on the in-house control system. Each week a report is created which identifies the sales revenue, the wage costs, purchases and recorded wastage. There is a target gross profit percentage for food of 76 per cent. Stocktaking is carried out once a week by the manager or an assistant. This helps to identify stock losses. These are typically very small (less than 0.5 per cent of revenue).

CURRENT TRENDS AND ISSUES AFFECTING SYSTEM

A major trend is the development of e-commerce based on information and communication technologies (ICTs). In simple terms, most items supplied to a hospitality operation will be mass produced in very large quantities in a limited number of locations. This enables food manufacturers such as Kraft and Heinz or brewers such as Guinness and Allied to take advantage of scale economies and keep their costs down. Two main things happen in the course of transferring goods from supplier sources to the operation. The most obvious is that they are physically transported; however, they are also broken down from large bulk quantities into the much smaller and specific amounts ordered by the operator. This is often the reason why operators do not order directly from manufacturers but use whole-salers who specialize in supplying both the range of goods needed and also the typical order sizes. This results in what has been called the 'supply chain'. In reality most operations do not depend on a single chain, i.e. they do not have a single source of supply, but many. Hence they have many chains that are interlinked, some of which are short (directly to source) and others which may have a number of intermediaries.

For a system to be as efficient as possible, the ideal would be for immediate feedback so that all output led to an adjustment in the flow of inputs into the system. However, complex supply chains reduce the immediacy of information and greatly reduce the efficiency. One of the reasons why restaurants hold 15 days of stock is that they cannot depend on goods being supplied when they want them. ICTs and the internet are significantly helping to overcome this problem. A good example is amazon.com. This website enables consumers to identify a wide range of goods, select want they want, pay online, check on delivery time and delivery status, etc. These same consumer marketing ideas are also being applied in relation to business-to-business (B2B) marketing in the hospitality industry. As well as using the internet to order items, check delivery times and pay for goods, hospitality operators can now also check their accounts with the supplier, facilitate goods returns and credit notes (see also Chapter 4), and identify what their typical order quantities have been in the past. When these ordering systems are then linked directly either to an operation's inventory management system or even point-of-sale systems, significant efficiency gains can be made – both in terms of lowering the administrative costs of purchasing and levels of stock held, as well as ensuring the continuity of supply.

Another major trend in the industry is the extent to which suppliers, especially food manufacturers, are 'forwardly integrating' into foodservice. This is to say, suppliers are taking on many of the activities that were formerly carried out by the foodservice operator. Simple examples of this are ready-peeled and cut fresh vegetables, prepared bread and pizza doughs, and so on. In some sectors of the industry, the role of the foodservice operator may radically change as a result of this trend. In the in-flight sector, for instance, food manufacturers such as Delta Daily Foods in The Netherlands are marketing 'food components' that can be 'assembled' in dishes by in-flight caterers almost in the same way that items are laid up on a tray. Likewise frozen meals, produced in a specialist factory by a frozen food manufacturer, are likely to replace the chilled meals previously produced in the flight kitchen. Some experts are predicting that only first-class airline meals will continue to be produced by in-flight caterers, and that all other meals will simply be assembled from items supplied by manufacturers.

SUMMARY

Procurement is concerned with the flow of materials *into* the operation; while control monitors their flow *within* the operation. These systems exist to ensure the operation does not have stock shortages or hold too much stock, prevent wastage of materials and monitor operational performance. Depending on the type of operation, such systems may be formal or informal. The volume, variety and value of stock items is a major influence on supplier selection, as well as helping to determine the nature of the procurement and production control systems. Good practice is concerned with effective supplier relationships and negotiations; stockholding as low as possible (although this may not be possible in some locations or for some types of goods); and suitable production controls for the type of production kitchen (see Chapter 11).

CASE STUDY: BIGFOOT AND SUPPLIERS

Bourdain (2001, p. 87), in his highly personal account of life as a chef in New York, recounts many of the acts of downright malpractice perpetrated by restaurant suppliers. His hero 'Bigfoot' was adept at handling such issues:

> Nothing made him happier than discovering fraud, deception or even a simple white lie. Once, after years of ordering shrimp from a reputable seafood purveyor, Bigfoot discovered a hastily applied label indicating net weight. When it peeled off, he realised the company had, for years, been printing their own fake labels – cheating him out of a few ounces of shrimp every five pounds.

Bigfoot's response was to take a polaroid photo of the incriminating label and send it to the supplier instead of payment for his next order, and likewise thereafter for nearly a year! In the UK it is probably best if the local Trading Standards Officer were informed.

Bigfoot also paid his suppliers on time – 'an unusual thing to do in [the New York restaurant] business ... Given this, pity the poor soul who sent Bigfoot a second-best piece of swordfish [or any other commodity].' Bourdain goes on to show how he would phone his supplier in these circumstances and demand immediate restitution. Likewise Bigfoot would weigh, count and record every delivery without fail.

Further study

Two possible sources of supply for a small catering operation are the supermarket and the cash-and-carry warehouse. What are the advantages and disadvantages of these two sources of supply?

Bibliography

Bourdain, A. (2001) *Kitchen Confidential: Adventures in the Culinary Underbelly*. London: Bloomsbury.

Jones, P. (ed.) (1990) *Restaurant and Foodservice Management*. Halifax, NS: Mount Saint Vincent University, Open Learning Programme.

Reid, R. and Reigel, C. (1988) 'Foodservice purchasing: corporate practices', *Cornell Hotel and Restaurant Administration Quarterly*, May, 25–9.

Turner, Michael (1991) *Food and Beverage Management*. London: Hotel and Catering International Management Association.

Recommended further reading

Davis, B., Lockwood, A. and Stone, S. (1998) *Food and Beverage Management*. Oxford: Butterworth-Heinemann, chapters 7, 9, 13–16.

Dittmer, P. R. and Griffin, G. G. (1999) *Principles of Food, Beverage and Labor Cost Control*, New York: John Wiley & Sons, sixth edition.

Stores

After completing this chapter you will be able to:

- *identify the two main purposes of the stores system*
- *describe how different types of materials need to be stored*
- *describe the layout and design of loading bays, dry stores, refrigeration units and cellars*
- *explain four key storage processes*
- *identify current trends in storage.*

INTRODUCTION

All operations that process materials have areas designated for the reception and storage of their inputs or 'raw materials'. In the hospitality industry, there are storage areas to support a wide range of operational systems – food production, food service, housekeeping, front office and administration. Depending on the size of the operation, the 'stores' may be a primary system, that is to say a separate designated area for the storage of materials, or a subsystem of the other systems, such as store cupboards and refrigerators in the kitchen, or shelving and coolers in the bar. This chapter looks at storage as a primary system.

For many years, the stores has been overlooked as a system. Lawson (1978) explains, 'stores tend to be regarded as non-revenue-producing areas, and consequently are reduced to the minimum [in size]'. But as he points out, inadequate or unsuitable storage may result in poor control of stock and stock rotation, pilferage, food deterioration and abuses of foodstuffs. It is therefore essential to have infrastructure of the right size and design (the 'transformational inputs'), as well as proper processing procedures.

PURPOSE OF SYSTEM

Storage is clearly a materials processing operation, along with the information processing required to support the system. Storage can be defined as the physical holding and handling of all products and materials necessary for the successful operation of the business. As well as providing an appropriate space in which physically to locate goods, the stores function has two main purposes.

The first is to ensure materials are available when needed by the systems that require stored goods as inputs. This requires two main processes to be carried out. The first of these is the purchasing process, which ensures the right level of stock is held (as discussed in the previous chapter). The second process is the storing process itself, which is designed to ensure that each particular type of material is held under the best possible conditions.

The second purpose is to ensure that storage adds value to the business. There is no point in operating a system that does not do this. But value is not the same as profit. So while the stores function may be a cost to the business, this needs to be offset by the value of holding stock so that other parts of the business can be profitable. Certainly, the stores function must be operated so that it is not unnecessarily costly. Purchasing the right amount of materials and storing them correctly helps in this. But the stores must also control the flow of outputs. So the stores also has a control system designed to monitor the flow of outputs, establish stock levels and ensure there is no pilferage, fraud or theft.

It is clear from this overview of the purpose of the system that successful stores performance can be measured by:

- overall value of stock held

- comparison of stock ordered with stock used, commonly known as the stocktaking process

- monitoring storage conditions against set standards, such as temperatures of storage areas etc.

- continuity of supply.

GENERIC SYSTEM CHARACTERISTICS

A systems diagram of the storage function is illustrated in Figure 4.1. The inputs are comprised of those materials that may be needed by the operation. These vary widely in type, and are typically considered as consumables and non-consumables. The former includes all those materials that are literally 'consumed', i.e. eaten or drunk by customers (or staff). All food and drink items fall into in this category. Non-consumables include all other types of materials, such as cleaning agents, stationery and small-scale equipment.

The storage of non-consumables is relatively straightforward, as they typically may be stored under normal conditions, at ambient temperature. Some cleaning agents must be stored in well-ventilated areas to avoid the build-up of toxic fumes and kept separate from others to avoid the possibility of a chemical reaction.

Consumables, on the other hand, may require a variety of different storage conditions depending on their perishability or 'shelf-life', i.e. the length of time they may be stored safely without deterioration. Dry goods, such as canned foods, packet items and jars, are stored like non-consumables, under ambient or cool, well-ventilated conditions. Perishable items such as dairy products, fresh meat and

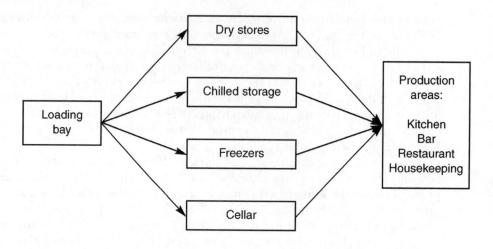

Figure 4.1 *Storage system*

fish, and fruit and vegetables need to be refrigerated. Chilling reduces enzyme action and bacterial growth, which either cause the food to deteriorate or allow pathogens or poisons to grow on the food, or both. Frozen products obviously have to be kept in a freezer.

Figure 4.1 also shows that the transformation infrastructure is made up of two main areas, comprising the space needed to receive goods, such as a loading bay, and the designated space for the physical storage of materials. The three key processes in the system are the receiving process, stores maintenance process and the materials issuing process.

In general terms, the outputs are the same as the inputs except for one difference. Goods inwards are usually purchased in bulk, whereas they are issued to receiving departments broken down into appropriate order sizes.

SYSTEM TYPES

Storage is clearly a back-of-house activity. Storage areas are usually located away from front-of-house, near to an entrance into the building, with good access for vehicles such as vans and trucks.

The size of receiving and storage areas is determined by the scale of the operation, often measured in terms of the number of covers served, the type of operation (in terms of the operational processes and technology in use) and the frequency of delivery. Thus a fast-food restaurant may have a smaller storage area than a 60-cover à la carte restaurant, because although it serves many more customers per day, the fast-food restaurant has a limited range of pre-prepared foodstuffs delivered daily, whereas the restaurant receives deliveries of a wider product range of fresh foods once or twice a week.

Subsystem 1: the receiving dock or loading bay

Not all operations have a designated receiving area. There may be just a back door into a corridor leading to the stores or kitchen. But assuming the scale of the operation justifies it, the minimum requirement for such an area is floor or counter space for the temporary storing of items, along with equipment such as scales for checking items and trolleys for moving goods.

In larger operations, there may be a proper loading bay. This would consist of an exterior raised platform so that trolleys could be wheeled off lorries directly (see the Abela Flight Catering case study in this chapter). The provision of this platform often depends on the building design and its location. It should be approximately 2.5 m deep, to allow palleted goods to be unloaded, and a minimum of 3 m wide, assuming only one lorry delivers at a time. As this is an access point for large vehicles, it is common practice to store large-scale waste adjacent to the dock for collection by lorry (see Chapter 6). Table 4.1 illustrates the size and scale of a receiving dock or loading bay.

The platform should be covered to protect goods and employees from the weather and well lit to ensure safe handling. The entrance should have some form of screening, such as an air strip or electronic opening, to prevent insects and other unwanted items from entering the premises. Other desirable features include a window overlooking the area from an administrative office for control and security purposes; and a completely separate employee entrance for safety and security reasons.

Subsystem 2: alternative forms of physical storage

As we have seen, the nature of the stored materials may include non-consumables, dry goods, perishable and frozen. Hence there are a wide range of different physical storage systems.

Type of operation	sq. ft.	Space needed sq. m.
Fast food	40–60	3.7–5.6
Restaurants		
200–300 meals/day	50–60	4.6–5.6
300–500 meals/day	60–90	5.6–8.4
500–1,000 meals/day	90–130	8.4–11.9
Institutions		
300–1,000 meals/day	80–100	7.4–9.3
1,000–2,000 meals/day	120–150	11.1–13.9
over 2,000 meals/day	150–175	13.9–16.3
Large hotel with extensive F&B	175–200	16.3–18.6
Health care facilities		
up to 50 beds	50	4.6
50–100 beds	50–80	4.6–7.4
100–200 beds	80–130	7.4–11.9
200–400 beds	130–175	11.9–16.3

Table 4.1 *Loading bay* (adapted from Scriven and Stevens, 1999, and Birchfield, 1988)

Dry stores

There are three main ways in which dry goods, either consumables or non-consumables, may be stored: shelved, binned or palletized.

Shelving is used for items that are individually packed in some way, such as packets, jars or cans. There are three types of shelving. Fixed shelving is permanently fixed to the wall or floor; static shelving is self-standing on legs; and mobile shelving is self-standing but on wheels or castors. All types of shelving are made either from wood or metal, sometimes covered with plastic. It is important that these materials can be easily cleaned.

Bins are used to store items that may be delivered in paper or cardboard containers but need to be protected from infestation either by insects or rodents. Typically flour and rice are stored in this way. The bin comprises a large metal container, often on castors, with a firmly fitting lid. The term 'bin' is also used to describe how bottled wine is stored.

Palletized storage occurs in very large-scale operations, such as in-flight catering. A pallet is a wooden platform that can easily be moved by a fork-lift truck on which goods are stored in bulk, usually in boxes or cases. Very large quantities of items can be stored in this way, in a stores area that resembles a warehouse.

Table 4.2 illustrates the size of dry stores in different types of foodservice operation.

Refrigeration

Chillers are designed to hold stored materials at a temperature of between 1°C and 3°C, whereas freezers hold frozen goods at a temperature of −20°C.

There are two main types of chiller or freezer unit used for storage (other units,

Type of operation	sq. ft.	Space needed sq. m.
Fast food	50–125	4.6–11.6
Restaurants		
200–300 meals/day	200–250	18.6–23.2
300–500 meals/day	250–400	23.2–37.2
500–1,000 meals/day	400–1,000	37.2–93.0
Institutions		
300–1,000 meals/day	200–300	18.6–27.9
1,000–2,000 meals/day	400–1,000	37.2–93.0
over 2,000 meals/day	1,000–2,500	93.0–232.5
Large hotel with extensive F&B	3,000+	279.0+
Health care facilities		
up to 50 beds	150–225	13.8–20.9
100 beds	250–300	23.2–27.9
400 beds	700–900	65.1–83.7

Table 4.2 Dry stores (adapted from Scriven and Stevens, 1999, and Birchfield, 1988).

such as display chillers and coolers, are discussed elsewhere) – self-standing cabinets or walk-in. **Cabinet chillers** or **freezers** have a front opening door with interior shelving. They are versatile since they can be located anywhere in the storage area (of the food production unit) and are relatively low cost to buy and maintain. Typically they have either one, two or three compartments, each with its own door. The 'net capacity', i.e. usable interior space, is typically 21.5 cu. ft (0.6 cu. m) for a single compartment chiller, 46.5 cu. ft (1.3 cu. m) for a double-door unit, and 70 cu. ft (2 cu. m) for a three-door. This net capacity tends to ignore the unusable space within the chiller that is taken up by lights, fitments, evaporators, tray slides, and so on.

Walk-in chillers or **freezers** are usually made from urathene foam, 10 cm thick, sandwiched between two sheets of metal such as unpainted or painted aluminium or steel or stainless steel. Units are either prefabricated from panels of standard sizes or built in situ. Prefabricated units are less costly to install than purpose-built chillers, but the latter may have a longer working life. The refrigeration system, which comprises a condenser, evaporator and expansion valve, may be mounted on top of the unit (if ceiling height permits), or on the side; or remotely, in some other area of the building or the exterior. Remote refrigeration systems are less efficient but have the advantage that the heat and noise of the system is located away from the working area.

A third type of freezer is the so-called **'chest' freezer**. Chest freezers are large containers with a lid that opens on a hinge at the top. They are an older design than cabinet units and cheaper to manufacture. Items should be stored in baskets that fit inside the freezer to allow easy access to items lower down. The major problem with this design is the difficulty of accessing items, which impedes both stock turnover and stocktaking.

The net capacity of a walk-in unit is considerably less (roughly 50 per cent) than its total cubic capacity, as space has to be left for a person to access stored items. This usually means that items are stored on either side of the chiller, with an aisle running down the middle from the door to the back of the unit. Further space may also be rendered unusable due to fans, evaporators, lights, and so on. Despite this, large walk-in chillers are considerably cheaper to operate than several cabinet chillers. Borsenik and Stutts (1997) cite an example of one walk-in that while it stores 900 kg of food, the equivalent of five single-compartment cabinet chillers, is over eight times less expensive to operate.

In planning the amount of refrigeration needed it is usual to take into account the combined amount of chilled and frozen capacity required. The total will be based on the scale of the operation, the frequency of supply and the sales mix; whereas the balance between chilled and frozen capacity depends on the menu, purchasing policy, style of operation and nature of raw materials. A rule of thumb is that 1 cu. ft of space will hold 25 lb of food and that a casual dining restaurant will require 1 to 1.5 cu. ft, whereas a fine dining restaurant may require up to 5 cu. ft (Katsigris and Thomas, 1999). So for a casual dining operation that serves 100 covers a day, with deliveries every two days, the refrigeration capacity needs to be:

100 (covers) × 1.5 cu. ft = 150 cu. ft

150 cu. ft × 2 (days' storage) = 300 cu. ft

300 cu. ft × 2 (net capacity is 50 per cent) = 600 cu. ft

600 cu. ft + 25 per cent (spare capacity) = 750 cu. ft

| Size of operation (seats) | Walk-in | | | | Cabinet | | | |
| | FREEZER | | CHILLER | | FREEZER | | CHILLER | |
	Number	Size*	Number	Size*	Number	Size	Number	Size
Under 50	0		0		1	2 door	2	2 door
50–100	1	9×12	1	9×12	1	3 door	3	2 door
100–175	1	9×15	2	9×12	2	2 door	3	3 door
175–250	1	9×20	2	9×15	2	2 door	3	3 door
250–500	1	9×20	3	9×15	2	3 door	4	3 door
500–750	2	9×15	3	9×20	2	3 door	5	3 door
More than 500	2	9×20	4	9×20	3	3 door	5	3 door

Table 4.3 *Refrigeration* (adapted from Ley, 1980)
* sq. ft

Table 4.3 provides a rough guide of the refrigeration needs for different sizes of operation.

The efficiency of operating and maintaining refrigerated storage is affected by many factors:

- Amount of insulation. Over time, door seals and rubber 'grommets' may wear and lead to tiny but continuous leaks.

- Efficiency of air flow. Fans assist air flow to ensure a consistent temperature throughout the unit.

- Items stored in the unit. Any item placed in the unit that is above the temperature of the refrigerated space will raise the overall temperature in the unit.

- Number of doors and frequency of opening. Normal usage is assumed to be six to eight openings per eight hour shift. Heavy usage (12 openings or more) increases the heat load by 50 per cent (Borsenik and Stutts, 1997). If units are subject to heavy usage, plastic strip doors may reduce heat gain by up to one-third.

- Surrounding environment. Refrigeration should not be placed near sources of heat, including direct sunlight. Energy savings can be achieved if walk-in chillers and/or freezers are located adjacent to each other (by 6 per cent according to Borsenik and Stutts, 1997) or if access to the freezer is through the chiller (by nearly 19 per cent).

- Efficiency of the evaporator. As this is cold, air moisture will freeze on it making it less efficient. Most units have an automatic facility that defrosts this component every 12 hours, either using a hot gas defrost system or electric resistance wires.

Additional features of refrigeration units may include:

- self-closing, cam-lift door hinges – most doors will be self-closing to prevent heat gain, but the cam-lift allows the door to stay open if it is opened past a 90 degree angle

- door ramp to allow trolleys to be wheeled in and out of the unit

- internal door opener so no one can be locked in the unit by mistake (or otherwise!)

- foot pedal door opener to allow a person carrying an item in both hands to access the unit

- freezer alarm system that activates if the interior temperature rises above $-10°C$

- wall protectors to prevent damage by trolleys

- air vent to relieve pressure when doors are opened or closed.

Cellar

A cellar is typically thought of as a storage area below ground. Historically they were built in this way so that food and drink items could be stored under consistently cool conditions irrespective of the outside temperature. Nowadays, the availability of coolers and air conditioning means that a cellar does not have to be built below ground level. All alcoholic drinks may be stored in the cellar for security reasons, but fortified wines, such as sherry and vermouth, and spirits, such as whisky and gin, may be stored in a highly secure dry store, as they do not require cool temperatures.

Cellars, like other storage areas, should have washable or wipeable walls and ceilings. Floors should be scrubbed to kill fungus or mould regularly, but not using a chemical agent such as bleach or disinfectant, as these may contaminate the stored items. Ventilation is important not only to help prevent damp and fungoid problems, but also to vent any CO_2 (carbon dioxide) build-up from any leaking gas cylinders (used to pump beer from kegs in the cellar to the bar).

SYSTEM PROCESSES

The stores is just one part of the total operation. Its processes are part of the operation's control system, as described in Chapter 3 (this is an example of simultaneous multiple containment).

Receipt of goods inwards

We identified that larger operations typically have a loading bay, equipped with scales etc., for the receipt of goods. Whether this exists or not, it is essential that goods are inspected at the time of delivery in order to ensure that:

- goods delivered match the quantity of goods ordered

- goods delivered match the quality specification

- prices charged match the quoted prices (if accompanied by an invoice – see below)

- there is no opportunity for malpractice by the delivery person.

To enable the stores person to keep abreast of all this, they may be provided with copies of purchase specifications (often in the form of a manual), copies of the original order, price lists, scales (to weigh goods), temperature probes (for checking refrigerated items), a calculator, a jemmy (for opening wooden or cardboard containers), a knife (for cutting into fresh produce such as fruit) and even a bar code reader (if there is a computerized inventory control system). And so that the stores person has enough time to inspect the goods properly, supply is often organized so that deliveries are only made during specified hours and staggered to ensure only one is dealt with at a time.

The paperwork or documentation that accompanies a delivery is typically of two types. In some cases, goods are delivered with an **invoice** which not only lists the goods but also prices them; in other words, it serves not only as a checklist but also as the bill. In other cases, the order is supplied along with a **delivery note**, which is an unpriced list of goods. In such cases, the supplier issues an invoice separately, sometimes on a weekly or monthly basis, often covering more than one delivery. Whichever system is in use, the stores person will be asked to sign a copy for the receipt of the goods. If they are not satisfied that goods of the correct type or quality have been delivered, they may be rejected. This may mean that the delivery note is adjusted to show goods as returned, or, in the case of invoiced delivery, a credit note will be completed by the delivery person to ensure correct invoicing subsequently.

Once goods have been received and the paperwork completed, it is essential that goods are moved to their appropriate storage space as soon as possible. Depending on the size of operation, trolleys, carts, conveyor belts or fork-lift trucks may be used for this purpose. Swift transportation ensures that goods, especially chilled or frozen products, do not deteriorate and that they are placed in a more secure area than the loading bay. In some cases, at this stage, the stores person may also have to date the delivered items (to ensure stock rotation), price items, apply tags to meat or even add bar codes.

While it is regrettable, malpractice at this stage is not unknown. There are a great many ways in which fraud or theft can be carried out by an unscrupulous supplier or dishonest delivery person. A skilled stores operative should check to see that:

- the quality of goods, such as fresh fruit, is as good in all the layers of a box, and not rely on inspecting just the top layer

- tins and packages are not damaged or 'blown'

- product weights have not been increased by adding excess water, packaging, ice, etc. (for example, stones in bags of fresh potatoes)

- the delivery person does not illicitly remove items from the loading bay or stores area, especially when goods or packaging (such as empty beer barrels) are being returned.

Of course, some problems may be the result of an unintentional error. Where such problems occur regularly or malpractice is discovered, management are well advised to change the supplier.

Safe and secure storage

The basic aim of the storage system is to ensure no loss of value in goods purchased. Such losses may be of two types, spoilage or theft.

Spoilage can be prevented by adherence to the following basic principles:

- Stock rotation – goods are used in sequence, older items first, to ensure they are consumed while still in prime condition.

- Stock separation – goods that might contaminate each other, even if just by odours (such as fish tainting dairy products), must be stored separately, if not in their own fridge, at least in sealed containers on separate shelves.

- Sanitation – to avoid cross-contamination, the stores area must be kept clean and the stores operative must comply with good hygiene practices.

- Temperature monitoring – the temperature in each main type of storage area (ambient, chilled and frozen) must be monitored to ensure it is maintained correctly, and if a fault is detected it must be repaired immediately.

- Safe handling – items must be handled and transported safely to avoid breakages.

- Prevention of infestation – insects and rodents must be prevented from entering storage areas through the maintenance of floors, walls and ceilings, the closures and screens on windows and doors, and specific equipment such as ultraviolet fly killers.

The **security** of goods may be threatened by anyone who gains access to the stores. The best way to ensure good security is to employ honest workers, select honest suppliers and design the physical storage area to be totally secure. In most cases, further control systems are put in place in order to deter, prevent or detect dishonest practice (as well as aid financial control of the business and prevent spoilage). Security systems include:

- Bin cards – it should be clear from the previous discussion that stock is not simply ordered at random. Nor is it stored at random. It is quite common, especially in operations that have standard requirements, for goods routinely to be placed in the same shelf location in the dry store, chiller or freezer. In some cases, the shelf may be labelled with that item. This makes it easy to remember where to find things and to take stock. In operations that require a 'perpetual inventory' to be kept, bin cards may be used. Such a card is kept at the storage point of each stock item. It records when and how many items were added to stock (and price if known), and when and how many items were issued. While it is time-consuming to amend bin cards, they do provide a way of controlling stock movements and afford documentary evidence of what the stock level is at any given moment. Nowadays, this system tends to be used only in cellars, for the control of wines and liquor. The computerization of inventory control, linked to bar codes, has also made it possible to have a 'perpetual inventory' without bin cards.

- Stocktaking – this is the physical alternative to perpetual inventory, namely a physical count of all stock items on a regular basis. Its main purpose is to calculate the cost of raw materials (i.e. stock at last stocktake + purchases –

stock at this stocktake = stock consumed). It also provides information about what needs to be ordered and enables a cross-check against bin cards and budgets. Physically taking stock can be time-consuming and labour intensive. It typically involves one person counting the stock while a second person records the information on a standard stock record form. Hence operators have to choose between their need for timely and accurate stock information and the cost of collecting the data. It is usually done at least once a month, and more frequently in high-volume operations or for high-value stock items.

- Locks and keys – another obvious security measure is to ensure goods are stored in a space that is locked when not in use. In many cases, goods are only issued from stores at limited times of the day, for example first thing in the morning and mid-afternoon. This is so that they can be kept secure for the rest of the day. Only authorized individuals should be issued with keys, and locks should be replaced if keys go missing. For a higher level of security, it is now possible to install computerized locks that record who used the lock.

- Rubbish compactors – storage areas produce a large amount of paper waste in the form of cardboard boxes and packaging materials. In order to prevent the 'scam' of items being stolen secreted in waste bins and then retrieved once the bins have been placed outside the premises, a waste compactor may be used. They also facilitate waste handling and recycling (see also Chapter 6).

- Employee entrance security – all hospitality operations should have a single entrance for use by employees. In larger operations, this entrance may be staffed by a member of the security team, whose role is to ensure only authorized personnel are allowed access to the building, as well as monitor what is being brought into or taken out of the premises.

- Premises surveillance – while access to the storage area should always be limited and controlled, a further deterrent is provided by the use of closed-circuit television (CCTV). This provides a 24-hour record of all personnel movements.

- Separation of ordering from payment – since there are a number of ways in which a person responsible for ordering goods could dishonestly collude with a supplier, it is usual for those employees to have no responsibility for paying invoices. Payment is typically assigned to the control or accounts department, part of whose role is to monitor supply procedures.

Issuing stock

In small operations, the storage area is part of the production area, so that all stock is 'in-process'. In larger operations, with separate stores, the stock is held until required by the production departments. This issuing process needs to be controlled to facilitate ordering, stockholding, cost allocation and financial control.

Usually stock is issued on the basis of a requisition form from the receiving department, signed by an authorized person, such as the Head Chef, Bars Manager or Head Housekeeper. Requisitions may be general purpose or designed for specific purposes or departments. At some stage the requisition will be priced – either by the storekeeper when the goods are issued, or more probably by the control office when it receives its copy.

In some cases stocks are issued without a requisition. These 'par stocks' are a standard list of items that are routinely issued, used and the unused stock returned, usually on the same day. This happens everyday in hotels when room attendants' trolleys are prepared with a par stock of cleaning materials. It may also be how temporary bars, in banqueting and outdoor catering, are stocked.

Stock valuation and stocktaking

The main technique for measuring food and beverage costs is the valuation of stocks and purchases. The choice of valuation method, particularly in times of rapid inflation, can have significant implications for profit and asset reporting. There are four textbook methods of stock valuation, which can be summarized as:

- FIFO (first-in first out) – which tends to give the highest value to stocks and to inflate profits.

- LIFO (last-in first out) – which tends to undervalue stocks, with a more realistic profit valuation.

- AVERAGE – which tends to overvalue stocks and consequently overstates profit. It has the advantage of being administratively convenient.

- STANDARD – which is a sophisticated technique forming the basis for a comprehensive cost control system.

These stock valuation methods can all be used for the valuation of issues from stores. The use of any one of these methods facilitates the preparation of a stores reconciliation which will accurately identify any loss (possibly through pilferage) from the stores. Computer-based stock control systems may utilize one or another of these methods. However, if used in manual stores issue systems, they present a burdensome administrative task.

There is an alternative method of stock valuation that is administratively far simpler, and is commonly used in many foodservice businesses. This involves valuing stock using the most recent price paid for a commodity – also known as the current price. However, this method has a significant disadvantage, namely that it does not permit an accurate stores reconciliation to be prepared. Thus, managers can choose a more complex method of stock valuation that permits accurate measurement of stores losses, or a simpler (and cheaper) method of valuation and forfeit an accurate control over the stores.

All businesses need to measure the costs of commodities accurately on this basis at least once a year, for the purpose of preparing annual accounts. The most widely used approach is the 'opening stock, plus issues, minus closing stock' model used for the purpose of profit measurement. Physical stocktaking of this type is usually done by a firm of external stocktakers, but this may cost a business up to several hundred pounds for the production of one stocktaking result. Apart from the production of annual accounts, almost all businesses produce a periodic operating statement, usually on a four-weekly basis, which, of course, requires the measurement of food and beverage costs. Production of accurate consumption figures, based on stocktaking results, has a high cost of control, particularly when external stocktakers are employed. Frequent external stocktaking is usually only considered necessary in chain operations when turnover is very high and the chance of fraud is considerable: for example, in managed pubs and travel catering. An alternative option for chain operations, where the possibilities of local fraud are less significant, is to get local management to undertake periodic stocktakes, with an annual or six-monthly validation by external stocktakers. Large single-unit catering operations will often have their own food and beverage control department, which undertakes periodic stocktakes, sometimes with the co-operation of other staff.

Investigating stock control problems

Stocktaking serves a number of purposes. First, it establishes the value of stock according to one of the methods described above. Usually there will be some target stock value based on the level of sales turnover. This ratio aims to ensure that there are no stock-outs, while also keeping the stock 'investment costs' to a minimum. This is often expressed as the number of days' stock held on average, i.e. sales revenue for the stocktake period divided by the average of the opening stock value plus closing stock value. Second, the level of stock turnover can be established by analysing categories of foodstuffs or single items. This ensures that within the overall target stock level, the different levels of sales for items is recognized. Slow-moving items can be identified and appropriate action taken – either by returning them to the supplier or using them up in 'specials' and modifying the menu as part of the menu analysis process. Finally, stocktaking compares the actual value of the stock held with the value of the stock calculated from the stock record system. This enables the actual food cost or gross profit percentage to be established for comparison with the target, if necessary. In the event that stocktaking reveals a discrepancy between the stock records and actual stock held, this is deemed a usage variance. If there is a discrepancy between target food cost and actual food cost, but no physical stock discrepancy, this is likely to be a policy variance or production control problem. The manager needs to carry out a systematic investigation of the causes of the problem.

In this section we shall review the causes of physical stock discrepancies and what to do about them. Stock shortages may be due to 'ghost' supplies, poor stock rotation, breakages or ullage, theft or unauthorized consumption on the premises. In fact there are so many different ways in which usage variances may occur that we can deal only with the most frequent causes here. So-called **'ghost' supplies** refers to goods for which the operator is charged but which are never received. This can occur in a number of ways: the supplier can supply the correct stock but overcharge, the supplier may charge the correct price but under supply, the delivery person can deliver less than the full order or substitute inferior goods for those specified. **Poor stock rotation** leads to waste, as perishable items may deteriorate before they are used and tins or jars may be retained beyond their 'use-by date'. New deliveries should always be stored behind existing stocks to ensure the older items are used first. **Breakages** also create losses. Management should ensure that staff are trained in the safe handling of materials and that the proper equipment is provided for transporting items. Obviously, if goods are stolen there will be a stock discrepancy. **Theft** may be carried out by trespassers on the premises, who do not have authorization to be there, or by dishonest employees. Employees in particular, may engage in one specific form of theft, namely **unauthorized consumption**, i.e. eating or drinking items that have not been provided for them.

SYSTEM ADOPTION

As discussed at the beginning of the chapter, for an operation to designate a storage area as a primary system it needs to be sufficiently large to justify its establishment, use of space and staffing.

CASE STUDY: LITTLE CHEF, A27, SUSSEX

Stand-alone restaurants provide good examples of storage, as they have to ensure adequate supply due to their isolated location. Compass Roadside operations made up of Little Chef table service restaurants and Burger King fast-food outlets are prime examples of this type of operation in the UK. The Little Chef on the A27 in Sussex is two miles from the nearest town, situated in a large detached property originally built as a pub and used as a steakhouse restaurant in the 1980s. Thus the unit contains a relatively large amount of space back-of-house compared with purpose-built Little Chefs. There is no loading bay at the rear, as there are only two deliveries a week, all stacked on one or two pallets.

The storage area comprises a dry store, walk-in chiller, walk-in freezer and various storage cabinets located in the food production area. The dry store is 3 m by 2.5 m in size and 15 cu. m in capacity. This is small for the number of meals served per day, but a high proportion of materials used in this type of operation are pre-prepared chilled or frozen foods. The dry store is equipped with laminated wooden shelving 54 cm deep. Most items stored here are canned (such as soup, fruit and baby food), bottled (such as juices, water and sauces) and packet items (such as cereals, salt and custard). The walk-in chiller and walk-in freezer are connected, with access to the latter through the chiller. The chiller is 2.5 m by 1.4 m, while the freezer is slight deeper (2.5 by 1.60 m). Total cubic capacity is 15 cu. m. Both are equipped with metal wire shelving, allowing the air to circulate. The bottom shelf is just 12 cm off the floor, with three further shelves each 40 cm apart. The chiller is used for the storage of fresh salad and vegetable items. The freezer stores meat, fish, frozen vegetables and bread. In addition to this fixed storage space, adjacent to the kitchen there are two self-standing cabinet refrigerators, one for desserts and the other for dairy items, as well as a chest freezer for ice creams. These have the standard capacity of 0.6 cu. m. Finally, there is also a large cleaning store, in which cleaning agents and cleaning equipment are kept. COSHH regulations are displayed on a notice board drawing staff's attention to the correct use of materials.

In such a small operation there is no stores person. The manager is responsible for all the stock. She or a colleague check all supplies as they are delivered to the back door before they are stored in the appropriate location. A company checklist detailing the shelf-life of all items is on display back-of-house. All team members have access to the stores. Only if the unit is experiencing stock loss problems will the manager institute issuing controls. Most main course items are pre-portioned, so production control is simplified. Loose items, such as baked beans and frozen French fries, have to be portioned by the team members and these cause the most stock variation.

CASE STUDY: ABELA FLIGHT CATERING, HEATHROW

In some industry segments the stores may be very large indeed, reflecting the large-scale nature of the operation. Many hospitals and school meals services now operate with a cook-chill system (see Chapter 9), producing meals in bulk for as many as 5,000 customers a day. In-flight production kitchens may be even larger, providing up to 20,000 trayed meals per day. The Abela unit at Heathrow averages 16,000 meals a week. The stores area comprises four main sections – the receiving dock (loading bay), dry stores and bonded store on the first floor, and production stores on the ground floor.

The receiving dock is 6 m by 12 m, with space for one vehicle to unload. There is an office for the Receiving Clerk, a temporary chilled storage area of 60 sq. m and a dry store of 220 sq. m. All goods are checked and weighed on arrival, then transported directly to the main stores or production stores. They are only stored in the temporary storage if capacity is unavailable elsewhere. All fresh produce arriving at the dock is taken directly to the production stores on the same floor. There are two 300 cu. m capacity freezers for frozen goods, and three 200 cu. m chillers for fresh vegetables, dairy produce and meat.

The dry stores and bonded store are approximately 800 sq. m, with the latter taking up one-third of the total space. Most goods are stored in bulk on pallets and moved by fork-lift truck. There are two 250 cu. m freezers for holding frozen foods in this main store. A feature of a flight catering unit is the bonded store. This is an area for stock items, mainly alcohol, cigarettes and perfume, on which no British sales tax (i.e. VAT) will be paid, as they will be served or sold to airline passengers as duty-free items. This area has to be physically separated from the other stores and be totally secure. British customs and excise officers can inspect the bonded stores at any time. At Abela there are three shelves, the top and ground level shelves hold pallets, while the middle shelf is set aside for individual stock items. These are arranged by airline rather than item, as in effect the stock is owned by the airline and Abela is merely providing warehousing for it. Stocktaking is carried out by Abela at least once a month, and may also be carried out by any of the airlines at any time.

Abela has approximately 120 separate suppliers, ranging from mainstream bulk suppliers of dry goods to specialist suppliers of ethnic speciality foods. In some cases the airlines nominate suppliers of specific items. As menus may change once a month for each of the different airlines, items are not stocked to par. There may be as many as 4,000 separate commodity items stored. A total of 18 staff are employed in the stores function.

CURRENT TRENDS AND ISSUES AFFECTING SYSTEM

The three major factors affecting the storage of materials have been technological, legislative and environmental.

Technological trends

Over the last hundred years, extending the shelf-life of perishable items has been a major concern of the food industry in general. Bottling, canning and vacuum-packing are all ways of preserving food anaerobically (without air). An alternative is to chill or freeze them, so that bacteria cannot grow. These methods may be combined together, along with other processes such as heat treatment, radiation or pasteurization that are designed to remove any bacteriological contamination.

As well as preserving fresh foods, alternative products have been developed that simplify storage and reduce labour in the kitchen. This usually involves creating a powder of some kind which can be rehydrated with water or some other liquid in order to make a soup or sauce. There has also been a shift from preserving foodstuffs in more or less their raw state towards preparing them as meal items ready for sale. Many catering operations now buy in complete dishes directly from a supplier rather than prepare them fresh on their own premises.

Legislative issues

All hospitality operators have a duty of care to both their customers and employees.

As far as customers are concerned, the storage of materials must ensure that these materials are not contaminated in any way. With respect to employees, the storage area must be set up and maintained so that it complies with the Health and Safety at Work Act.

Refrigeration and the environment

Many hospitality businesses throughout the world are still using refrigeration systems that predate the new generation of CFC- and HCFC-free units, despite international initiatives and legal sanctions. Refrigerator coolants (and aerosols) used to emit chlorofluorocarbons (CFCs) into the atmosphere. These in turn release free chlorine far above the earth that ultimately attacks the protective ozone layer. Scientists have linked the resultant harmful ultraviolet rays with increases in the incidence of skin cancer. When it was first identified, the potential danger, was ignored due to the conflict of interest with industrial manufacturers. Only when scientists discovered the hole in the ozone layer did the world begin to wake up to the need for remedial action and that this could only be effective through inter-national partnership. The Montreal Protocol in 1987 committed 28 nations to begin phasing out the manufacture of CFCs.

Technological advances have produced alternatives to these hazardous chemicals that are cheaper and more efficient, and it is now a relatively easy task for main-tenance engineers to carry out the necessary conversion. As already noted, safe collection and disposal of the CFCs and HCFCs is essential to prevent the gases from escaping into the atmosphere. Clearly, when buying new refrigeration units or air-conditioning plant, managers should buy only CFC- and HCFC-free equipment. Energy savings of 10–50 per cent are possible with modern equipment.

SUMMARY

This chapter has looked at storage as primary system. It has identified it as mainly a materials processing operation, along with the information processing needed to operate the system effectively. Key performance aspects in this system are to hold the right value of stock to ensure continuity of supply but not excessive overhead costs, and to ensure the safe and secure holding of items to prevent contamination, waste and illicit acts. To achieve these goals, the stores person carries out processes associated with receiving goods, stocktaking and issuing goods.

The wide range of materials includes consumables and non-consumables, some of which may be perishable. This requires four main types of storage condition – dry stores, chilled, frozen and cellar. Each type of storage employs a variety of methods to provide the right conditions. Dry stores may have fixed, static or mobile shelving, bins or palletized containers. Refrigeration (chilled or frozen) may be contained in cabinet, reach-in or walk-in units.

Further study

Obtaining access to stores may be problematic. However, where it is possible to do so, compare and contrast the size and nature of storage areas in different types of restaurant operation.

Bibliography

Birchfield, J. C. (1988) *Design and Layout of Foodservice Facilities*. New York: Van Nostrand Reinhold.

Borsenik, F. D. and Stutts, A. T. (1997) *The Management of Maintenance and Engineering Systems in the Hospitality Industry*, New York: John Wiley & Sons.

Katsigris, C. and Thomas, C. (1999) *Design and Equipment for Restaurants and Foodservice*. New York: John Wiley & Sons.

Lawson, F. (1978) *Principles of Catering Design*. London: The Architectural Press.

Ley, S. (1980) *Foodservice Refrigeration*. New York: Van Nostrand Reinhold.

Scriven, C. and Stevens, J. (1989) *Manual of Equipment and Design for the Food Service Industry*. New York: Van Nostrand Reinhold.

Recommended further reading

Katsigris, C. and Thomas, C. (1999) *Design and Equipment for Restaurants and Foodservice*. New York: John Wiley & Sons.

CHAPTER 5
Maintenance and engineering

OBJECTIVES

After completing this chapter you will be able to:

- *identify the four main functions of the engineering system*

- *describe heating systems, ventilation systems, lighting and electrical service systems, waste water systems and swimming pools, building transportation systems and fire safety systems*

- *describe the work processes of hospitality maintenance engineers*

- *identify current trends in maintenance and engineering systems.*

INTRODUCTION

The average UK hotel costs £80,000 per bedroom to build, while a restaurant investment can vary between £100,000 up to £1 million. It is important therefore that this costly capital outlay is protected, by ensuring that the physical infrastructure is well maintained. Furthermore, both customers and staff expect the building to be habitable and serviceable. In developed countries we tend to take for granted our power supply, water and sewage system, and other technologies. These are present in our homes, offices, shops and factories, as well as in hotels and foodservice operations. As they tend to be so reliable, we often forget that they need to be managed and controlled. In the commercial context, the operations manager is not only concerned to ensure continuity of supply (i.e. no breakdowns, or threat to either people or the building) but also about the cost of provision and the environmental impact (see also Chapter 6).

Maintenance and energy costs are not an insignificant proportion of total operating costs in the industry. Borsenik and Stutts (1997) suggest that, on average, energy represents 4.4 per cent of operating cost and maintenance 5.3 per cent in American hotels and motels; while 3 per cent of sales is spent on energy and a further 3 per cent on maintenance in the US foodservice sector. However, energy consumption varies widely. For instance, they identify cafeterias and full menu restaurants as registering above-average energy consumption, limited menu restaurants and quick service restaurants as average, while coffee shops and pizza restaurants have lower than average consumption. This is in part due to the different uses energy is put to within each type of operation, such as food production, sanitation, refrigeration, lighting and heating/ventilation. It also reflects the geographic location of the unit, its siting (whether stand-alone or adjacent to other properties), the age of the building, scale of the operation and its opening hours.

PURPOSE OF SYSTEM

Maintenance and engineering systems are materials processing operations, along with the necessary information processing needed to support these systems. We identified in the Introduction to this chapter that hospitality operations should be 'habitable and serviceable'. In other words, they should have systems to:

- maintain a comfortable temperature

- provide adequate lighting

- deliver power and water

- remove waste

- ensure personal safety

- assist movement within the property (by having equipment such as lifts and escalators)

- ensure the correct functioning of equipment.

The engineering function has four main purposes. The first is to ensure continuity of supply. It is important that all these systems operate continuously. In some countries, this is not always easy. For instance, the electrical grid may shut down, thereby depriving hotels of power, so most have their own generator that kicks in when this happens. The second purpose is to ensure that these systems work properly. A systems failure has the potential to be catastrophic, for instance an electrical fault may cause a fire, or a burst pipe result in flooding. Third, the systems must work efficiently. Poorly controlled systems and poorly maintained equipment may result in higher than necessary energy costs. Finally, it is increasingly the case that energy consumption is an environmental issue, and systems need to be designed and managed in such a way that their impact is minimized.

It is clear from this overview of the purpose of maintenance and engineering systems that successful performance can be measured by:

- continued supply of power and other services necessary to deliver products and services to customers

- maintenance of a safe and healthy environment

- economic management of the physical infrastructure

- minimization of environmental impact.

GENERIC SYSTEM CHARACTERISTICS

To achieve the desired outputs of this system, there are three main 'inputs', that connect the hospitality operation with the environment. These are:

- one or more sources of power, e.g. electricity, gas, solar, etc.
- water supply
- drainage system.

These inputs are connected to several technological systems that are often inter-related. These typically include:

- A heating system
- A ventilation system
- A lighting and electrical service system
- Waste water system and swimming pool
- Building transportation system
- Fire safety system.

In this chapter we shall look at each of these six systems in turn.

SYSTEM TYPES

Heating systems

The heating system and its energy consumption will vary according to the geographic location of the property and the nature of its construction. Location is important in terms not only of the average overall temperature but also the level of variation in temperature both every 24 hours (the difference between day and night temperatures) and over the year. Building construction is important, as it can greatly affect both the loss of heat from the building if cold outside and the gain of heat from the exterior on a hot day. Different types of wall (brick, wood, etc.) and glass, plus their thickness, have different heat transmission coefficients. For example, a window made from a single thickness of glass transmits almost twice as much heat as one that is double-glazed (two panes of glass with an airspace between them). Another factor is the number of windows and doors in a building and the frequency with which they are opened. For instance, in a 'normal building' with a floor area of 100,000 sq. ft and windows in half the total wall space of 8,000 sq. ft, energy savings of 34 per cent can be achieved by reducing the windows down to only 1,000 sq. ft (Borsenik and Stutts, 1997).

Borsenik and Stutts suggest a number of factors that influence the selection of a particular heating system. These include fuel availability, fuel storage requirements, fuel conversion efficiency, system cost, heat recovery capability, temperature and moisture quality, labour implications (skills needed and costs) and hazard potential and insurance.

The basic components of a heating system are a heat plant, i.e. source of heat, and a heat transference system. This will be regulated by a control network of some kind.

Heat plants

There are a wide range of different heat plants depending on the type of fuel used. **Coal-fired furnaces** used to be quite common, but required someone to replenish them with coal and produced a fairly large amount of pollutants. Today it is possible to install coal stokers that mechanically feed coal and air into the combustion chamber, but it is still necessary to manually remove the clinker (i.e. residue of burnt coal). Another type of heat plant is fuelled by oil. There are several types of **oil-fired furnaces**, depending on the grade of oil used. These are much more efficient than coal-fired boilers, at around 87 per cent efficiency compared with 70 per cent. The third type of boiler is **gas-fired**. These have an efficency rating of about 80 per cent. Less common forms of heat plant are based on solar panels, heat pumps and geothermal sources. In some cases, furnaces are connected directly to a heat transference system and hence they are known as 'boilers'.

Heat transference systems

Heat can be transferred in four forms within a building – as hot water, steam, warm air or radiant heat. **Hot water systems** transfer heat through pipes to radiators, convectors or underfloor radiant systems. Although very common, this system has some disadvantages: it requires the water to be treated to minimize corrosion to the pipes, valves and pumps in the system, leaks can cause considerable damage, and it is more costly to maintain than some other systems. **Steam transference systems** are similar to hot water systems and are typically connected to radiators or convectors for in-room heating. The steam may also be used to heat hot water, via a heat exchanger, for bathrooms and kitchens. **Warm air distribution systems** have the advantage that they can also be used for air conditioning. Air is blown through ducts into rooms and removed via other exhaust ducts for recycling through the system. As well as being heated, the air can have moisture added to it in order to control humidity and it can be filtered to maintain air quality. The main disadvantage of this system is the space required for ducting and ensuring an adequate air flow to every room. Finally **radiant heat distribution systems** provide heat through heated wall or ceiling surfaces. While hot water or steam may be used as the heat source, most radiant systems are electric.

Heat control systems

The most common form of heat control is the **thermostat**. This operates locally by sensing the air temperature around it and switching on the heating system if the temperature is below the required level. Interior temperatures of buildings are typically maintained at between 65 and 68°F, but this may vary significantly if the thermostat is inaccurate. One degree variation in heat may increase heating costs by as much as 3 per cent (Borsenik and Stutts, 1997). In some cases, larger areas may be controlled by zone thermostats. In addition, sensors outside the building, known as anticipators, may measure the exterior temperature and override interior systems if it is rapidly warming outside. Increasingly, control is now **computerized**.

This enables not only thermostats, but also time switches, heat plant controls, ignition systems and safety devices to be interlinked. Such computerization enables greater central control over the heating system. For instance, hotel room thermostats may be set according to their letting status (i.e. sold or unsold) or their usage (i.e. occupied or unoccupied): heat plant efficiency may be monitored and adjustments made to fuel and air flow; water chemistry can be monitored in hot water or steam heat systems; maintenance may be scheduled; faults identified; and energy consumption managed. The latest generation of computerized controllers, or building energy management systems (BEMs), 'learn' from past activity about the performance of the building and are able to optimize the starting-up and shutting-down procedures of all elements of the heating and ventilation systems.

Ventilation systems

People's perception of air temperature is a function not only of how hot the air is but also the level of humidity (i.e. water content). A high humidity prevents the air absorbing sweat from the body, and hence increases the perceived temperature. A humidity level of 50 per cent is the most comfortable. Another effect is the rate of air movement – the greater the movement the lower the perceived temperature. An ideal air movement rate inside a building would be between 12 and 20 feet per minute. But ventilation is not only about the temperature, it is also about removing smells and pollutants, such as tobacco smoke, from the air that we breathe.

The simplest form of ventilation is achieved by opening an exterior window, allowing air to flow in from outside. However, most modern buildings have some kind of mechanical system for achieving air flow. These are of two kinds:

Air cooling systems

The simpler type is an air cooling system based around an evaporative cooler. Such systems simply reduce air temperature, either by blowing cool air or by increasing the water content of hot, dry air, or both.

Air conditioning

The more sophisticated approach is air conditioning, which not only cools air but may also heat, filter, humidify or dehumidify it. The typical air-conditioning system comprises filters, pre-heaters and pre-coolers, humidifiers and dehumidifiers, fans and system air supply.

There are many different types of **filter**, each of which is suitable for a different circumstance. A dry filter is essentially a disposable mesh or screen, typically made of fibre glass. While it removes larger air particles such as dust, it is ineffective at removing smells or smoke. In some cases, such filters may be treated with oil or chemicals to improve their effectiveness. In cases where the air needs to be humidified and smoke is a problem, water spray filters may be used. Impurities, including dust and some pollen, are removed by a very fine spray through which air is passed. The purest type of filter is electronic, comprising electrically charged screens. These are costly to install but have a low operating cost and low air resistance. In some instances, special types of filter are used. For instance, grease filters are placed in the exhaust hoods of food production areas.

Humidifiers add water to air. Two types have been identified above – the eva-porative cooler and the water spray filter.

There are also two types of **fan**. Axial flow fans resemble the propellers on an aircraft. These are typically used for removing the air from a room to the outside. They are relatively cheap to install and operate efficiently, but are ineffective in a large, complex building. Centrifugal fans are rotating cylinders which draw air in through their central core and discharge it out through their surface. Although more costly to install and operate, these fans provide greater control over air distribution and are commonly used in large public areas within buildings.

Lighting and electrical service systems

Most modern buildings are supplied with electrical power. This is used for two main purposes: as the source of energy for all forms of electrical equipment and for the lighting system.

Electrical systems

A typical electrical system comprises supply wires to the exterior of the building, some kind of electric meter that measures usage, a master control switch, trans-former (if it is necessary to reduce the voltage), wiring circuits, circuit breakers (or fuse boxes) and an emergency generator (which starts up automatically if the mains supply is interrupted for any reason). Each element of this system needs to be maintained to ensure continuity of supply and safe operation. For hospitality operations, buildings are usually wired with **'parallel' circuits**, that is to say dif-ferent circuits for each part of the building and for different types of electrical equipment. The longer each circuit (due to resistance within the wires) or the greater the number of appliances attached to it, the greater the likelihood of voltage drop, which means that energy is used wastefully. To protect the circuit and the equipment attached to it, each circuit will usually be fitted with a **fuse** or **circuit breaker**.

Lighting systems

Lighting is typically the second highest user of electrical power in most buildings (electric motors are the highest). The ouput of a lighting system is measured in lumens, which represents the quantity of light that illuminates an area at a specific distance. The further away the surface area from the light source the less intense the light. The amount of lumens produced varies according to the size and type of lamp (i.e. source of light) and the light fitting in which it is placed.

There are a variety of types of **lamp**, which range in efficiency between 5 per cent and 35 per cent, since they give off (unwanted) heat as well as light. One of the most common types is the incandescent lamp, which glows when electricity flows through a filament wire. These lamps come in a variety of shapes (such as standard, reflector, globe, etc.), with a variety of bulbs (clear, frosted, coloured, and so on), different types of fitting (screw, bayonet) and different wattages (25, 40, 60, 75, and so on, up to 1,500 watts). This type of lamp creates a warm light and brings out shades of red, orange and yellow. This makes it particularly suitable in res-taurants, as it brings out the best in red meats and wine, as well as people's flesh tones. A standard bulb may have a life of 750 to 2,500 hours, but less than 15 per cent efficiency. An alternative is the halogen lamp, which has many of the same characteristics of the incandescent lamp. Despite the fact that its initial cost is higher, it lasts longer and produces more light at a lower wattage.

The other main type of lamp is electric-discharge lamps, the most common of which is the fluorescent tube. In this case, light is generated by electrons being passed through mercury gas. This produces white light very efficiently (16–26 per cent) and it has a long working life (16,000–24,000 hours). The interior glass bulb coating may be coloured to produce different types of light, but red-colour-emission fluorescent lamps are less efficient. Light output is also affected by the air temperature, working best at 80°F. Modern versions of this type have enabled the straight tube to be bent into a variety of shapes (U, circles, double-folded, and so on). Wattage ranges from 4 to 110 watts. Other types of lamp, similar to fluorescent, are high-intensity discharge lamps, such as mercury, sodium or metal halide lamps.

Lighting design requires an understanding of the performance characteristics of different types of lamp, along with the amount of light required for the use the lighted space will be put to. For instance, there are industry standards with regards to the amount of light needed for kitchen work areas, bathrooms, fast-food restaurants, hotel lobbies, and so on. Factors which influence lighting design are the size and shape of the room, colour and texture of surfaces (walls, floor and ceiling), type of light fittings and room cleanliness. Lighting may be direct (all light directed outward from the fixture), indirect (all light reflected onto a wall or ceiling) or a combination of both direct and indirect lighting (semi-indirect is 10–40 per cent reflected, diffuse lighting has 40–60 per cent reflected light, and semi-direct has 60–90 per cent reflected). In the hospitality industry direct lighting is typically found back-of-house, whereas public areas usually have some form of indirect lighting.

Waste water systems and swimming pools

In most developed countries, water is supplied suitably treated for consumption through a mains supply pipe. Likewise waste water and sewage is removed by mains drainage pipes.

Water distribution systems

There are two basic ways of piping water around a property. The first is the **upfeed system**. This system depends on the pressure created by the mains supply to force water around the building. In some cases, this might be assisted by a water circulating pump. However, this system will not work in tall buildings above five floors, as the pressure will almost certainly be too low. In this case, the **downfeed system** is required, whereby water is pumped to a storage tank at the highest point in the building and then gravity-fed to where it is needed. Very tall buildings would have supplementary tanks located at different levels feeding off the main tank.

Whichever system is installed, it is important to maintain as far as possible a constant water pressure. This is to ensure that there are no sudden fluctuations in hot and cold water pressure, which could lead to the shower in a hotel room running hot when the toilet in another room was flushed. Balancing the system involves ensuring the right diameter of pipe in combination with its run (i.e. length), the use of valves to control flow and the number of fixtures (water taps or cisterns) attached to the pipe. For instance, 5 toilets can be serviced by a 1.5 in water pipe at 35 gallons per minute (gpm) pressure, whereas 20 toilets require a 2 in pipe at 62 gpm (Borsenik and Stutts, 1997).

Water supplies in hospitality businesses

Utility companies provide most hospitality businesses with their water supply, though wells bored into aquifers may be the source in remote areas. Within the UK, cold water supplies for drinking and cooking are taken directly from the mains. For all other purposes the source will be an intermediate storage tank containing either cold or hot water. Each operation will have its own particular systems and standards, but the ideal temperatures of hot water are:

Guest Room   50° Centigrade
Kitchen (general) 60° Centigrade
Sterilizing   80° Centigrade
Laundry   80° Centigrade.

Note that the removal of waste water is controlled by local regulations. Roof and site drainage water is usually separated from sanitary waste, and kitchen waste is often passed through grease filters before entering the waste system.

Drainage systems

Drainage is typically a gravity flow system, although in special circumstances waste may be macerated and pumped. Drainpipes are either **soil** pipes, which handle all kinds of waste, including that from toilets, or **waste** pipes, which remove any kind of waste water except toilet waste. Fittings inside the building, such as toilets, baths and sinks, are connected to drainpipes that usually run down the outside of the building. This is because they require venting above the building's roof line. To prevent odours from the sewer escaping into the building, all waste water typically flows from the fixture through an S-bend trap.

Swimming pools

A swimming pool is a feature of many hotels, especially resort properties. They come in all shapes and sizes, and may be located inside or outside the property. There are a variety of different types of pool. The type selected will depend on factors such as local ground conditions and water table, weather conditions (especially if air temperatures go below freezing) and local building codes. The most durable and costly type is made entirely from reinforced steel and concrete, lined with a water-resistant plaster and finished with tiles. Since these pools can crack if the water in them freezes, they must be drained during periods of cold weather. Less costly, less likely to crack in freezing conditions and possibly easier to maintain are semi-concrete pools, where the pool bottom is concrete and the side walls are either stainless steel or fibre glass. A lower cost alternative to tiling is vinyl lining, which is available in various thicknesses. The lowest cost type of pool is an above-ground pool, usually made with steel walls lined with plastic.

The basic maintenance equipment for a pool is its **filter**. This removes impurities and ensures that the water remains clear. Pool water should be cycled through the filter at least once every day, and more frequently if the pool is heavily used, there is heavy rainfall or full sun, or it is contaminated by airborne particles. There are many different types of filter, and operators are advised to follow closely the manufacturer's advice with regards to cleaning and maintenance. In addition, surface debris must also be removed. This is usually achieved by the incorporation of a **weir** all round the pool over which the water spills, allowing it to be strained. This may also be linked to the filter. Finally, pools are typically treated with **chemicals** designed to kill waterborne bacteria. The use of these disinfectants varies widely with conditions. The two most common types are chlorine and bromine, which come in liquid, powder, solid or gas forms. Typically, chlorine is used in swimming pools at a level of two parts per million, while bromine is more suitable for heated spas at one part per million. If the natural **pH** of the water is not slightly alkaline (7.2 to 7.6) chemicals may also be needed to adjust this to within these levels. Finally, **algae growth** may need to be controlled by using algicides; and water colour can be treated by adding conditioners.

Building transportation systems

What is a building transportation system? Quite simply it is all those pieces of equipment that are used to move people or things from one place to another inside a building – machinery such as lifts, hoists, escalators and moving walkways. Many hotels are now built in high-rise buildings, for instance the Hilton Park Lane hotel has 23 floors. Others cover very large areas, such as the Opreyland Hotel in Nashville and some of the larger hotels built recently in Las Vegas.

Vertical transportation

Employers, customers and goods are not necessarily moved up or down by machines – they can always use stairs, ramps or chutes. However, lifts and escalators are used where distances are great or there are large numbers of people.

Lifts can be used to move passengers or freight. There are two basic types. In the cable system the lift car is suspended from cables that have counterweights attached to the other end. The hydraulic system replaces the cable with an oil pump in the form of a plunger attached to the underside of the car, and is only used in buildings up to two or three storeys high. Both systems have a shaft that is fitted with guide rails for the car. There are two key safety issues. The first relates to ensuring the lift cars function properly and do not fall disastrously. Cars are usually controlled by elecro-magnetic brakes, which have proved very dependable. In cable systems, several separate cables are used with a margin of safety in case one should wear or break. The second issue is the danger the lift shaft creates should fire break out somewhere in the building. The shaft would naturally act like a large chimney, fanning the flames and spreading the fire from one floor to another. To restrict this, all shafts are constructed of fireproof materials and smoke or fire detectors are fitted at each floor to ensure the lift doors remain closed if a fire breaks out.

Escalators are essentially moving stairs. They are usually installed in pairs, one going up and the other coming down, typically at a 30 degree angle. The direction of travel may be reversed, for instance if large numbers of people are entering a convention area at the same time or if a fire breaks out. In the USA they are constructed in two basic sizes. The 32 in wide escalator can transport 4,000 passengers per hour at a speed of 90 feet per minute (fpm) or 5,000 at the higher speed of 120 fpm. The 48 in wide escalator can transport 6,000 or 8,000 passengers respectively. The driving machinery and control equipment is very similar to that utilized for lifts.

Horizontal transportation

Moving walkways are very similar to escalators in size and design, except that they have a continuous belt instead of separate steps. They move at speeds of up to 180 feet per minute and typically are fitted with an audible signal to warn people when they reach the end of the walkway.

Fire safety systems

We have seen that it is important to ensure the correct installation of equipment and energy sources so that they do not cause fires. However, in addition most buildings are fitted with systems that deliberately monitor the risk of fire and assist in its prevention or containment. Fire does not simply destroy materials by flames. It generates great heat that can melt materials or burn human beings; it creates smoke that can spoil large areas of a building not directly affected by the fire and prevent people from escaping; and it gives off gases that may asphyxiate people.

Fire detection systems

Most modern buildings incorporate various kinds of fire detection system. **Heat detectors** monitor the temperature. One type is activated when it rises above a fixed point, typically 25 degrees above the normal maximum anticipated temperature. A second type monitors the rate of change in temperature and would typically activate if it rose by 15 degrees in less than a minute. **Smoke alarms** detect smoke either through ionization or photoelectric cells. In some cases, this equipment can be combined to create a multi-sensory unit using microprocessor technology to monitor and measure the environment. Other types of alarm may include flame detectors that sense radiant heat, or alarms that can be activated manually by the person who discovers the fire outbreak.

To be effective, detection devices have to be located in the right place. This means at the right height, in sufficient numbers for the size of the space or building, and of the right specification for the type of fire that may break out. Generally buildings are divided into 'zones', each with its own detector. Modern systems have self-checking routines to ensure fail-safe operation.

Fire suppression systems

For a fire to exist there must be oxygen, fuel and heat. Fire suppression systems are designed to remove one or more of these factors to combat the fire. Fires of different types may be suppressed using one of three different approaches – water-based, gas (carbon dioxide) and dry chemical. In some cases, the fire suppression system is incorporated into the building and set off automatically by a sensor. In most cases, however, buildings are equipped with fire-fighting extinguishers carefully located at strategic points on each floor. Each type of extinguisher is usually colour-coded so that it can be selected easily to fight the right kind of fire. Water-based systems (colour-coded red in the UK) are suitable for general fires, but not electrical fires or burning liquids. These types of fire should be tackled with a CO_2

extinguisher (coded black in the UK). Powder extinguishers (blue) are also suitable for burning liquids, fat fires and electrical fires. Kitchens are also equipped with a fire blanket, which can be used to wrap around someone whose clothing has caught fire or lain over a deep-fat fryer fire (so long as it has been switched off).

Emergency escape

As well as means of suppressing a fire, buildings are also designed to allow occupants to leave the building safely. Escapes may either be external or internal. External escape has the advantage that occupants are less likely to be affected by smoke and fumes, but they can be slippery when wet or icy. In addition, access from each floor on to an external escape increases the number of exterior doors, thereby heightening the security risk. For this reason, interior or so-called 'protected' routes are preferred. Such routes have to be clearly marked with emergency signing, equipped with fire doors that automatically close in the event of a fire, and decorated with fire-retardant materials.

KEY PROCESSES

The technological systems we have been considering are generally 'closed' systems. That is to say, they operate without much interaction with their environment. Whatever interaction there is often mechanized, for instance the thermostat that controls room or water temperature. Hence, in their everyday function, these systems utilize processes that work 'automatically'. However, since no technology is completely fault-free and needs continuous monitoring to ensure that it is operating correctly, most hospitality operators will nominate employees to be responsible for engineering maintenance. In this section we shall therefore consider the processes or activities undertaken by maintenance engineers. These fall into two broad areas – maintenance, both preventative and remedial, and developing action plans in response to environmental issues such as energy management and improving water quality.

Preventative and remedial maintenance

Maintenance may either be carried by out an engineer in-house or by manufacturers, distributors or service companies on a contract basis. In most cases, there will be a policy of **preventative** maintenance designed to ensure that equipment is serviced on a regular basis to facilitate efficient operation and avoid breakdown. A programme of preventative maintenance includes:

- regular inspection, at predetermined time intervals, by the in-house engineer or contractor

- a system of record keeping, by the 'inspectors', recording their inspection and assessing the condition of the building fabric or equipment

- a programme of lubrication, adjustment, painting and cleaning

- a schedule of servicing for all major items of equipment, including the routine replacement of parts.

However good the programme of preventative maintenance, breakdowns may still occur, which will require a system of **remedial** maintenance. A key feature of this system is to establish in advance an appropriate speed of response in relation to the criticality of the breakdown. Breakdowns that may cause the operation to close down or endanger human health must be dealt with speedily, whereas non-threatening failures can be dealt with more routinely. Such breakdowns need to be reported to the engineers or contractors immediately by those staff who use that equipment or part of the building. In January 2001, a restaurant which was operated by a multinational fast-food company was fined £20,000 for a breach of health and safety when a customer was injured by a faulty hand drier in the toilets. It had been reported faulty three days earlier, but no action had been taken. There have also been cases of faults being incorrectly repaired by inappropriate and untrained members of staff such as chefs. All staff should report faults and not attempt to repair them.

To ensure maintenance policy is being carried out and as a record of good practice in the event of litigation, a system of record keeping is required. Typically an operation would have a general repairs record and equipment maintenance log books. The **general repairs record** identifies faults with floors, wall tiles, paintwork, plumbing, cupboards, fixtures, locks and keys. In some cases, this would be a multi-part book, with one copy going to the maintenance department as a requisition to have the work carried out. Management may monitor such a record to identify areas that require remedial treatment and thereby adjust their preventative maintenance schedules to reduce the level of remedial action. The **maintenance log book** typically lists all equipment, grouped together according to the frequency of routine and major inspections. It identifies the staff member responsible for carrying out the maintenance and records the dates of each past inspection, and is signed by the relevant person to confirm that the work has been completed, along with the due date of the next inspection.

Finally, maintenance may be improved if equipment is correctly used and the building space is properly occupied and regularly cleaned by employees. Equipment breakdown, in particular, may often be caused by misuse of an appliance. **Cleaning** ensures safe hygiene practices, improves employee working conditions and morale, and extends the working life of equipment or surface finishes. Cleaning routines should be carried out far more frequently than maintenance routines, as Fuller and Kirk (1991) emphasize: 'it is vital to ensure a rhythmic pattern of cleaning from hour-to-hour, day-to-day, week-to-week and section-to-section is established'. The labour and materials cost of cleaning requires that these resources are used effectively. Surfaces need to be analysed in terms of their composition, nature of soiling and the degree of hazard entailed in carrying out the cleaning. Such analysis determines the nature of the cleaning agent to be used, its level of concentration, method of application (by hand or by machine), frequency of cleaning and responsibility for the task. This information is typically incorporated into written cleaning routines for the operation.

Energy management

Many hotel and catering companies have recognized the danger of escalating energy costs and have sought to control consumption. It has been estimated by the UK's Energy Efficiency Office that 'with moderate improvement in efficiency and some rationalization in the use of equipment, savings in excess of 20 per cent are achievable'. Energy management programmes, designed to achieve such savings, are based on monitoring and targeting. Consumption is systematically recorded and targets for future consumption established against a set of specific energy-saving measures.

The first step in any energy management programme is an **energy audit**. By analysing and evaluating historic records and operating statistics, a measure of the energy performance of the entire building can be obtained. It is a more complex task to determine the energy performance of individual departments and this may require specific investment in submetering. The energy audit should encompass the following:

- Establish fuel consumption costs by collecting information in each billing period from the various energy supply companies. Energy consumption usually has to be converted into the same basic units (kilowatt/hour – kWh) in order to establish total energy costs, which can then be used to monitor usage over time.

- Break down total cost into energy cost centres, such as heating, air conditioning, hot water, lighting, refrigeration, equipment and swimming pool. This is only possible if supply can be separately metered to each of these areas.

- Match monthly consumption of energy to the average monthly climate.

- Match consumption to level of business activity, such as room occupancy, covers served or sales volume per month.

- Survey equipment usage to identify its power rating, its pattern of daily use and its diversity (the percentage of time the appliance is consuming energy when it is switched on). For instance, the diversity of cooking equipment is typically 50 per cent, but for refrigeration only 20 per cent.

As with an environmental audit, an energy audit requires the full involvement of employees. It will show where the energy is being spent, and highlight energy-saving opportunities. It should also quantify achievable energy targets. However, it is important to note that energy performance indicators are meaningless without an external comparator, such as the equivalent for other hospitality businesses and industry average data. Care must be taken in comparing one operation with another, as there are many factors associated with the construction, location and operation that can affect energy consumption, for example hotel facilities like leisure centres and swimming pools, and air conditioning. Another complication is that comparisons can only be made if the units of energy are standardized to kWh. In estimating costs, account must be taken of the different price per kWh of the various sources of energy used and of their relative efficiency.

An audit facilitates the development of an **energy policy**. Audit data can enable an operation's performance to be compared or 'benchmarked' against other units in the chain or industry averages. This allows a policy to be established with regards to choosing the most appropriate form of energy, selecting energy suppliers, investing in capital plant and equipment (see Chapter 6), creating best management practice and altering operational activity. Reducing energy costs may not be easy, as there is an element of fixed cost (i.e. energy) consumption that does not vary according to the level of business activity. However, in catering, the use of cooking equipment may represent 40 per cent of consumption that does provide some opportunities for ensuring efficient usage. Improvements may be made in a variety of ways: switching on an appliance just before it is required and switching it off immediately after use, loading equipment such as dishwashers and fryers to their correct capacity, opening oven and refrigerator doors for as short a time as possible, and selecting the most energy-efficient appliance for food production, such as a steamer for vegetable cooking.

Improving water quality

Most water supplies have been treated by the utility company before reaching the hotel, though those using wells will need on-site treatment. Quality levels are related to intended use. Thus lower quality water may be used in toilets and for gardening purposes, but non-potable and potable supplies must be physically isolated to prevent contamination.

There are three classes of pollutants:

- chemical, e.g. lead, aluminium, nitrates and pesticide residues, and chemicals causing 'hardness'

- bacteriological, as indicated by the presence of coliform bacteria and removed by chlorine-based disinfectants

- organoleptic factors (affecting taste, smell or colour).

An **action plan on water quality** should include three steps. First, an *identification of standards* applicable to the hotel and its location (e.g. World Health Organization and European Union standards), where appropriate, and national and local standards and codes. Aim for the highest of these standards. Check water supplies against these standards and, where they are not met, request remedial action by the utility company or, if the hotel has its own supply, take direct action.

Second, a *check on the functioning of the existing water plant* to ensure it is being properly maintained and can cope with present and anticipated demand. Take remedial action where necessary. Having identified all possible harmful chemicals and materials, ensure procedures are in place to prevent contamination of both water supplies and effluents. Common defects and their treatment include:

- suspended solids: filtration

- high salt content: desalination

- iron: potassium permanganate treatment

- acidity: increase pH

- corrosivity and scale: chemical treatment

- hardness: water-softening treatment

- high temperature: cooling

- bacterial contamination: chlorination and flocculation

- odour and taste: filtration through an active carbon filter.

Third, there should be an *assessment of the design and state of physical plant*, especially for sources of stagnant water, e.g. checking the inlet and outlet points of tanks are not too close together and that there is sufficient turnover. Ensure tanks are covered and all outlets are designed to prevent contamination from airborne particles, birds and rodents. Hot water tanks should be checked to ensure there is sufficient turnover. The temperature of water in storage tanks should be checked to ensure bacteria, such as *Legionella pneumophilia* (legionnaire's disease), cannot survive. Similar checks should be carried out on the system's pipework.

SYSTEM ADOPTION

The range in scale and type of building used in hospitality is enormous: everything from a multi-storey, city centre block housing a hotel down to a small kiosk selling burgers in a sports arena. It is not possible to illustrate such a wide range of building types here, so we shall illustrate an operation's approach to maintenance and engineering through the following case study.

CASE STUDY: FOUR SEASONS HOTEL, LONDON

The Four Seasons Hotel on London's Park Lane is a 196-room five-star hotel. The building is 11 storeys high, including a sub-basement and basement. The sub-basement and top floor of the building are given over almost exclusively to building plant, such as hot water boilers, water coolers and air-conditioning plant, lift plant, and so on. The basement comprises only back-of-house areas, such as staff changing rooms, staff restaurant, stores, cellar, laundry and a guest car park for up to 60 cars. On the ground floor there is the lobby, front desk, lounge restaurant, two retail outlets and two banqueting rooms, while back-of-house on this floor there is a loading bay, dry stores and administrative offices. On the first floor, there is the cocktail bar, main kitchen and four banqueting rooms, including a ballroom for 200 dinner guests. The decor of the whole hotel is exemplified by the striking interior design of the 90-seat Lanes restaurant, which has 'wood panelling, stained glass and marbling in midnight blue, bottle green and deep cranberry. A glass and marble central buffet, topped by an 81-element glass sculpture, is stunning. Stained glass borders around the picture windows frame views up Park Lane.'

There are 120 superior en-suite rooms located throughout the hotel that provide a combined bedroom and comfortably furnished sitting area. A further 41 deluxe rooms of the same size and features have full-length sliding windows overlooking Hyde Park and Old Park Lane. Since the ground and first floor of the building have a larger footprint than the other eight storeys, there is a second floor terrace running east–west along the length of the building. On these terraces there are 11 'Conservatory rooms', which have a glass-enclosed conservatory as well as a bedroom. There are seven Four Seasons suites, which feature French doors separating the bedroom from the parlour, as well as a balcony overlooking Old Park Lane or Hyde Park. The seven Apsley suites offer one or two bedrooms and a separate living room with private access from the hall. 'With two full marble bathrooms, a complete entertainment centre and dining seating for six, these suites are ideal for sophisticated social gatherings or vacationing families.' Five more suites of this design also provide panoramic views of Old Park Lane, Hyde Park and central London. The hotel also offers several one-of-a-kind luxury suites on the second floor, all opening out on to the terrace and some featuring glass-enclosed conservatories.

The hotel was built in 1970 and took three years to construct. The property has a reinforced concrete frame overclad with Portland stone. There are double-glazed windows in all guest rooms and some public rooms. Throughout the building air conditioning provides both cooling and heating. The boilers are gas-fired, and in case of a black-out there is an emergency electricity generator. A new CHP (combined heat and power) unit recycles waste heat in order to help heat water. The water system is a pressure-fed system designed to equalize pressure in all rooms. All the water tanks and plant are on the tenth floor. The fire control system is based around newly installed detectors that measure both heat and smoke in the atmosphere. A sprinkler system is installed in all public and back-of-house areas, but not in the bedrooms, which are protected by the provision of emergency hose-reels and extinguishers placed in corridors.

Maintenance and engineering in the property is managed by the hotel's Director of Engineering. He serves on the hotel planning committee, which comprises the General Manager and seven other senior staff. It routinely meets once a week. Reporting to the Director of Engineering are 17 permanent maintenance staff. These include mechanical engineers, electrical engineers, plumbers, painters/decorators, carpenters and general trades staff. These staff work either an early shift (7.00 a.m. to 3.00 p.m.) or late shift (3.00 p.m. to 11.00 p.m.), engaged mainly in routine maintenance. In addition there is 24/7 coverage from 'shift engineers' who have a wide range of skills so that they can deal with any emergencies. As well as in-house staff, the Director of Engineering is also responsible for organizing and monitoring specialist engineers employed on a contract basis to service and maintain large or specialist equipment and plant such as chillers, refrigerators and lifts. Likewise water quality is checked once a quarter by external consultants. In the event that an Environmental Health Officer comes to check the hotel, the Director of Engineering will accompany him or her around the building.

All guest bedrooms are subject to a twice-yearly routine maintenance check of 45 separate items. This list includes some items that are required by law or regulation, such as the descaling of shower heads, water temperature checks, electrical safety checks; and others that are carried out for maintenance reasons, such as the replacement of tap washers, and so on. The hotel generally has a five-year cycle of room refurbishment. On an annual basis, a capital budget is agreed for this purpose and rooms are scheduled for redecoration during low periods of demand.

As well as routine maintenance and refurbishment, the engineering team also has to deal with emergency problems. Typical problems include televisions with poor reception, overflowing baths and assisting guests with electrical equipment. For some events, there are well-established crisis response systems. For instance, guest baths may overflow as the pressurized system means that they fill more quickly than guests expect and the bathrooms were not designed with floor drains. Flooded bathrooms not only affect the guest in that room, but may also affect the room below if water soaks through the ceiling, as well as damaging electrical and telephone cabling. The shift engineer therefore knows precisely where to find footwear, pumps and other equipment specifically needed for this type of problem.

Four Seasons also has an environmental committee in all its properties. The committee is made up of members from every department in the hotel. As well as implementing corporate environmental initiatives, the committee also proposes its own. In London, all the gardens are organic, there are now energy light bulbs in back-of-house, and sensors switch off lights back-of-house. Every major piece of equipment purchased recently, such as the main dishwasher, has also been selected for its environmental features.

CURRENT TRENDS AND ISSUES AFFECTING SYSTEM

The three major factors affecting the maintenance and engineering systems have been technological, legislative and environmental.

Technological trends

Two key trends affecting the engineering function in hospitality have been changes to construction methods and the availability of new sources of power.

Legislative and environmental issues

Policy and procedure with regards to property and energy management have been greatly influenced by an increasing concern for the environment. This is looked at in detail in the next chapter.

SUMMARY

This chapter has looked at maintenance and engineering. It has identified it as mainly a materials processing operation, along with the information processing needed to operate the system effectively. Key performance aspects in this system are the continued supply of power and other services necessary to deliver products and services to customers, maintenance of a safe and healthy environment, economic management of the physical infrastructure and the minimization of environmental impact. To achieve these goals, the maintenance engineer carries out processes associated with planned maintenance and energy management.

The key technological systems, which are interrelated, are a heating system, ventilation system, lighting and electrical service system, waste water system, building transportation system and fire safety system. These are each configured in a range of ways according to the nature of the hospitality operation, its size and location, and other factors.

Further study

On a tour of any hospitality operation try to identify the type of heating, ventilation, water and drainage system.

Compare and contrast the lighting system in a fast-food restaurant with that in a pub.

Bibliography

Borsenik, F. D. and Stutts, A. T. (1997) *The Management of Maintenance and Engineering Systems in the Hospitality Industry.* New York: John Wiley & Sons.
Fuller, J. and Kirk, D. (1991) *Kitchen Planning and Management.* Oxford: Butterworth-Heinemann.

Recommended further reading

Energy Efficiency Office (1993) *Energy Consumption Guide 36: Energy Efficiency in Hotels.* London: HMSO.

CHAPTER 6

Environment and waste

After completing this chapter you will be able to:

- *understand how firms progress through a series of environmental initiatives*
- *explain the concept of equilibrium*
- *describe the characteristics of environmental systems*
- *describe an environmental management system*
- *explain the management of specific resources – water, energy, waste, the indoor environment*
- *understand the concept of a holistic approach to environmental management*
- *identify current trends in environmental management.*

INTRODUCTION

There has been growing concern over the last forty years about the state of our environment and the earth's ability to 'carry' the developmental activities of its population. The environmental problems that we face, such as population growth, excessive and wasteful use of resources and pollution, are in many ways all related and result from poor systems performance. The complexity of their interrelationship highlights the value of a systems approach when looking at environmental issues.

These environmental issues are complex and range from the global issues discussed in the press, such as global warming, to many local catastrophes and disasters. We know, for example, that there are now more hungry people than ever before, and the gap between rich and poor people is widening. Each year 6 million hectares of productive dry land turn into worthless desert and more than 11 million hectares are destroyed. Acid rain, apart from obvious cultural damage, may have acidified vast tracts of soil beyond repair. Burning fossil fuels gives off carbon dioxide leading to global warming. This is predicted to have a disruptive effect early in the 21st century, when raised sea levels will flood coastal towns and displace agricultural zones. These pressures are resulting in increased legislative and regulative pressure on businesses to manage their impact on the environment.

In addition to international and governmental pressures for change, we are also seeing the growth of the green consumer. Although this is having only a small impact at this point in time, businesses will need to monitor these changes in green consumerism. Businesses are subject both to the 'push' of governmental pressure, for example through the 'polluter pays' principle, and the 'pull' of the market, as increasing numbers of consumers express a preference for green products.

Hospitality businesses have responded to these pressures in a variety of ways. Some have simply incorporated environmental management and waste management procedures into their everyday activities. Some have developed new procedures, based on an environmental policy. Others have seen environmental management as a means of differentiating themselves, and have gone in for environmental or 'green' award schemes.

PURPOSE OF SYSTEM

The purpose of an environmental and waste system is to manage the exchange of materials between the operation and its environment, that is to optimize inputs, processes and outputs. In Chapter 1, we saw that the environment has a specific meaning in systems thinking. It defines anything that is external to the system and is separated from it by a boundary. It also implies an interest in the relationship between the two – that is, a concern about the nature of exchanges between the system and its environment. Much of environmental management is concerned with the nature of systems outputs, particularly those we consider as waste. However, it is becoming increasingly clear that in order to manage the impact on the environment we need to consider not only the outputs but also the inputs and processes. A basic analysis of a system indicates that there are two points of contact with the environment. All inputs into the system are drawn from its environment. All outputs (which includes both useful output, residue and waste) are returned to the environment (see Figure 6.1).

There is always a danger that the focus is on the wrong subsystem or system component. In the case of pollution control there was an exclusive concentration on treating *undesirable* outputs through pollution control – an expensive option. However, it was later recognized that looking at inputs and processes, which themselves contain hidden pollution costs, and innovating to eliminate all undesirable pollution (pollution prevention), can be more effective. Pollution is not simply an inevitable outcome, but a symptom. The cause may be close in time and space (e.g. the production process) or more remote (e.g. a design flaw), or both.

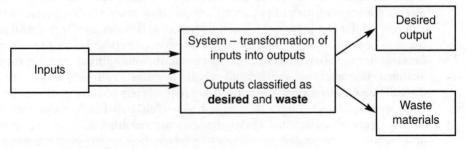

Figure 6.1 *Exchanges between a system and its environment* (based on Kirk, 1996)

Environmental equilibrium and sustainable development

With the exception of the energy inputs from the sun, our planet is essentially a closed system from an environmental point of view. In other words, the earth's resources are finite. More recently, concern has grown that the rise in consumption of resources is not linear, but curved positively, or exponentially. In systems thinking terms, exponential growth occurs when the system is driven by a dominant positive feedback loop. Since, in most cases, these resources are finite, demand will outstrip supply.

In addition to the exhaustion of finite resources, there has been much publicity over other environmental effects, such as:

- the harmful effects of chemical fertilizers and pesticides

- carbon dioxide emissions into the atmosphere leading to global warming

- the extinction of many species

- the transformation of once fertile land into desert

- the threats to human health and crop yields from damage to the ozone layer.

In systems terminology, the world is often considered to be in equilibrium, through the action of negative feedback processes. If man introduces processes that destroy this natural equilibrium, the stability of our environment will be threatened. In other words, any irreconcilable conflict between ecology and economy will destabilize the earth.

One of the main problems is that the causes of pollution are often not as clear as we would wish, and causes are often distant in time and space from their effect. Acid rain in one country may be caused by emissions in another unidentifiable country. Such acid rain may well be caused by sulphur dioxide emissions from coal-fired power stations, but it may also be caused by car exhaust emissions. The causation and relative contribution of possible sources are not known for certain. Any decision to legally force the power stations to reduce emissions of sulphur dioxide, which may subsequently prove to be unnecessary, has immediate economic repercussions in terms of driving up the price of electricity relative to gas.

An important concept in the development of environmental management is that of sustainability. The concept of sustainability is related to that of negative feedback. In any systems that we design or manage, we should try to ensure that we do not reduce any of the earth's finite resources, nor should we upset the balance of equilibrium in the earth's ecology. Economic processes take place in open systems. Resource-intensive business management is often too narrow in its view. Technological solutions must be multidisciplinary, since there is a complex system of interrelated tasks.

Sustainable development has been described as a new paradigm for management theory and practice. The World Commission on Environment and Development (WCED) (i.e. The Brundtland Commission) defined sustainable development as 'development which meets the needs of the present without compromising the ability of future generations to meet their own needs' (WCED, 1992, p. 49). A concrete result of the Rio meeting of the world's leaders was the development of the publication known as Agenda 21 (UN, 1993, pp. 9–479). This international agreement sought to limit unsustainable development through establishing voluntary targets for governments.

All companies now need to take an interest in the environment, and to consider the following questions:

- What do consumers value?

- What do environmentalists want?

- What are regulators demanding?

- What will the local community value?

- What does science suggest?

- Whose opinion counts most?

Current business managers have been trained to think of the environment as part of a raft of government regulations, that is, as an issue of compliance with laws and codes of practice. Most of these regulations and codes are about system outputs. There is a danger that managers will control the symptoms rather than modify their processes. In the USA and other countries, environmental responsibility has become part of the search for total quality. The parallels between aiming for total quality and cradle-to-grave environmental management can be seen through similar audit systems, such as ISO 9000 and ISO 14000. Other companies have already passed into a third stage of development, and many are now accepting the ethical case for developing sustainable strategies. For example, some companies now have environmental sections in their annual company reports. There is clearly an ethical case for the business world to protect the environment in the interest of future generations, and some businesses feel that they have a moral obligation to go beyond what is legally required and to move towards developing sustainable processes and practices.

Implementing an environmental management programme

The five main drivers for change towards sustainable development in an organization are:

- the need for compliance with legislative and fiscal requirements

- opportunities for financial savings

- consumer attitudes and pressure

- public opinion

- enlightened senior management.

Much of the early emphasis in environmental management was on manufacturing companies, as these were seen as the main producers of environmental pollution. It has taken much longer for the above drivers to come into play in the service sector, particularly in industries characterized mainly by small and medium enterprises (SMEs) that lack resources to respond to the challenge. As new measures of ethical performance come into force, shareholders, consumers and investors will exert increasing pressure on hospitality companies to improve their environmental performance. Meanwhile, green pressure groups will continue to exert their influence.

GENERIC SYSTEM CHARACTERISTICS

The characteristics of an environmental management system are:

- a written policy statement

- a set of targets against which to measure progress

- agreed specific actions

- monitoring results against targets.

An environmental management system (EMS) must be 'fed' from a variety of sources, including internal subsystems and the external environment. Some of these may be considered as 'tools' of environmental management that provide feedback, to which the EMS then responds. There is a need 'to establish structures and norms which will ensure that environmental performance is improved over time'. This may be achieved through the organization first assessing its own performance and then responding to the resulting data by setting targets or benchmarks (Stainer and Stainer, 1997). A possible model for effective environmental performance appraisal, in the form of a continuous loop, is given in Table 6.1.

1. define the environmental context and objectives
2. identify potential measures
3. select appropriate measures
4. set targets
5. implement measures
6. monitor and communicate results
7. act on results
8. review.

Table 6.1 *Environmental performance appraisal model* (James and Bennett, 1994)

SYSTEM TYPES

Companies often progress through a number of evolutionary changes in their approach to environmental management. The first stage of development is sometimes referred to as an '**end-of-pipe mentality**', where the concern is with:

- dangerous or toxic wastes

- disposal of waste materials

- waste of scarce resources.

This approach leads to an emphasis on waste minimization and waste recycling.

The second stage of development is based on an evaluation of an existing process holistically, through consideration of the input–transformation–output process. This leads to a consideration of the measurement of the ratio of input to output (**system efficiency**) and maximum use of resources. These considerations lead to better controls over purchasing, storage, production and service.

The third stage of development reflects the approach of a company that has an **environmental vision**, reflected in:

- holistic design systems

- environmental principles designed into the total organization

- consideration of all internal and external stages and the links between them.

An EMS may be seen as a hierarchy, starting with, at the highest level of the organization, a policy statement. Below this will be those operational systems that impact on the day-to-day management of all areas of a hospitality business: purchasing, food production, foodservice, rooms division, maintenance, transport, and so on. Achievements against targets will be measured against a regular audit of environmental performance.

The environmental policy and mission statements

All employees have to play their part in moving the organization towards sustainable development. The production and dissemination of clear environmental policy and mission statements, endorsed by senior management, is essential. These must include specific and attainable goals and targets, including performance targets, and details of the arrangements for monitoring, control and communication. The policy statement should also clarify responsibilities.

Whether issued as a new policy statement or incorporated into the company's mission statement, the environmental initiative must be linked to action and targets; hence the need, possibly, for an environmental strategy in larger companies, with a specific environmental manager or co-ordinator.

While no responsible company would aim at minimum targets, it is important to know what these are. Naturally, the organization has to meet local and national legal requirements and may wish to incorporate the requirements of a standard such as ISO 14001. Any existing company standards will have to be incorporated in the new policy, and the standards used by suppliers and recommended by trade bodies may also influence policy.

A policy should:

- be brief, two pages maximum

- be able to be understood by, and communicated to, all levels of the company

- be available to the public

- include a commitment to a progressive reduction of areas of environmental impact

- include a commitment to meet all current legislation

- aim to go beyond legal compliance

- indicate that individuals will be assigned direct responsibility

- indicate that an auditing programme will be set up to measure the implementation of the policy

- have a commitment to review the policy after a specified period

- be consistent with the health and safety policies of the company.

The environmental audit (EA)

The term 'audit' is usually associated with finance, and a financial audit involves the application of rigid rules. By contrast, environmental auditing is based on a balancing of facts and values, rather than just on financial measures. The purpose of an environmental audit is to assess the performance of an organization against prescribed targets related to inputs, processes and outputs.

Input measures include indicators, targets and measures of plant efficiency, materials quality and recyclability. It may be seen as much broader than simply material input and might include, for example, the effectiveness of training staff.

Process measures aim at percentage improvements in reducing waste in stockholding, processing and packaging.

Output measures record impact on, or damage to, the community, including waste, emissions and pollution.

Clearly, such an audit on the whole organization must be carried out at regular intervals, feeding back internal information for control of the EMS. As we saw in Chapter 5, audits of subsystems of the EMS, such as those of specific resources – water, energy, etc. – feed back into policies relating to the specific management of these resources.

Integrating environmental and operations management

At the highest level, organizations should integrate environmental issues with their corporate strategy, and the increasing regulatory and consumer pressures have encouraged this process within some firms. Similarly, environmental management should be more concerned with integrating environmental considerations with normal management functions in all areas of business than merely with the development of separate management systems.

The operations manager will be concerned with the purchase and management of the specific resources and should appreciate his or her responsibility for the environmental management of these resources, whether or not there is an overall environmental manager for the group. In some instances, the appraisal of operations managers will include performance in environmental management, a practice which has been adopted by some hotel chains.

The commercial and stakeholder advantages resulting from good management of water, energy, materials and waste, and the indoor environment are similar. They may be expressed in terms of who benefits and how. Hospitality business owners and managers, including operations and marketing managers, benefit because gains in efficiency mean fewer staff are required and operating expenses are lower. Resources can therefore be released for investment in improving or expanding the hotel's facilities, or adjusting room rates. This can lead to higher levels of repeat business. Guests benefit from the efficiency of the controls used to satisfy their needs and could also benefit in the long run from more competitive prices for environmentally friendly hospitality businesses. Finally, staff benefit from the associated training and empowerment, which in turn results in higher staff morale, increased job satisfaction, improved levels of productivity and lower levels of absenteeism and staff turnover.

KEY PROCESSES

Water management

Fresh water is becoming more and more scarce and conservation must be a high priority for all managers. There are several reasons why hospitality operations managers focus on the management of water consumption and water quality:

- waste water reduces the supply of what is often a scarce resource and adds to the hotel's costs

- a waste of hot water is also a waste of energy

- poor quality water supplies may pose a health risk to customers and employees

- such poor quality water often adds to the running and maintenance costs of equipment and reduces its life

- contaminated waste water is a hazard to the health of others in the community and increases the load on effluent plants.

Evaporated water is pure, but it then becomes contaminated with impurities as it passes through the cycle, for instance the nitrate-based chemicals from fertilizers that may only emerge from deep underground supplies up to a decade later. Other contaminants include phosphates and the acid rain that results from absorption of the sulphur dioxide in the atmosphere. Rivers are also used for waste disposal, which may accidentally rise to danger levels, despite stringent precautions, regulations and 'lateral thinking' solutions such as making companies draw their water from downstream. For all these reasons, water is usually treated before being used for drinking and cooking.

In addition to rivers and lakes (natural and artificial), water supplies come from wells that tap natural groundwater that has accumulated through seepage in underground structures called aquifers. In many areas demand is exceeding natural supply and aquifer water levels are falling.

Control of water consumption

Control of water consumption is accomplished by assessing current performance through conducting a **water use audit**, which relates the measure of water consumption to the time of year and the hotel's level of business and gives a detailed evaluation of efficiency. The performance is then compared with previous figures for the hotel or those of other hospitality businesses. Comparisons with other hospitality businesses' water consumption, obtained in cubic metres per customer per year by dividing the annual consumption of water by the average number of guests per day for the year, can provide a basis for benchmarking. However, in such comparisons, specific factors affecting consumption, such as indoor laundries and swimming pools, must be taken into account.

Reducing water wastage

Water costs account for typically 15–20 per cent of a hotel property's utility costs. Hot water wastage is most costly due to associated energy loss. Reducing water loss must not be at the expense of the comfort of guests, unless they specifically agree to certain measures. It has been estimated that the average hotel can reduce its water bill by 40 per cent. The main savings come from managing flushing systems, which account for 33 per cent of total water usage, compared to only 3 per cent for drinking or preparing food. The used water may be treated and reused in non-contact areas such as washing machines and lawn sprinklers. This is called a greywater recycling system and is quite invisible to the customer. Other savings may be made through rainwater harvesting and self-closing taps, and through adapted shower heads that reduce water usage while maintaining customer satisfaction. Table 6.2 gives some guidelines for good practice.

Energy management

Hotels were forced to look for energy economies when the cost of oil soared in 1973–4. Hotels use more energy, in terms of £ per square metre, than industrial buildings, naturally ventilated offices and schools. The benefits of good energy management to the environment include conservation through a reduction in the use of non-renewable energy resources; and also a diminishing of atmospheric pollution, global warming, ozone depletion and acid rain.

- Communicate to all employees the commitment to efficient water management, including objectives, goals and data on consumption, costs and trends.
- Train all staff to understand, operate and maintain the hotel's equipment and systems to maximize energy efficiency and minimize water wastage. Make this an ongoing process.
- Encourage staff to put forward their ideas and proposals to save water.
- Encourage guest participation.
- Both in the building design and landscaping of a new hotel, and on an ongoing basis, invest in building, equipment and systems to improve efficiency, including water collection from building roofs and waste systems.
- Analyse consumption patterns by department and determine where the most significant savings can be made. One of the most important areas is guest bathrooms and from related sewer, chemical and energy costs.
- Introduce regular measures of efficiency, particularly in areas which are major water consumers, e.g. boilers, chillers, cooling towers and air handlers.
- Set and continuously monitor targets for each department.
- Scan the market continuously for improved technology that can be applied in the hotel.
- Give a high priority to utility conservation projects, at least on a par with interior decoration.

Table 6.2 *Water management for reduction of waste*

The principle of energy management is to minimize the amount and cost of energy used by the hotel without any perceived loss of comfort to the guests unless this is done with their consent, for instance if they agree that they do not need fresh towels every day.

Energy in existing buildings may be saved by implementing the following measures:

- a review of the mix of energy sources used

- a review of tariffs used or other contractual arrangements with energy supply companies

- staff training leading to practical steps that can be taken to reduce energy consumption

- a programme of capital investment in the building, plant and equipment in order to reduce energy consumption.

These measures would form part of an energy audit (as discussed in Chapter 5).

It has been estimated that a typical hotel releases about 160 kg of carbon dioxide into the atmosphere per square metre of floor area. Fossil fuels represent the most abundant energy source at present, though within this category there has been a tendency in recent years to switch from solid fuels to natural gas to reduce the output of sulphur dioxide. The ideal, renewable source of energy is the sun, and some writers insist we must move to solar energy, incorporating solar technologies such as photovoltaics that convert energy from the sun directly into electricity. This gives increased efficiency, more flexible use, better storage and dramatically reduced costs. Solar energy is particularly suitable for new hotels in sunny climes. Renewable energy may be derived from the wind, hydroelectric, wave, tidal and geothermal power, but these sources account for only a very small proportion of the world's energy supplies.

For the programme to be successful, someone within the hospitality business should be given managerial responsibility for energy use. In many cases this will be the individual responsible for both building and maintenance and possibly the total environmental management programme.

Materials and waste management

A waste management scheme will reduce the amount of waste produced, partly through recycling, where feasible, and thus also make savings in resources such as time, materials and money. For economic reasons, such a scheme will concentrate first on achieving maximum waste minimization and only then on disposal of the residual waste.

As in the other environmental management programmes, problems must be viewed holistically, waste management being perceived as a process affecting all stages of an operation from design to production, and aimed at maximizing the value of all resources. Figure 6.2 illustrates how such a policy reduces costs at every level, including the landfill (or tipping) costs that involve financial payments, loss of materials and degradation of the land.

Every employee must make their personal contribution to waste management, including product and services designers, those responsible for purchasing, stock

Figure 6.2 *A waste management hierarchy* (based on Kirk, 1996)

control, operations and sales management, with the aim of achieving the best possible financial return. As with other environmental management programmes, the first stage is the design of a waste audit.

It is, however, inevitable that some waste will occur, unless there is appropriate, local, multi-sector co-operation to close the waste loop. Management of this waste must be carried out within the constraints of the hotel's legal duty of care in a prioritized manner, as follows:

1. reuse the material if possible
2. if not, collect for possible recycling
3. if this is not possible and the material has potential energy value, donate it to local incineration or power generation schemes
4. if none of the above options is possible, consign to a landfill site.

Invisible waste

A holistic approach to waste management must take account of waste that is not measurable as an 'output', for example the excessive use of detergents and cleaning fluids. This is often called 'invisible waste' and can be detected by means of a more comprehensive input–output analysis, combined with measures of efficiency, including comparisons with industry standards or other hospitality businesses in a chain.

Specific categories of solid waste

Particular attention should be paid to levels of food waste. It has been found that around 15.5 per cent of edible food is wasted in hotels and restaurants. A flight kitchen may produce as much as 10 tonnes of waste per day. Paper is another commodity where waste can be minimized by reducing consumption, and reuse and recycling where necessary. An analysis of present use, including purchases and waste, should yield some solutions to the problem. It is essential that waste effluents which contribute to environmental pollution are minimized or eliminated altogether, thus promoting sustainability locally and globally. Noise pollution must also be avoided in the interests of the local community.

Recycling

The advantages to the environment of recycling are obvious. However, there are also financial advantages, including a reduction of the cost of waste disposal and the cash value of some of the products of recycling. Table 6.3 identifies some common recyclable materials and the resulting products.

Aluminium: e.g. cans and foils with high waste value, made into new aluminium products.
Steel cans: the tin coating is removed and the steel melted down for steel-based products.
Paper: separated into different qualities; the high grade paper is treated and made into boxboard, tissue, printing and writing paper, newsprint and liner-board.
Glass: usually clear glass is separated from coloured glass. The glass is crushed and treated, then melted, the molten glass being made into new containers, fibre glass or glass beads for reflective paint.
Plastic: plastic goods require careful sorting. The plastic can then be melted and remoulded into drainpipes, insulation, rope, carpet backing and many other goods.
Frying oil: This has a commercial value and may be collected by manufacturers for a variety of uses, including the base for cosmetics.

Table 6.3 *Recyclable materials* (Based on Kirk, 1996, pp. 117–18)

Management of the indoor environment

What do we mean by indoor environment? We define it as the ambience customers, employees and visiting professionals experience within a hotel or restaurant. This comprises air quality and levels of lighting and noise. These can impact upon the comfort, health and well-being of customers.

The Health and Safety at Work Act 1974 and the Health and Safety at Work Regulations 1992 provide the main legal requirements within the UK. These are supplemented by the Control of Substances Hazardous to Health Regulations 1988. Each country will have its own regulations covering health and safety. The UK regulations cover, in particular, the dangers of occupational lung diseases caused by exposure to dust, smoke and chemicals.

Comfort is a subjective experience, even though attempts may be made to measure it objectively in terms of temperature, purity of air, humidity, ventilation and noise levels. When we look at comfort holistically, it will become clear that the above factors affect one another – ventilation and acceptable temperature, for instance. A comfortable temperature will also depend on people's level of activity and what they are wearing. There is no absolute optimal temperature defining comfort, but rather a range of temperatures known as the 'comfort zone', within which most people will feel comfortable under defined conditions.

Other factors that interact within the bedroom environment system are bedroom temperature, ventilation and energy loss – arising from guests opening their windows if too hot. The need for individual control of temperature and ventilation by the guest will be obvious.

Operations managers have a responsibility for reducing to a minimum the risks to guests, other visitors and employees from a variety of hazards. There are five groups of chemical hazards:

- toxic (e.g. herbicides and pesticides)

- flammable (solvents and fuels)

- explosive

- corrosive

- infectious.

Software may be used to create, update and monitor a database of all potentially harmful materials, chemicals and substances in the hotel. In the UK, under the Chemicals (Hazard, Information and Packaging) Regulation 1993, manufacturers of hazardous chemicals must provide data sheets giving the information necessary to build up such a database. The principle which should be applied to dangerous materials is that of substitution with a safer alternative or, if this is impossible, ensuring safe handling, use, storage and disposal procedures are in place.

Air quality

Poor air quality can affect both the comfort and health of guests and staff. The parameters by which air quality may be measured are (i) the proportion of normal air gases and (ii) pollutants. Concern has been expressed over the effects of mechanical ventilation and air conditioning on indoor air quality. The competing claims of energy conservation and ventilation have resulted in poor levels of the latter. This can cause headaches, mucosal irritation of the eyes, nose, throat and respiratory problems. Table 6.4 gives the principal potential sources of air pollutants.

Air quality can be analysed by diagnostic screening to identify problems that can then be eliminated. Comments from staff and guests and objective measurements should be used over a time-frame, as single measures can be misleading. The three ways to improve air quality are:

- eliminate or reduce the pollutant source

- filter or purify the air

- ventilate or dilute pollutants.

Thereafter, monitoring and evaluation are essential for maintaining high air quality.

Noise

The most common sources of irritating noise are traffic, including aircraft, construction, industry and other human activities such as entertainment and sport. Noise can have many effects on the health of guests and employees, from migraines to sleeplessness. Noise can also impair employees' creative and productive performance. New hospitality businesses should be designed to physically separate noise-producing activities from noise-sensitive ones. Existing hospitality businesses should carry out a noise audit, based partly on an analysis of complaints, taking steps to change procedures and, where necessary, invest in noise control facilities.

Combustion products, including gases such as carbon dioxide, nitrogen oxides, sulphur dioxide or hydrocarbons; and suspended particulates from boilers, cooking stoves, vehicle engines, etc.

Chemical vapours from cleaning solvents, pesticides, paints and varnishes, and photocopier emissions.

Building materials that may include toxic substances, e.g. formaldehyde in foam insulation, textile finishes, pressed wood, fibre glass or mineral fibres, plasticizers, etc.

Tobacco-smoking products. Employers are legally obliged in the UK to control passive smoking. Designated smoking areas should be located nearest to the extract point of the system and non-smoking areas nearest to the ventilation inlet.

Radon gas and radon products which can be released by the soil beneath the building or by stone (especially granite), cement or brick building materials.

Methane gas from the decomposition of any nearby landfill facility or from leaks in the gas distribution system.

Water vapour that may result in high humidity and mildew, discoloration, odours and damage to materials.

Odours, both chemical and naturally arising odours from human activity.

Asbestos, in older buildings, capable of producing asbestosis and cancers.

Dust and particulate matter, causing allergic reactions, damaging equipment and decor, and increasing cleaning costs.

Airborne micro-organisms, such as *Legionella pneumophilia*, normally associated with moisture in air-conditioning and ventilation systems.

Table 6.4 *Potential sources of air pollutants* (based on Kirk, 1996, pp. 89–90)

Light

The properties and quality of light available within different areas of a hotel or restaurant have important effects on the overall experience of guests/customers and the efficiency of staff. The intensity of light for detailed work should be between 500 and 1,000 lux (or lumen per square metre), a measure of 'illuminance'. Only 200–300 lux is necessary for non-detailed work. Corridors and public areas require an illuminance of between 100 and 250 lux. Within bedrooms, the overall illuminance will vary according to the number of lighting units, with the most important factor being the degree of control that the guest has over lighting. Artificial light can cause distortions, for example in the colour of foods, and therefore lighting effects must be tested. Types of fluorescent lighting, in particular, must be tested with furnishings, crockery and food to check for any undesirable colour distortion.

Non-ionizing radiation

The most common sources of radiation in hotel operations are microwave radiation from microwave ovens, visible radiation associated with lasers in printers and ultraviolet radiation used in sun beds. Radioactivity (ionizing radiation) is rarely found in hospitality businesses, other than emissions of the radioactive element radon from certain types of building materials. Microwave radiation in the form of heat can affect the eyes, producing symptoms similar to a cataract. Regular checks on microwave ovens for leakage should be carried out to ensure that any exposure is below the recommended maximum exposure level of 100 watts per square metre.

Laser printers have built-in protection against this form of radiation, which can damage the retina of the eye and burn the skin. Staff should be trained to limit their maintenance activities to that recommended in the handbook and leave repairs to the manufacturer.

The holistic approach to environmental management

We shall now look in detail at a couple of approaches to environmental management.

Environmental management of pollution involves dealing with a complex set of interacting issues and emergent systems. It is only possible to achieve effective management of specific resources by treating these issues in a holistic way. By considering all these factors as a system and recognizing how all the parts of a hotel system interact, it should be possible to make sensible decisions that allow the hotel to obtain the optimum benefit to the environment while at the same time posing no threat to the financial viability of the hotel.

Let us consider the example of waste management. Treating the operation as a whole, and taking into account interactions between design, purchasing specification, production planning, stock management, waste management and waste disposal, it is often possible to gain both environmental and financial benefits, utilizing these savings to finance environmental initiatives with no immediate short-term payback. This holistic way of viewing the environmental management system is shown in Figure 6.3.

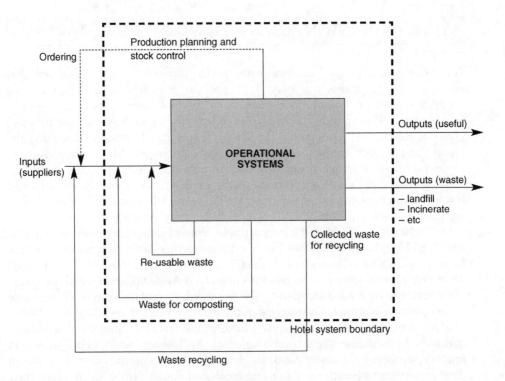

Figure 6.3 *An environmental management system* (based on Figure 6.7 of Kirk, 1996)

Some authors have expressed the view that the whole economic and business system has to be redesigned to integrate with the natural environment. They advocate the redesign or start-up of a business so that it maintains a holistic relationship between economy and ecology, and is not therefore limited to 'end-of-pipe' remedies such as reducing existing emissions. Many companies in the hospitality industry have attempted the design or redesign approach.

Apart from hospitals, hotels have the highest environmental impact of commercial buildings, due to the amounts of energy, water and other resources they consume every day of the year. Indeed, 'the construction industry, in general, consumes half of the resources produced on the planet every year, and is directly and indirectly responsible for about 40 per cent of emissions' (Rada, 1996). One of the most obvious commercial advantages of an environmentally designed new hotel or restaurant is that it will have lower operating costs than a conventionally designed structure. Rada suggests that the main principles of environmental design are:

- *minimizing the use of resources*, the advantages of which cascade down into reduced maintenance and technical equipment costs

- *thinking of a building as a complete system* rather than as a collection of engineering disciplines

- *multifunctional use of parts, features and systems*, which has the twin advantages of reducing costs and increasing functionality.

SYSTEM ADOPTION

For many years, people involved with service industries have considered that environmental concerns are only applicable to industrial and manufacturing business – what are commonly thought to be the polluting industries. However, more recently this view has been challenged by bodies such as the International Hotel & Restaurant Association, the World Travel and Tourism Council and the Hotel Catering International Management Association (HCIMA). The reasons lie in the fact that, although hospitality and tourism businesses are often small and consume relatively small proportions of the earth's finite resources and produce low levels of emissions and waste, they are the world's largest industry in terms of turnover and job creation.

Jones (1999) reveals how the International Hotels Environment Initiative (IHEI) and World Wildlife Fund (WWF) are working together to develop benchmarks for hotel chains. Other schemes include the Green Globe certification (USA) and Green Gum Tree classification (Australia), the Green Leaf Award (Canada) and the Green Tourism Business Award (Scotland). The hotels which make up the IHEI were able to demonstrate considerable progress in the first five years (Green Hotelier, 1998).

Many hotel groups now operate globally and can be categorized as multinationals. In their case, the dictum 'think globally, but act locally' is not so easy in practice, as there is an understandable desire to develop policies that are uniform throughout their operations. Of course, such companies also wish to adapt their practices to local cultures and competitive conditions. If they seek to introduce a world-wide corporate standard, they may find this does not always fulfil the legislative and regulatory demands of the individual countries in which they operate. These hotel groups will also be influenced by competitive pressures, for example the strategic and practical approach on environmental issues taken by suppliers and competitors.

As an example, in the Veneto region of Italy, hotels noticed a sharp downturn in business in 1992, following an excellent year in 1991. They discovered that this was due to northern European visitors' dissatisfaction with the region's attitude to the environment. Steps were taken to remedy the situation, including the formation of a consortium to demonstrate and promote green values. The Hotel Ariston in Milan implemented an environmental policy and increased its occupancy by 15 per cent, while the general occupancy for Milan hotels went down by 25 per cent.

In some parts of the world, water is a critical resource. This is true for many parts of the Asia Pacific region. The Mandarin Oriental in Jakarta, Indonesia, has been able to reduce its water consumption by 13 per cent, through the use of practical measures, such as reduced-flow shower heads (Clements-Hunt, 1995).

In the mid-1990s, a number of the top hotel groups in the world founded the IHEI, and this group has been responsible for spearheading and developing many new approaches to environmental management. For example, in 1997, the Scandic Group of hotels opened a 194-room hotel in Oslo, Norway. This hotel incorporates features such as natural wood and fibres in the construction (each room is 97 per cent recyclable), individual computerized bedroom heating controls, low energy light bulbs, submetering of energy and water and segregated waste bins in each bedroom (paper, organic waste, metal/plastic) (Green Hotelier, 1997a). In the same year, the Hong Kong Shangri-La became the first hotel in the Asia Pacific region to be awarded ISO 14001 (Green Hotelier, 1997b).

A lot of the emphasis of environmental management focuses on the large international chain hotels. However, there is much that small independently managed hotels can do. An example is the Kings Manor hotel.

CASE STUDY: KINGS MANOR HOTEL, EDINBURGH

A member of Best Western Hotels, the world's largest group of independent hotels, the Kings Manor is a three-star, 68-bedroom hotel, situated 4 miles from Edinburgh city centre. Family-owned and managed since 1976, the Kings Manor was among the first environmentally friendly hotels in Scotland.

Its owner and director is a strong believer in the need to preserve resources for future generations. It is due to his commitment and enthusiasm that the company successfully introduced a programme of environmental management, leading to the accreditation of the Silver Green Tourism Business Scheme Award and now awaiting ratification of the Gold Award.

In 1992 the hotel developed a formal environmental policy in close co-operation with the local authority and various environmental action groups. As stated in its environmental policy statement, 'it is our intention to create a positive attitude towards Environmental Issues through Company-wide involvement at all levels – Ownership, Management, Staff, Suppliers and Guests'. As such, the policy covers aspects ranging from legislation, to indoor air quality, to transport, to communication.

Currently headed by the assistant manageress acting as environmental management co-ordinator, the programme evolved over a period of years. Initial measures involved maximizing lighting efficiency through energy-saving designs; installing automatic flush systems in all public toilets; operating a recycling programme of all glass, aluminium, paper and cardboard; replacing all of the windows with double-glazing over a period of eight years and introducing a towel-saving initiative.

Following the expansion of the hotel and the addition of a swimming pool and leisure centre, built under the consultancy of the Shetland Environmental Agency, three condensing boilers were installed in the totally computerized heating plant to maximize energy-efficiency levels. Today the hotel boasts a 95 per cent energy efficiency rate.

Further examples of the management's effort and commitment to preserve resources include the re-utilization of ancient cobbles and slates, found when digging the foundations of the actual building (previously a convent); the recycling of old bedroom units as office units; the supply of used duvets, soap bars, candles and bed units to charity organizations and of toner and printer cartridges to the local primary school and the Lifeboat Institute.

As well as being active within the company, the Kings Manor has launched and supports a variety of other initiatives involving the local and broader community. In association with the Wildlife Trust, of which the hotel is a corporate member, and with the help of primary school children, a millennium tree will be planted and a bat box erected, while the money obtained from the recycling of aluminium cans is used to sponsor a child in an African country.

The hotel practises the principles of responsible purchasing by buying, wherever possible, local, fresh produce, avoiding disposables and considering environmentally friendly products above others. It also actively encourages the use of public or alternative transport. By providing secure and adequate storing facilities, such as bike racks, the number of staff cycling to work has increased considerably.

The successful implementation of such a comprehensive environmental management programme as the one in place at Kings Manor has relied on the management's commitment and determination to make it work, as well as on the enthusiasm and co-operation of staff. Through the direct involvement of employees in the development of new measures and the provision of relevant and adequate training, high levels of motivation were achieved, awareness raised and staff participation ensured. The reinvestment of environmental savings in the improvement of staff facilities further contributed to high morale.

The examples cited above are just some of the initiatives undertaken by the hotel. While some measures were regarded as simply good housekeeping practice, others involved a significant capital outlay. The benefits, however, by far outweighed the costs. Aside from the tangible cost savings, the business has benefited in terms of enhanced image, overall raising of standards as well as improved community and staff relations. Further, the company's corporate efforts in safeguarding the environment have generated a 'feel-good factor' among staff of all levels. More importantly, while benefiting the environment, such efforts have contributed towards the wider endorsement of environmental responsibility among operators of the hospitality industry.

CASE STUDY: THE ORCHID HOTEL, MUMBAI[1]

The Orchid Hotel is situated in Mumbai, India. Uniquely, it offers the finest in luxury and state-of-the-art technology in an environmentally friendly context. There are five categories of bedroom: deluxe rooms and suites, executive rooms and suites, club private rooms and suites, Orchid suites and Presidential suites. But in keeping with the hotel's environmental commitment and Ecotel certification, every room is a 'green' room.

The Orchid also offers a variety of cuisine in the four restaurants. The Boulevard is a 24-hour coffee shop with a wide selection of Indian and international cuisine. The Coffee Bar brews 18 different varieties of coffee specially blended using fresh coffee beans. 'Vindhyas' serves authentic Indian meals in a traditional style. Mostly Grills is a fusion restaurant, serving a range of barbecued dishes in the open air on the hotel's rooftop. There is also Merlins Bar and Cascades, a cocktail bar on the rooftop, along with a rooftop swimming pool, state-of-the-art fitness centre and a same-day laundry/dry-cleaning service.

It would seem, therefore, that the Orchid has many of the features and outward appearance of a typical 'Western' hotel. But the Orchid is different, as its mission statement explains: 'ORCHID, Asia's first 5 Star ECOTEL Hotel, is committed to enhancing the guest experience while setting a new standard of environmental responsibility by conserving natural resources, educating, enlightening and motivating our staff, and cultivating community relationships.'

As evidence of this commitment to sustainable development, the hotel has Ecotel certification. The Orchid can demonstrate environmental friendliness in all aspects of its construction and operation, ranging from the civil engineering and architecture, to its use of water and energy. Even the cement that has gone into the construction of the Orchid is environmentally friendly. The Portland Pozzalana Cement (PPC) contains 15–20 per cent fly ash, as compared to Ordinary Portland Cement (OPC). The internal partitions are constructed from wall panels made of fertilizer waste, the efficiency of which have yet to be demonstrated. Conventional walls are made of red brick, which depletes the topsoil. These wall panels are also reusable, but do not require curing, plastering and recuring.

Two materials were used for the external walling and the wet-walling structure of the hotel. Autoclaved Aerated Concrete (AAC) is eco-friendly, as it is manufactured using approximately 60 per cent fly ash. Another brick substitute, it has excellent thermal insulation properties and a better sound absorption coefficient than ordinary bricks. The second material was Siporex, a structural material of steamcured cellular (aerated) concrete. Using this eco-friendly material saves up to 40 per cent on cement and up to 50 per cent on steel compared to reinforced cement concrete.

The hotel's façade has been deliberately designed with depressions and protrusions. These play an important role, since the majority of the dead walls remains in the shade, thereby reducing the surface radiation. The building is also designed with 72 rooms facing the atrium. These rooms are not directly exposed to the external elements, thus reducing the overall heat load.

---

1. This case study was written by Professor Peter Jones, based on information from the Orchid Hotel's own website: www.orchidhotel.com

Lighting in the atrium has been achieved by skylights, constructed from double-layered domes to reduce heat load and noise levels, yet also maximizing natural light in the atrium space. The swimming pool is located on the rooftop and is 4 feet deep. This acts as an insulator from the heat. KoolDeck is applied around the swimming pool deck to reduce the glare and the surface temperature so that one can walk barefooted around the pool.

At the Orchid, energy-efficient low energy fluorescent lighting is used, which provides as much light as ordinary bulbs, yet consumes substantially less energy. One 10W PL lamp is as bright as a 60W incandescent bulb, whereas the power consumption of the PL lamp will be just 25 per cent of the consumption of the ordinary bulb. Furthermore, room lights come on only when a key card is inserted, so there is no chance that lights or the air conditioner remain on once the guest leaves the room.

The hotel claims ozone depletion levels have been reduced to 99.55 per cent as it uses the more eco-friendly alternative R22, instead of CFC, refrigerants, in its air conditioning. The mono screw chillers, which have the smallest number of moving parts, operate on a stepless efficiency range of 10 per cent to 100 per cent. Attached to the air-conditioning system is the STL (stored energy) tank, used to store cold energy during off-peak hours. This stored energy is then used during the peak hours/periods, thus reducing compressor overloading and cutting power consumption. The heat generated from the air conditioners provides hot water to the guest rooms, laundry, toilets and kitchen.

Even the mini bars used in the guest rooms save up to 40 per cent energy, as they are equipped with 'fuzzy logic', which senses the load inside the refrigerator and cools it accordingly. An added advantage is that these mini-bars are CFC-free.

The Orchid has taken steps to reduce air pollution by installing air scrubbers in the boiler outlet connected to the chimney. The boiler produces a high amount of carbon dioxide fumes, which pass through the scrubber and are emitted through the chimney (as clear white fumes instead of the dark/black fumes usually seen). When the fumes pass through the scrubber, they are sprayed with water, dissolving the carbon dioxide, which settles down in the shower traps and clear fumes are emitted in the air. The consumption of water is 300–600 l per hour for 1,000 cu. m of gas, reducing the fume gas temperature from 250°C to 50°C. The water utilized in the air scrubber is recycled water from the sewage treatment plant (STP). A similar equipment, installed in the kitchen exhaust system, is the 'air washer', which works on the same principles.

The Orchid believes in the three 'Rs' theory of 'Reduce, Reuse, Recycle'. They are taking special care to conserve water by employing a number of techniques. All taps contain special aerators, which increase the water's force and reduce outflow, thus saving water. Using these aerators saves up to 50 per cent of water.

The toilets are fitted with Geberit Concealed Cisterns. These uses only 6 litres of water per flush, as against 15–20 litres in conventional flushes. Likewise, the men's urinals are equipped with infrared detectors to ensure a definite flush after every use, thus avoiding unwanted flushings of timer-set systems.

The Orchid also recycles waste water. Employing the latest technology, waste water is treated and then reused in areas like the air conditioning and gardening. However, to ensure the cost-effective use of this water outdoors, the gardens are drip-irrigated.

The hotel's window frames, master control panels in each guest room and shutters are constructed from rubber wood. After producing sap, the rubber tree is cut down and, because it is a soft wood, is not normally used for any other purpose. However, by impregnating the wood with an unleachable type of timber preservative chemical and seasoning in a kiln to ensure dimensional stability, it can be used. This process also gives the wood a natural timber look.

Much of the interior of the hotel has walls made from medium-density fibre wood (MDF), which is manufactured using cotton stalks. The cotton bush, which grows to a height of 5–6 feet, is cut down after yield and is usually rendered useless. With the help of advanced technology, the waste stalks of the bush then go through a manufacturing process that involves chipping, sieving, washing and cooking of the fibre chips. After this lengthy procedure, MDF is produced, having all the features of natural wood.

The triple-glazed windows throughout the property comprise a hermetically sealed double-glazed unit and an added reflective glass. This triple-glazed window blocks the heat of the sun from entering the room and helps in conserving the air-conditioning energy. An added advantage of this unit is that it prevents fabric and furniture colours from fading, as the triple-glazed glass prevents the infrared rays of the sun from entering the room. These windows also help in effectively cutting out the noise pollution from India's busiest airport, situated nearby.

Ozonetek is a company providing a range of products based on ozone technology in the areas of drinking water treatment, air treatment, waste water and effluent treatment, swimming water treatment and cooling tower water. A state-of-the-art technology, it was developed in India after five years of in-house R&D. It produces ozone by controlled high excitation to split molecules and recombines them to form ozone. This ozone is very unstable and reduces to oxygen in 60 minutes in air and 20 minutes in water.

One of their products, 'Aquazone', employs ozone to treat drinking water. It destroys all micro-organisms including bacteria, virus, spores, mould, fungi, etc., producing water that is absolutely safe, pure, fresh and healthy. This avoids the need to use chlorine to purify the water. When drinking water is treated with chlorine, the residual chlorine is also consumed and there are fears that chlorine may be a highly carcinogenic chemical. On the other hand, ozone, having half the life of only about 20 minutes, reduces to oxygen, leaving no trace of toxicity in water. This makes it the most environmentally friendly treatment known today. Aquazone water can be used for drinking, cooking and washing fruit, vegetables, meat, poultry and seafood, and to destroy surface bacteria for healthier preservation. Ozonized water can also be used for disinfecting anything, and is colourless and odourless.

'Airozone' deodorizes air and cleans industrially polluted air. It also reduces cigarette smoke and pollen levels in the air. It does this by using ozone to oxidize toxic chemicals present in the air. The result is clean, pure, fresh and healthy air to breathe. The Orchid pursues this method in its air-conditioning plant.

Common pollutants in swimming pool water are bacteria introduced by the bathers and from the surrounding area. Normally this is also treated by chlorine, but chlorine causes irritation to the eyes, nose and throat, and leaves a heavy smell in the water and on the body after a swim. A pool treated with ozone will minimize the use of chlorine by 30 per cent to 100 per cent of the normal recommended dosage for club, hotel and public pools. Ozone also has a micro-floccolant property, producing crystal clear and sparkling water that is clear blue in colour.

Another benefit of ozone treatment is that cooling tower water can also be freed completely from any chemical treatment and subsequent downstream pollution control. Ozonization prevents scaling, while removing existing scale from the condenser, which increases its efficiency. It also destroys all micro-organisms, preventing fouling of heat exchange due to algae, ends blow downs (the need to clean heat exchange surfaces with high pressure water) by increasing the cycle of mineral concentration, which drastically reduces water consumption with very little waste discharge, and reduces the corrosion rate by almost 50 per cent.

The Orchid Hotel management believe that employee education is most important to establish and maintain its 'green' objectives. In order to ensure the committed participation of the staff, it has assembled a 'green team' headed by an Environment Officer who is responsible for training, conducting refresher courses, solving 'green' problems and generally creating and keeping alive an awareness of the environment. He or she also holds competitions every month – coining slogans, sketching and even eco-friendly Antakshari. Employees are encouraged to come forward with new ideas. All this helps to keep staff morale high, while ensuring that the hotel's standards of 'Reduce, Reuse and Recycle' are maintained.

CURRENT TRENDS AND ISSUES AFFECTING THE SYSTEM

Such is the complexity and regional diversity of the global hospitality industry that it is very difficult to identify clear trends (Jones, 1999). Indeed, the very word 'trends' implies a degree of stability which is rapidly being supplanted by 'complexity' or 'chaos'. Nevertheless, recent apparent trends may give some clues about the directions in which environmental management within the hospitality industry will develop in the 21st century.

Legislation

There are specific waste regulations covering the disposal of different forms of waste. As these vary from country to country, we shall not look at them in any detail. However, it is essential to keep up to date with local requirements. One particular example is the disposal of packaging. Within the EC regulations on packaging – The Producer Responsibility Obligations (Packaging Waste Regulations) 1997 – there is a line of responsibility reaching down to the end business user. This has affected the fast-food industry in particular.

Although some people in the hospitality industry take their environmental responsibilities very seriously, others are only willing to act if there is some compulsion. Legislation is being, and will continue to be, used to change the behaviour of businesses. For example, in the UK we have seen legislation on waste disposal, energy use and on a reduction in the use of packaging materials. These have all affected the hospitality industry.

Green marketing

Marketing has been blamed for contributing to environmental damage simply because it produces increased consumption, particularly of raw materials. There is therefore likely to be an increasing emphasis on the social dimension of marketing, mainly in reaction to consumer pressure. There is a sense in which customer needs must be viewed holistically over time. Marketing decisions in future will have to take account of ecological factors if sustainable development is to become a reality.

Welford (1994, p. 26) asserts that it is in this functional area (of marketing) that a company's commitment to sustainability will be judged, particularly by the consumer and wider public. Some companies, such as The Body Shop and Tesco, have been proactive, rather than reactive, and this is likely to become a trend. Hospitality businesses will have to undertake new market research and strategies to inform customers of their environmentally friendly products and services. Marketing will have to be included within the company's holistic approach to environmental management. Despite consumer pressure relating to the environment, sometimes firms will have to face the challenge that arises when consumers' wants do not coincide with the long-term interests of the environment. This challenge can be met, at least in part, by marketing strategies that educate and inform on environmental issues and benefits.

Although some experts stress exclusively the rights and expectations of shareholders (Reinhardt, 1999), businesses in the 21st century will increasingly have to meet the demands of other stakeholders, such as customers, employees and the local community. For this reason, it is necessary to make public at least part of the results of the environmental audit.

Finally, there is likely to be an upsurge in green branding. This may be adopted by chains, such as the subtle highlighting of 'eco' in the Grecotel chain's logo. Alternatively, it may appear in the shape of awards given by professional bodies (such as the Green Globe scheme) or by local tourism organizations (such as the Scottish Tourist Board's Green Tourism Business Award).

Local and regional co-operation

Hospitality businesses can only optimize their contribution to global sustainability through local and regional co-operation. This can take many forms. Welford (1994, pp. 28–9) advocates the development of environmental networks, including multi-sector networks, among small businesses, voluntary organizations and the public sector. As other companies, through promotion, become aware of best practice in this kind of initiative, expanding numbers of such networks will enable controlled and sustainable growth to occur.

A global integration

The IHEI is one example of global co-operation within one industry, involving the sharing of environmental information and examples of best practice. The WCED is an example of an initiative to introduce inter-sectoral and international co-operation. However, to meet the global environmental challenge, there will need to be a meeting of minds, a consensus world view on the integration of economics and the environment. A fundamentally new paradigm relating to economics and development is more difficult for many economists and business experts to accept than was Einstein's assertion that time is relative for scientists in the early twentieth century. Even a shift from short-term to longer-term perspectives is proving unpalatable. But this time the stakes are much higher.

This approach is reactive rather than proactive and does not address the added value of environmental management. It involves only a 'cost-effective' consideration of compliance, rather than a 'cost-benefit' or 'value-added' approach. There is no encouragement either to go beyond strict compliance, or to attempt to influence future legislation. The guidelines suggested by Piasecki *et al.* (1999) are therefore neither holistic nor entrepreneurial. The language of compliance used by Piasecki is that of the manager seeking only to minimize the costs of this inconvenience without extinguishing a creative approach to other aspects of the business. These weaknesses arise from an unimaginative response to regulation that is perceived purely in terms of cost. By contrast, the entrepreneur, or enlightened senior manager, actively seeks competitive advantages from the creative use of imposed legislation and regulation, and attempts to influence other stakeholders and competitors and to influence future legislation in alignment with the company's environmental investment programme.

SUMMARY

This chapter has reviewed the response of the hospitality industry to pressures (from government, pressure groups and consumers). These responses vary from total indifference, to a cost-based approach. Other organizations have taken environmental management to the heart of their business and reviewed all business processes accordingly.

From a systems perspective, environmental management is concerned with all aspects, starting with the inputs to the business, the design and management of all processes and the output or waste from the system. Environmental management should start, with a policy statement and then conduct an audit, to establish current performance. This usually leads to a number of planned and measurable changes, designed to improve performance.

Areas of the business covered by an environmental policy should include:

- water management

- energy management

- materials and waste management

- indoor environment.

Although hospitality businesses were fairly slow to get into environmental management, a range of high-profile initiatives have promoted environmental awareness. A number of countries and/or regions have also developed environmental awards or grading schemes as a means of promoting their initiatives. In the future it is likely that we will see more of these developments, impelled by intergovernmental agreements, such as Agenda 21.

Having said that, many companies are at an early stage of development. Initially it is often possible to link environmental management with financial savings. Plans that result in lower consumption of energy or water or reduced costs of waste disposal are relatively easy to sell to the boards of companies. Beyond those changes, however, other changes may cost money to implement, with less tangible returns, and are often based on marketing or public relations benefits that are hard to quantify. This differentiates between those companies who only respond to a particular business case and those who take an ethical stance on environmentalism and sustainability.

Further study

Using sources such as hotel guides, tourist destination literature or websites, identify hotels and restaurants which use reference to environmental management as a marketing or promotional device.

Can you find any examples of grading or classification schemes based on environmental practices?

When you next visit a hotel or restaurant, see if you can find any obvious areas where environmental management is being used, or could be used:

- notices in guest bathrooms about reducing the frequency of laundering towels and sheets

- the use of low-energy light bulbs

- separate waste bins for paper and other refuse

- electric vehicles for grounds maintenance.

Bibliography

Clements-Hunt, P. (1995) 'Asia on stream', *Green Hotelier*, 1, 6–7.
Green Hotelier (1997a) 'Scandic opens "recyclable" hotel', *Green Hotelier*, 8, 6.
Green Hotelier (1997b) 'Shangri-La's path to ISO 14001', *Green Hotelier*, 8, 30–1.
James, P. and Bennett, M. (1994) *Environmental-Related Performance Measurement in Business: From Emissions to Profit and Sustainability?* Berkhamstead: Ashridge Management Research Group.
Jones, P. (1999) 'Operational issues and trends in the hospitality industry', *International Journal of Hospitality Management*, 18, 427–42.
Kirk, D. (1996) *Environmental Management for Hotels*. Oxford: Butterworth-Heinemann.
Piasecki, B. W., Fletcher, K. A. and Mendelson, F. J. (1999) *Environmental Management and Business Strategy: Leadership Skills for the 21st Century*. New York: John Wiley & Sons.
Rada, J. (1996) 'Designing and building eco-efficient hotels', *Green Hotelier*, 4, 10–11.
Reinhardt, F. L. (1999) 'Bringing the environment down to earth', *Harvard Business Review*, July–August, 149–57.
Stainer, A. and Stainer, L. (1997) 'Ethical dimensions of environmental management', *European Business Review*, 97(5), 224–30.
UN (1993) *Report of the UN Conference on Environment and Development*, Vol. 1. New York: UN.
WCED (1992) *Our Common Future (The Brundtland Report)*. Oxford: Oxford University Press.
Welford, R. (1994) *Cases in Environmental Management and Business Strategy*. London: Pitman.

Recommended further reading

Blowers, A. (ed.) (1993) *Planning for a Sustainable Environment*. London: Earthscan.

Brown, M. (1996) 'Environmental policy in the hotel sector: green strategy or stratagem?', *International Journal of Contemporary Hospitality Management*, 8(3), 18–23.

International Hotels Environment Initiative (1993) *Environmental Management for Hotels*. Oxford: Butterworth-Heinemann.

Kirk, D. (1995) 'Environmental management in hotels', *International Journal of Contemporary Hospitality Management*, 7(6), 3–8.

Kirk, D. (1998) 'Attitudes to environmental management held by a group of hotel managers in Edinburgh', *International Journal of Hospitality Management*, 17, 33–47.

Webster, K. (2000) *Environmental Management in the Hospitality Industry: A Guide for Students and Managers*. London: Cassell.

PART C

ACCOMMODATION SERVICES

This part of the book has two chapters that cover the provision of accommodation within the hospitality industry. There are two main systems that make such provision. Housekeeping refers to the system that is designed to provide clean and comfortable rooms for occupation by customers on a daily basis. This is essentially a back-of-house operation, one with which the guest rarely comes into contact. On the other hand, the other system – front office – is one that typically has a high degree of customer contact, dealing as it does with advanced reservations, check-in and check-out, and customer enquiries.

Front office

After completing this chapter you will be able to:

- *identify the main purposes of a front office system*

- *describe different types of front office*

- *explain the key processes in front office operations*

- *identify current trends in these systems.*

INTRODUCTION

The front office of any hotel is a central focal point for the whole operation at a number of different levels. For the customer, it represents the first and potentially last contact point with the operation. From making the reservation, through arrival in the hotel, throughout the stay and on departure, the front office will provide the guest with personal contact, information and a range of services that are likely to represent the majority of their contact with the operation. Its position at the most important entry and exit point of the hotel makes it the most easily accessible location for the guest during their stay in the hotel, and as the home for the telephone switchboard, it is also a central communication point. For hotel employees, the front office provides a focal point for all information about the guests as well as any activities, such as meetings, conferences and tour group arrivals, which are taking place in the hotel on a daily basis. For the hotel business, the front office is responsible for the sale of the hotel's most valuable resource, its rooms, and ensuring that these generate the optimal level of revenue. The front office is also the main centre for the collection of all hotel revenues as guests charge their meals, drinks and other services to their hotel bills, and will probably handle the processing of all cash. This makes the front office crucial for collecting key information on the performance of the business and for producing a range of reports for management use. This unique position within the hotel imbues the staff working in the area with a high profile and status, which is not always well received by other sections of the hotel's employees.

PURPOSE OF SYSTEM

The prime purpose of the front office system is to provide an interface between the guest and their access to hotel bedrooms and related services. The front office handles all stages of the guest cycle, from taking the reservation, through greeting the guest on arrival, dealing with their luggage, providing a point of information and access to hotel services during their stay, to preparing the bill and taking payment on departure. After departure, the front office will also maintain records of the guest and their stay, in order to encourage them to make a return visit and to improve service.

The front office also provides a central point for the collection of information and charges related to the guest's use of hotel services during their stay, so that an accurate and complete bill can be prepared ready for their departure. This activity also involves the collection and preparation of data related to the revenue of the hotel from its varied sales activities, and so provides useful information for managerial decision-making. As well as acting as the central point for the collection of hotel revenues from guests paying their bills on departure, the front office will also be responsible for handling revenues paid in by other departments of the hotel, such as restaurants and bars.

A third important purpose of the front office system is to maintain control over the hotel's room inventory and to optimize the revenue and profit potential of these assets. This activity occurs at a number of different levels. First, it involves the taking and monitoring of advance reservations to ensure that hotel rooms are available for guests who wish to book in advance. The decision as to whether to accept an advance booking involves consideration of the expected level of occupancy, i.e. whether there are rooms available for sale on the nights requested, and the rate at which the room is to be charged. Second, it involves the day-to-day allocation of appropriate rooms to arriving guests. This will depend on the type of room requested and the data on available clean rooms provided by the housekeeping system. At any time, the front office system should be aware of the status of every room in the hotel, i.e. whether it is clean or dirty, occupied or empty, by whom and for how long and at what rate. A 200-bedroom hotel operating at an annual average occupancy of 75 per cent will handle nearly 55,000 room nights in a year and will need to maintain accurate records about each one, representing a complex and significant information processing task.

It can be seen from the above description that the front office system involves all three types of operations process – materials processing (e.g. guest luggage), customer processing (e.g. on check-in and check-out) and information processing (e.g. advance reservations). These processes will be described in more detail in the next sections.

GENERIC SYSTEM CHARACTERISTICS

Figure 7.1 provides a simple diagram of the front office system. The diagram shows how the system revolves around two key elements – customers and rooms. Customers arrive tired and leave refreshed, having used the hotel's accommodation. In

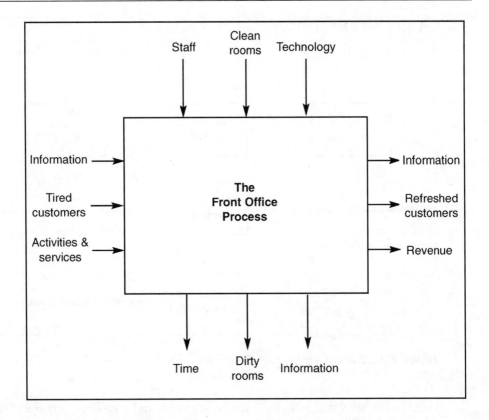

Figure 7.1 *A simple diagram of the front office system*

so doing, they convert clean rooms to dirty rooms, which then become the main inputs to the housekeeping system described in the next chapter.

Inputs

The most important input to the front office system is the supply of the customers who will use the hotel. These may come from a wide variety of sources and can be segmented in many different ways, but in simple terms can be split into segments based on the dimensions of group v. individual, leisure v. business and domestic v. international v. local (see Figure 7.2).

Each of these different permutations will place particular demands on the front office system. While a large booking from a tour company for a coach party may simplify the booking process, it places heavy demands on the registration and luggage transport processes when the group actually arrives. Some hotels have separate reception areas specifically for handling group arrivals, while others may register the guests and hand out keys on the coach while the luggage porters are already moving cases to their rooms. Some hotels have created guest-recognition programmes so that frequent business guests can bypass the traditional check-in procedures completely.

The other required inputs to the process are information, about the guests as well as the hotel and the surrounding area, and a range of activities and services pro-

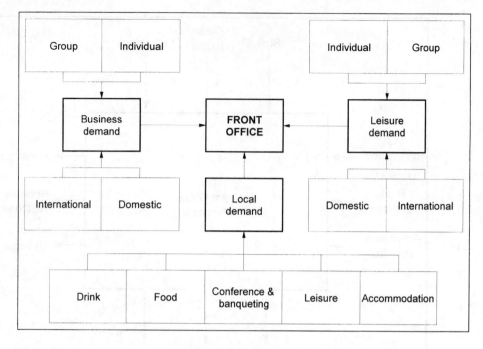

Figure 7.2 *Customer segmentation in hotel front office*

vided by the hotel that will satisfy the guest's needs and raise charges that will form part of their bill.

Transforming inputs

One of the key transforming inputs to the front office system is the transformation of the room stock from clean to dirty by the action of the guest's stay and back to a clean and ready state by the housekeeping process. The configuration of the room stock in terms of the numbers of different types of rooms – with single beds, double beds, king-sized beds, suites and so on – should reflect the particular demand patterns for the hotel based on the market segmentation, as discussed earlier. As demand patterns alter, it may be desirable to change the hotel configuration, but this might prove difficult, particularly if it requires physical modification to the property.

The other transforming inputs to the system will be the staff who carry out the tasks required by the various processes within the front office and the technology, increasingly computer based, that will facilitate the achievement of these tasks, as discussed later.

Processes

The front office deals with a seemingly complex set of processes that can be simplified by distinguishing them against two key dimensions – the stage in the guest cycle and the type of process (see Figure 7.3). The stages in the guest cycle are identified as pre-arrival, arrival, in residence, departure and after stay. The types of

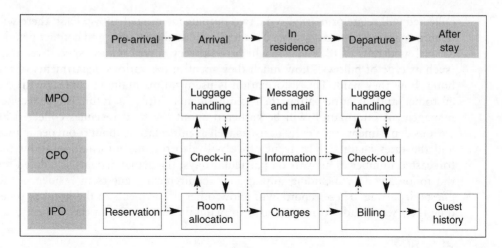

Figure 7.3 *Materials, customer and information processing operations in the front office*

process involved are the same as those discussed in Chapter 2 – customer, materials and information processing.

[The diagram clearly illustrates the importance of the interfaces between the types of processes and the stages in the guest's stay. The information required at check-in has been taken during the reservation process and is passed on to the billing process, where charges are added and payment received. The information is then stored on departure for use in future marketing or during the guest's next stay.]

The materials processing operations of luggage handling and mail and message handling depend on accurate information being available on the guests and their rooms. The customer processing operations afford the vital link between the guest and the materials and information processing operations, providing the front-of-house to the other back-of-house processes.

A key process not shown on the diagram but linking many of these operations, and indeed linking to the rest of the hotel's operations, is the telephone switchboard process.

Outputs

Refreshed (and hopefully satisfied) customers constitute the main output of the front office system. In recent years, there has been increased recognition of the importance of retaining customers and developing loyalty to the specific hotel and indeed the chain, should it be part of one. It is to be hoped, therefore, that the output of the departing customer will become an input to the system on some future occasion.

A second output from the front office system is revenue. The majority of the hotel's turnover will be collected either in cash, by debit card, credit card or account through the front office. Not only will all the room charges be collected here but also any other services that the guest has made use of during their stay, such as mini-bar, restaurant, office services, car parking and so on. The front office is also likely to provide other departments with their cash floats on opening and to handle payments received at their close of business.

A third output from the front office system is information. The information collected will relate primarily to the two outputs mentioned above. First, there will be information about customers. This will include their names and contact details, as well as details of their stay – which room they stayed in, any special requests (such as type of pillows), how much they spent in the various departments of the hotel, how they paid. This information is useful in maintaining contact with the customer and in anticipating their requirements during a future stay. Second, management information will be gathered about the total revenues collected by various departments on a daily basis, as well as information about room occupancy and the rates charged. The front office will also provide information about the forecasted number of arrivals on particular days, the actual arrivals scheduled for the following day, including any special requirements, guests in residence and guests departing. These reports will allow other departments in the hotel to schedule their workloads correctly and help maintain the security of the property.

Boundary

Within a large hotel, the front office and the housekeeping department will come under the responsibility of the Rooms Division Manager. Within the front office itself there may be a number of different sections, including reservations, reception, mail and information, concierge, telephone, night audit, guest relations, business services, cashiers and exchange. As the size of the hotel decreases, the number of different sections is also likely to decrease. In a small hotel, there may be only one person handling all these duties.

Although, in general terms, the work of the front office is easy to identify, boundary issues arise in a number of areas:

- Reservations. Particularly in chain budget hotels, advance reservations will be dealt with by a central reservations department and not at the hotel level. It can indeed prove difficult to book directly by merely walking in to such properties.

- Porter services. Many hotels find it difficult to justify the expense of full-time luggage porters. It may be possible to draft staff in from other departments in the hotel to take on this role when required. Some hotels, for example, ask their leisure centre staff to carry guests' luggage, but this may not present the image the hotel is aiming at.

- Restaurant cashiers. Some hotels will use their front office staff, particularly receptionists or cashiers, to act as restaurant cashiers, preparing bills and taking payment in the restaurant itself. Changes in technology however, have meant that the restaurant staff themselves can now easily handle this function.

- Business services. While some hotels will place this responsibility in the front office, those with a high percentage of conference business may locate these services in the conference office, as this may well provide the highest demand.

Interaction

As an important central function within any hotel, the front office will interact with most other departments. In particular, the interface will be most frequent with housekeeping and the customer-serving/front-of-house departments. The link with housekeeping is important to maintain control of the room stock – which rooms are dirty or out of order and which are clean, which are empty and which are occupied and by how many guests. This information is essential to ensure that rooms are allocated properly as guests arrive. The link with other customer-serving departments is important to ensure that all charges are appropriately made for any services that the guest has used, such as laundry, bars, restaurant, photocopying, and so on. Another important link is to the accounts department, where those guests who have arranged an account with the hotel, such as companies or frequent stayers, will be passed for invoicing. The front office is a primary source of information about what is happening on any particular day in the hotel and will receive enquiries both internally and externally.

Occupying a prominent position on entering the hotel and taking responsibility for the switchboard, the front office is commonly the first point of contact for external contacts, both residents and non-residents.

Process choice

It can be seen from the previous discussion that the majority of processes in the front office rely on contact with the customer, either face to face or via the telephone. The nature of the interaction with the guest will be predictable, but the detailed requirements will vary from individual to individual. For the majority of these processes, the job shop will be the most appropriate process type (see Chapter 2), but it may be possible to build in elements of mass customization. The 'ideal type' of layout for a job shop is the process layout and this is typically how the front office is organized in large hotels, with separate desks for reception, cashier, keys and information, concierge, transport, and so on. In smaller hotels, the activities will be combined into a smaller number of sections and the staff will need to be increasingly multi-skilled.

Typically the desks in the front office will present a high barrier between the customer and the member of staff, and transactions will be carried out standing up. While this may be necessary for security reasons with cashiers, who may be handling large amounts of cash, for other processes it may represent an unnecessary barrier. Some hotels have replaced their high counters with low desks where the guest and staff can be seated. The latest design for Courtyard by Marriott, for example, incorporates 'a walk-around front desk, enabling more interaction with guests' (www.marriott.com).

There are, however, some possible exceptions to this. Night audit, for example, who will ensure that all charges are entered onto guests' bills prior to making up the bill for departure, and who will reconcile the charges made and revenue received, are a back-of-house function that will more likely work on a batch process basis. Where advance reservations are taken centrally for a hotel that is a part of a chain, the reservations call centre may now be operated more as a production-line operation with standardized procedures and standardized scripts for the reservation agents.

SYSTEM TYPES

There is a key distinction within the front office between manual systems, proprietary or mechanical systems and IT-based solutions. Although primarily a distinction between information processing systems, it can be extended to the customer and materials processing operations as well. Manual systems are largely paper based, utilizing forms designed for a particular unit. A hotel may, for example, create its own booking form or it may enter them directly into a bookings diary. A proprietary or mechanical system would include the Whitney system. This uses forms printed on no-carbon-required paper that fit into purpose-designed racks. The slips are completed on guest registration and placed in the appropriate slot in a room board. This then shows which rooms are occupied and by which guest. IT-based solutions can be stand-alone systems carrying out functions such as reservations and billing independently, or they may be fully integrated into a property management system that can also link with electronic point of sales (EPOS) terminals in each department, the key system, the telephone system and even automatic sensors in the mini-bars in the bedrooms.

The decisions about which system types to introduce in a particular hotel operation will be influenced by the following factors:

- Size. While a small operation with only a few rooms can quite easily rely on simple paper-based manual systems, the complexity of large hotel operations means that a computer-based system is much more effective and efficient. Before computer systems were widespread, the Whitney system and similar systems from other makers were the most sophisticated available and were used successfully even in the very largest hotels. It is doubtful, however, whether any hotel would now think of installing such a system, and it has largely disappeared.

- Ownership. While independent hotels have the option of adopting whatever system they prefer, most chain hotels will now be based on computer systems and are likely to be linked to a central reservations office and to head office for transferring performance data on a regular basis.

- Service level. The hotel's level of service will influence the way that front office systems are designed and implemented. In a budget hotel, it is perfectly acceptable for all reservations to be handled by a central office; it is acceptable that the room will be paid for in advance and that no charges can be made to the bill; it is acceptable that there will no luggage porter service etc. In a luxury hotel, a higher level of personal service will be expected. The guest will expect to be escorted to their room; they will expect the concierge to be able to obtain tickets to the theatre at short notice; they will expect their car to be valet-parked and so on. While the budget hotel customer expects systems to be computerized and would find out-of-hours check-in by computer and credit card a novelty, the traditional full service hotel may well hide its computers in the back-of-house so as to preserve an image of personalization and traditional values, yet at the same time maintaining its position at the leading edge of the technology.

KEY PROCESSES

Information processing operations

The information-processing operations within the front office system span all stages of the guest cycle, extending both before arrival and beyond departure. In order to illustrate the complexity of the information-processing task, the following section describes in some detail the functionality of a Micros Fidelio property management system (PMS), one of the industry market leaders. A property management system is 'a computer system that links together all different parts of the hotel. It can be used to gather information from all those systems, such as the phones, restaurant and bar, to calculate guests' bills and even monitor stock and staff performance' (Davies, 2001).

CASE STUDY: MICROS FIDELIOXPRESS FRONT DESK MANAGEMENT SYSTEM (FDM)

The FidelioXpress FDM is a full-featured property management system designed specifically for smaller to mid-size independent and chain hotels. It automates property management operations such as room reservations, room assignments, guest check-in and check-out, and other front desk activities. It can improve the accuracy of charge posting and balancing guest accounts. It can confirm reservations over the internet and provide information key to making critical operational decisions. The basic software consists of eight standard modules.

Reservations

This is used to create and manage guest reservations both for individuals and groups. It includes the following features:

- single or multiple room reservations
- arrival and departure dates selected from a drop-down calendar
- a display of up to 14 days of room availability
- days on which particular room types are sold out shown in different colours
- automatic calculation of rates based on room type, rate code, arrival date and number of guests
- quick location of existing reservation by name, company, confirmation number and dates
- attachment of messages to reservations awaiting guest arrival
- ability to create group bookings and rooming lists
- ability to pre-assign rooms to guests
- confirmation of the reservation via e-mail, fax or internet.

Rooms

This module facilitates the management of the hotel's rooms and floor plan. The features include:

- display of the hotel floor plan by floor/wing
- display of real-time room status information for both housekeeping and front desk
- colour-coded room status
- schedule of rooms for future maintenance
- tracking room status discrepancies.

Front desk

This module is used to manage guest check-in and registration. It includes the following features:

- lists all guest arrivals for the current day
- prints registration cards
- allows the fast retrieval of guest arrivals – swiping the credit card pulls up the reservation details
- provides access to and editing of guest in-house data
- tracks all guest activity for the length of their stay
- performs room moves.

Cashier

This module is used to manage guest bills and perform check-out procedures. It includes the following features:

- location of any guest by name or room number
- management of all aspects of the guest's bill, including debits, credits, adjustments, transfers and voids
- viewing or printing detailed or summary bills
- quick check-out
- ability to perform a fast group check-out
- foreign currency exchange.

Night audit

This module is used to balance the day's activity and complete the hotel's accounting functions for the day. It includes the following features:

- performs routine tasks such as posting room charges, changing non-guaranteed rooms to no-shows with a single touch

- processes no-show reservations and deposit payments
- automatic posting of certain charges
- automatically sets status of occupied room to dirty
- batch prints registration cards for the following day
- prints customized reports automatically
- automatic data back-up
- performs full audit without closing the system down to other users.

Back office

This module provides an integrated system for managing the hotel's financial and statistical information. It includes the following functions:

- guest stays are listed by guest, company, group, travel agent and room number
- revenue totals are shown by guest, company, group, travel agent and room number
- sets up accounts for regular, corporate and travel agent clients
- tracks payments of accounts receivable
- produces ageing report of accounts receivable
- prints statements and reminder letters.

Reports

This module allows access to all system reports, which can be customized. It produces reports on reservations, groups, deposits, room rates, front desk, housekeeping, back office, travel agents and audit, as well as producing customized marketing letters and mailing labels.

Set-up

This module allows the system to be customized for a particular hotel operation. In addition to the basic system, links can be established to other systems that will, for example, send individual and group confirmations by internet fax; automatically authorize credit cards and check credit limits during a guest's stay and track settlement; integrate with electronic room locking systems; connect to other internal and external systems.

Adapted from http://www.micros.com/products/hotels/hotel-management/, May 2002)

It can be seen from the above description that the key processes are concerned with the following activities:

- Taking reservations and the need to be able to identify quickly and accurately whether rooms are available and at what rate. The agent then needs to take the customer details, which subsequently form part of the hotel's guest database. Reservations need to be confirmed.

- Room status and allocation. On arrival, while the guest is completing any registration formalities, they must be allocated an appropriate room dependent on the current status of the hotel's room stock. It is important that the room status data is as accurate as possible to avoid any delays and to ensure that guests are not given rooms that are dirty or already occupied.

- Billing. All charges that are incurred during a guest's stay need to be added to their bill. The information must be both accurate and timely. On departure, the bill will be printed for checking by the guest and then either payment made or transferred to an account.

- Audit. The information recorded during the day needs to be checked for accuracy and reports prepared of the day's activity. Overnight, the status of all rooms must be reset, all room charges need to be posted and preparations made for the following day's departures and arrivals.

- Reporting. At any stage of the front office process, reports will be required to inform management and other departments of the day's business and to provide control information on business performance.

- Guest history. Once the guest has departed, they become a potential repeat guest and can be targeted with marketing materials to encourage them to return. If they do return, then information on their previous stay can be used to enhance the level of service offered during their current stay, so encouraging customer satisfaction and further repeat business.

Materials processing operations

The materials processing operations to be found in the front office are very simple and are only concerned with the short-term storage and transport of luggage, mail and messages, and cash. Depending on the type of hotel, they could also extend to car parking and shuttle bus or limousine services.

The key processes here are transport and storage. Any differences in these processes depend on whether they are undertaken for individuals or groups and the level of security required. The transport of luggage for an individual guest is relatively straightforward, once the room number has been assigned. Processing the luggage for a group that arrives together can, however, be more difficult. The main problem is in ensuring that the right luggage is delivered to the right room and that any changes in rooming instigated at check-in are communicated to the porters who will be delivering the items. Some hotels, for example in the development of the Post House concept, have removed the delivery of luggage from their services, assuming that the guest will be able to deal with their own bags and/or by providing trolleys to make it easier. Most hotels, however small, will find some way of helping infirm guests even if they do not normally provide the service. The transport of cash raises particular issues in terms of security. While individual transactions are of little concern, it is when cash is batched together for transport to the bank that problems could arise. Many hotels will outsource their cash collection to a specialist firm.

Many guests will require their luggage and other possessions to be stored for short periods on arrival or departure. Procedures should be in place to ensure that the property is stored securely and that the correct luggage is returned to the guest, normally by some form of ticket system. The secure storage of valuables for guests is commonly conducted through the front office, which can provide a safe-deposit box service where keys are held both by the guest and the front office. Many hotels have, however, introduced a self-service system with individual safes in the guest bedrooms that can be programmed with access codes by the guests themselves.

Depending on the level and type of hotel, the front office will provide a range of transport services, from shuttle buses at airport hotels linking to the terminals, to organizing taxis or hire cars. This is another area of hotel operations that is commonly outsourced to a separate company.

Customer processing operations

There can be no doubt that the high-profile position of the front office within a hotel places particular pressures on the employees working in this area. Research conducted by Barrington and Olsen (1988) found that the complexity of the front office service was most affected by the process of dealing with others, the task significance, the task identity and autonomy. Dealing with others was concerned not only with the constant pressure of handling customer demands but also with the need to work closely with other members of the team and with other departments. Task significance was concerned with the extent to which the job is likely to affect the lives or well-being of others. Task identity is to do with the extent to which a job requires the completion of a whole and identifiable piece of work from start to finish, while autonomy is the degree to which the job is performed without supervision.

The customer contact role has immediate impact both on the customer receiving the service and on the employee delivering it, and it is widely recognized that this can create considerable stress for both parties (for a fuller description of the nature and complexity of managing service, see Jones and Lockwood, 1989). Companies therefore spend considerable time and effort ensuring that this 'service encounter' has the best chance of success. The dyadic nature of the service encounter makes it almost impossible to supervise directly, although some telephone interactions can be 'overheard' in real time or recorded for later assessment. This has encouraged a range of responses. Some companies, such as Disney, have turned to a strongly scripted interaction, where staff are encouraged to repeat the same carefully structured routine with each customer and so ensure a consistent standard. At the other extreme, some companies, such as Ritz Carlton, have favoured an empowerment approach, where, within certain guidelines, staff are encouraged to respond in the most appropriate manner to ensure the guest's ultimate satisfaction. Whichever approach is adopted, there will be a need for customer service training.

CASE STUDY: FORTE'S COMMITMENT TO EXCELLENCE

In 1998, Granada's Forte hotel group (composed at that time of Le Meridien, Heritage, Post House and Travelodge brands) launched their 'Commitment to

Excellence' training programme. The programme, consisting of 20 hours training over a 12-week period, was delivered to all 47,000 permanent and temporary employees. It covered everything from how employees should respond to customers and handling crises to body language and teamwork. The emphasis was on encouraging a more open and empowering culture across the group. The company wanted customers to receive a predictable rather than a random experience, which would keep them coming back.

Having trained all existing staff, the attention then moved to the recruitment and induction process for new staff. All candidates have to answer questions designed to reveal how they would respond to customers. In addition to completing a specially designed application form, all applicants undergo a further screening test made up of 25 multiple-choice questions that ask how they would feel or behave in a range of situations, including how they would respond to an unhappy customer.

(Adapted from Anon, 2000)

However, concern has been expressed recently about the standard of customer service received, especially in limited service hotels in the USA (Brudney, 2001). Brudney reports being very disappointed by the lack of warmth in the greeting, the limited eye contact, and in particular the lack of interest shown in the guest and their requirements for onward reservations or suggestions for places to eat. The reaction to his concerns from the industry would seem to suggest that the prime cause is a lack of recognition of the importance of the front desk's role and the increasingly poor pay and conditions to be found as staffing levels are reduced to cope with business downturns.

Key systems

An interesting area of change in the front office has been in the area of the management of room keys. In the earliest examples of inns, there was no need for room keys as the bedrooms, and indeed the beds, were shared by a number of different guests. Over time, however, the need for security and privacy has grown so that a lockable door is now an essential requirement. Mechanical locks with completely different keys for each lock would be unworkable in all but the smallest hotels, so mechanical locks sharing the same basic structure and providing suites of keys, including masters and sub-masters, were introduced. Mechanical locks and their associated keys are problematic if a guest should leave with a key. The key will have to be replaced for the incoming guest and the 'lost' key, with its large room identifier attached, presents a potential security problem.

Many hotels have therefore moved to electronic locks that are programmed to respond to an electronic code on a plastic card that can be changed for each new incoming guest. The key cards are programmed using a terminal at reception when the guest arrives and have a unique code, which the door lock recognizes. If the key is lost, a new key and code can be issued. A range of master and sub-master cards can be issued to room attendants who need access to a given section of rooms, or to housekeepers or managers who need access to all rooms. The following section describes some of the features of the VingCard system.

CASE STUDY: ELECTRONIC LOCKS AND ROOM KEYS BY VINGCARD

The VingCard Compact 2100 is designed to meet the needs of small to medium-sized properties. The system consists of a system controller based in the reception area of the front office and a card encoder base that writes each cardholder's personal code on a standard magnetic stripe card. The system controller can be removed from the base station and plugged into any lock in the hotel to repro-gramme it or to view or download the last 100 openings from the lock's entry log, providing an audit trail of which card allowed access to the room and at what times. The card encoder takes three steps to issue a card – key in the room data, key in the check-out time and swipe the card to give to the guest.

The controller sits on the front desk and is stand-alone, i.e. it needs no wiring connection from the locks to the controller. When the guest uses the card in the lock for the first time, the lock checks that the card is valid for that door and that it is within the time given and then automatically recodes itself for the new card and the duration of the guest's stay.

The card can be configured for four different guest 'types':

- standard guest access with a short lock-open time

- handicapped guest with an extra delay on lock-open times

- deadbolt override in family rooms enabling one guest to open the door even if it has been deadbolted from the inside by another room guest

- handicapped guest with deadbolt override combining both features.

Employees using the card can be grouped by section, zone or building, and up to 23 different user groups can be programmed, allowing different shift patterns and supervisory levels.

The system can handle four different lock types:

- guest door with access limited to an individual guest and specific employee groups

- service doors, such as linen cupboards, giving access to a single employee group

- service common doors allowing access by several employee groups

- global common doors, such as perimeter doors or night entrances, allowing access to all guests and employees.

A number of special purpose cards are also available:

- fail-safe key cards that are kept in a locked safe for use in the event of total system failure

- emergency key cards that open all doors and override deadbolts

- lock-out cards that will invalidate the current guest key card for any room.

The system can be linked directly with any property management system, allowing check-in and key coding to be carried out from the same terminal, speeding up the process and reducing keyboard errors.

(Adapted from www.vingcard.com/Products/VC2100/extra.htm, May 2002)

CURRENT TRENDS AND ISSUES AFFECTING SYSTEM

Although the front office does not immediately appear to be an area that would be at the forefront of operational trends, it does display many of those described in Chapter 2.

Production-lining

Computer-directed interaction. Many of the processes carried out in the front office involve entering data onto computer-based forms. These forms constitute a type of production-lining, in that the task becomes computer directed. The computer is programmed to accept entries in a particular sequence only. The user is directed to ask for specific information before being moved on to the next field. In this way the interaction is always consistent and collects all the required information, but it may lack flexibility and the sequence may appear inappropriate at times. Systems of this nature are also likely to be monitored and record the number of calls taken, the time taken on each call, and so on.

Decoupling

Decoupling is the notion of separating back-of-house or back office operations from front-of-house operations. Examples of this trend can be seen in the front office system, particularly in relation to the reservations process and the out-sourcing of some functions. In small independent hotels, the scale of operations may require that front office staff must be multifunctional and carry out reservations, reception, cashiering and telephone tasks. In larger properties, there will be an opportunity to specialize and split the tasks into separate roles. In this case, a specialist team of staff would only deal with taking reservations. This should lead to a more efficient and more effective reservations process. Taking this one stage further, the majority of budget hotel chains have removed all reservations tasks from the unit level and created central reservations offices that handle all the bookings for all the hotels in the chain. This again gives opportunities for econo-mies of scale and scope, but also allows a chain-wide perspective on bookings to be taken, which may lead to more strategic decision-making to enhanced revenue management.

Another process in the front office that can also be decoupled is the whole of the accounts receivable and debt recovery process, which can be outsourced either to head office or to a specialist company.

Self-service

There are many examples of the introduction of self-service into the front office system. These include:

- Booking via the internet. Increasing numbers of hotels, both large and small, independent and chain, now have the facility to establish availability, take reservations details, accept payment and provide confirmation automatically through the hotel's own website, the chain's central website or a third-party booking agent.

- Check-in by terminal and credit card. The French hospitality company Accor, with their Formule 1 budget hotel chain, were one of the first hotel companies to install computer terminals, rather like bank cash machines, that would allow guests to check in out of hours and gain access to the hotel and their room using their credit card and the issuing of an electronic key. While many airlines have installed similar machines at airports to allow express check-in, there has been limited uptake in the hotel industry in general to provide a similar express service within the hotel lobby.

- Information through the TV screen. One of the most frequently used services of the front office is the provision of information about the hotel's services and its locality. This information can now be easily provided through the TV in the guest bedroom.

- View the bill on the TV. Similarly, it is now possible to link the hotel's accounting system to the TV in the room, so allowing the guest to view their bill. If the guest has already registered their credit card or the bill is being charged to a company account, the guest could also agree the payment and effectively check-out without any need to call at the reception desk. If the rooms were equipped with printers or fax machines, then a receipted bill could also be delivered, or it could simply be sent on by mail following the guest's departure.

- Direct dial telephone and fax. Obviously, the introduction of direct dial telephones has drastically reduced the number of calls that need to be handled by the switchboard operator. Similarly, introducing fax machines into guest rooms would allow those business clients to self-serve their own faxes rather than relying on the office services of the hotel's front office.

- Morning call. Early morning calls used to be taken by the porter or receptionist and involved the switchboard operator ringing round the rooms at appropriate times. This system was superseded by an automatic function that could be programmed to ring the guest room with a recorded message at the required time, but increasingly rooms are equipped with alarms, either through the telephone or through the TV system, that can be programmed by the guests themselves.

Micro-footprint

A recent development noted in the USA is the Mobile Zip-in Check-in programme at the Newark Gateway Hilton (Siguaw and Enz, 1999). Guests using the hotel's airport shuttle bus can register with their credit card or HHonours card using a card reader on the bus. This is relayed to a dedicated workstation at the hotel's front desk so that their room can be allocated and the key be ready at the front door when the shuttle bus arrives at the hotel. A less sophisticated but equally effective system operated by the Marriott US Postal Service Conference Centre uses a set of pre-allocated room keys and a simple voucher imprinter to offer the same shuttle bus express check-in.

Yield management

One of the key developments in front office systems has been the introduction of yield management or revenue management. This is based on the premise that, due to the nature of the cost structure of hotels with high fixed costs and low variable costs, increases in revenue result in more than proportionate increases in profit, especially in the rooms operation. It is imperative then to ensure that the best combination of hotel occupancy and room rate is achieved. Jauncey *et al.* (1995) define yield management as 'the maximization of room revenue through the manipulation of room rates in a structured fashion so as to take into account forecasted patterns of demand'. Although yield management is seen as a modern trend, for many years hotel reservations managers have recognized the need to optimize rate and occupancy; the difference, as suggested by Sigala *et al.* (2001), is that over recent years IT has provided better information to support and guide the decision-making process. This has led Jones (2000, p. 88) to recognize the strategic role of yield management in his definition:

> a system for hotel owners to maximize profitability through their senior management in hotels identifying the profitability of market segments, establishing value, setting process, creating discount and displacement rules for application in the advanced reservations process and monitoring the effectiveness of these rules and their implementation.

Jones (1999) has also provided a useful model to describe the yield management system (see Figure 7.4). The model clearly differentiates between two parts of the advance reservations process – the decision support system in the lower box and the decision-making system in the upper box. The decision support system, comprising the human resources taking the reservations and the technology that facilitates this process and analyses the information on demand patterns as it comes in, feeds into the decision-making process. The decision-making process, guided by senior management's strategic perspective, is made up of a series of rules that determine the number of rooms that can be sold on which dates and at what rate, taking into account the possible displacement of demand from multi-night bookings. This operational decision-making can either be done 'manually' by the reservation agents or automatically through the computer system.

There is, however, only limited evidence that implementing a yield management system does make a clear impact on profit performance. This is partly due to the sensitive nature of data collection in this area, but also because of the difficulty of isolating the benefits of yield management from the many other variables that could have an effect. Jones (2000) tentatively suggests that yield management may improve yield performance by around 4 per cent in the UK, based mainly on improvements in achieved room rate rather than the better management of occupancy, and primarily during periods when demand is strong.

Integration

The development of modern database applications, including property management and point-of-sale systems, has greatly increased the efficiency with which the tasks of taking reservations, handling charges to guest accounts, etc. can be handled. However, many hotels have not been able to take advantage of all the benefits

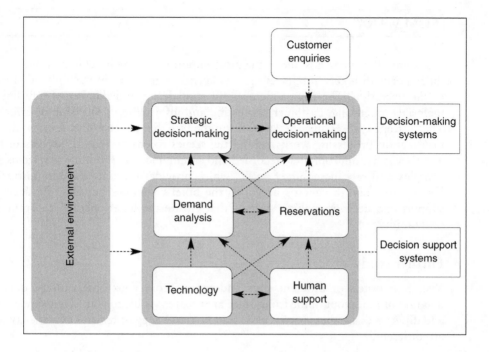

Figure 7.4 *Yield management system* (adapted from Jones, 1999)

that these systems provide, because of the time and effort involved in developing the interfaces between the systems that allow them to communicate together effectively and reliably. The basic problem is finding a common language that the various systems that have been added over many years of operation can use to transfer data. Translating data between old systems and new ones can add significant cost to their introduction, as well as causing possible delays and increasing the risk of system failures. The Hospitality Information Technology Integration Standards (HITIS) are being developed to make sure that in future all systems will be able to communicate through the adoption of international hospitality specific standards. Further information on the progress being made to developing robust standards can be found at www.hitis.org.

ASPs

One of the most recent developments in front office systems is the introduction of Application Service Providers (ASPs). Closely linked to the concept of outsourcing, the ASP provides software based on their own external server, which the hotel accesses through the internet or similar link. The hotel therefore does not need to invest in powerful computers within the unit but only requires a 'thin client'. All maintenance of the system, upgrades or repairs are conducted by the supplier at their own premises. The hotel pays a regular service fee, but does not purchase or license the software, so avoiding large one-off payments.

SUMMARY

The front office system is one of the most important in any hotel operation, as, for the majority of hotels, rooms revenue will generate more profit than any other part of the operation. The front office system is made up of a number of interlinked materials processing, customer processing and information processing operations. The customer processing operations form the face that the customer sees, while the information processing works behind the scenes to ensure that all aspects of the guest's stay are appropriately recorded and communicated. Front office systems are complex and rely increasingly on IT, which provides not only the administrative systems to assist the guest's access to the hotel's facilities but also the decision support and decision-making systems that ensure the hotel operates to optimum profitability.

Further study

Visit four hotels of different sizes and types. From your observations, draw a diagram of the layout of the front office area that is visible to you. What similarities and differences are there between the four layouts? Suggest reasons why the layouts are different.

Visit www.hotel-online.com and find Brudney's article on customer service in American limited service hotels. Next find his follow-up article entitled 'America's front desk fights back!' from January 2002. Compare the perspectives of the senior executives and the unit managers. In what ways are their views different? Suggest reasons for the differences. Can the two views be reconciled?

Bibliography

Anon (2000) 'Immaculate reception', *People Management*, 9 November, 46–8.

Barrington, M. N. and Olsen, M. D. (1988) 'An evaluation of service complexity measures of front office employees in the hotel/motel industry', *Hospitality Education and Research Journal*, 12(2), 149–62.

Brudney, D. M. (2001) 'Front desk fails to catch America's hospitality spirit', www.hotel-online.com, November.

Brudney, D. M. (2002) 'America's front desk fights back', www.hotel-online.com, January.

Davies, A. (2001) 'Property management systems', www.caterer.com, 8 August.

Jauncey, S., Mitchell, I. and Slamet, P. (1995) 'The meaning and management of yield in hotels', *International Journal of Contemporary Hospitality Management*, 7(4) 23–6.

Jones, P. (1999) 'Yield management in UK hotels: a systems analysis', *Journal of the Operational Research Society*, 50(11), 1111–19.

Jones, P. (2000) 'Defining yield management and measuring its impact on hotel performance', in Ingold, A., McMahon-Beattie, U. and Yeoman, I. (2000) *Yield Management: Strategies for the Service Industries*, second edition. London: Continuum, 89–97.

Jones, P. and Lockwood, A. (1989) *The Management of Hotel Operations*. London: Cassell.

Sigala, M., Lockwood, A. and Jones, P. (2001) 'Strategic implementation and IT: gaining competitive advantage from the hotel reservations process', *International Journal of Contemporary Hospitality Management*, 13(7), 364–71.

Siguaw, J. A. and Enz, C. A. (1999) 'Best practices in hotel operations', *Cornell Hotel and Restaurant Administration Quarterly*, 40(6), 42–53.

www.micros.com/products/hotels/hotel_management/
www.vingcard.com/Products/VC2100/extra.htm

Recommended further reading

Ingold, A., McMahon-Beattie, U. and Yeoman, I. (2000) *Yield Management: Strategies for the Service Industries*, second edition. London: Continuum.
Verginis, S. and Wood, R. (eds) (1999) *Accommodation Management: Perspectives for the International Hotel Industry*. London: Thomson Business Press.

Housekeeping

After completing this chapter you will be able to:

- *identify the main purposes of a housekeeping system*

- *describe different approaches to housekeeping*

- *explain key processes in housekeeping operations*

- *describe the design and layout of bedrooms*

- *identify current trends in these systems*

INTRODUCTION

If the front office of a hotel is one of the most sought-after areas in which to work, with its high visibility, high customer contact, fashionable uniforms and perceived status, then the housekeeping area is one of the least admired. This is primarily due to the 'back-of-house' nature of the operation. It involves a series of physically demanding tasks, and very little contact with customers, other than cleaning up the 'mess' that they leave behind. It is seen as a low skill, low pay occupation, comprising largely repetitive tasks. It is also one of the most important areas of any hotel and is fundamental to successful operations.

According to Falbo (1999), the cleanliness of a room remains one of the few basics that can make or break a guest's willingness to return to that hotel. There is little doubt that while a clean room will not necessarily make an immediate impact on a guest, a dirty room certainly will. In a research study conducted by Hartline and Jones (1996), housekeeping employees had a direct influence on perceived service quality and word-of-mouth recommendations. However, they argue that it is more likely to be their performance in terms of the service outcomes – a clean room or hotel – that makes the difference rather than the service process – how friendly they were.

In a standard hotel stay, the guest will spend more time in their hotel room than in any other part of the hotel (even if they are asleep for a large part of that time), and it is the housekeeping system that is responsible for ensuring that the room meets the appropriate standards.

PURPOSE OF SYSTEM

According to Branson and Lennox (1988, p. 1) in a book first published in 1965, housekeeping may be defined as 'the provision of a clean, comfortable and safe environment'. This definition emphasizes that the housekeeping system is not necessarily confined to what might be thought of as the housekeeping department. It includes all those processes involved in providing the customer with the accommodation or space to meet their needs. This space involves hotel bedrooms but can be extended to any part of the hotel property – the public areas, restaurants and bars, conference and banqueting and leisure areas.

In particular, the housekeeping system serves five key purposes:

- The prime function of the housekeeping system is to provide clean rooms for the hotel to sell to its guests, and to service those rooms for the duration of the guest's stay. In an airport hotel, this may require the room to be 'turned round' more than once in 24 hours, but in a university residence or hostel the guest may stay for many weeks.

- To provide cleaning services as required throughout the hotel, ranging from all types of floor coverings, to walls, furniture and soft furnishings. This could extend to all areas of the hotel, although it is common for the cleaning of the kitchen, and indeed restaurants, to be managed within these departments.

- To provide all areas within the property with clean linen and uniforms as required, and to provide laundry and dry-cleaning services to guests.

- To provide security for hotel property, including the hotel's own infrastructure, furniture and fittings, but also extending to guests' belongings and indeed the guests themselves.

- To maintain decorative touches throughout the property through the provision of flower arrangements or other decorations.

GENERIC SYSTEM CHARACTERISTICS

Figure 8.1 provides a simple diagram of the housekeeping system with the key focus on room servicing.

Inputs

The main inputs to the housekeeping system are dirty rooms (which have either been vacated by a customer or are occupied for more than one night), the clean linen and towels used to make the bed and dress the bathroom, the cleaning materials used to clean and polish surfaces and the guest amenity supplies, such as shampoo, shower caps, tea and coffee, used to replenish room stocks.

Transforming inputs

The main transforming inputs, which remain largely unchanged by the process,

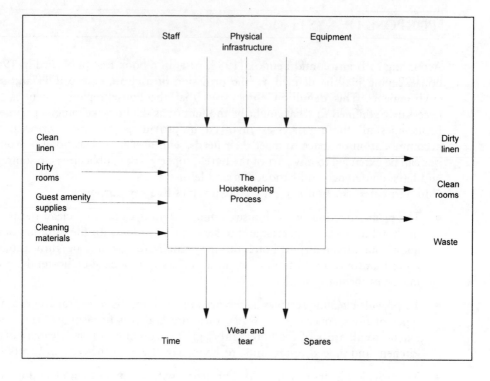

Figure 8.1 *Housekeeping: simple system diagram*

include the physical infrastructure of the building, the equipment used (vacuum cleaners, trolleys, laundry machines, and so on) and the labour force. In the majority of hotels, the housekeeping department is likely to employ the single largest group of employees. While the labour force provide their time and effort to the process and will be restored 'automatically', the equipment and infrastructure will require spare parts (cleaner bags, light bulbs) and need repairing as they suffer the wear and tear of use.

Processes

The main processes used in the housekeeping system will be room servicing, cleaning, asset protection, linen handling, decor and design, and room status communication. The first four of these processes are principally materials processing operations, while the latter two are information processing operations. As housekeeping employees do come into direct contact with the guest, albeit in a fairly limited way, there are also elements of customer processing in the system. The dominant process, however, is clearly materials processing.

Outputs

The main outputs from the housekeeping system are clean rooms, dirty linen and waste. The waste is partly generated by the process of room and general cleaning, but also derives from the guests themselves and their use of the room and other amenities.

Boundary

Establishing the boundary of the housekeeping system is a difficult issue and varies from property to property. Following the initial definition of the housekeeping function as 'the provision of a clean, comfortable and safe environment', the boundary should include all areas of the property – both internal and external and across all departments within the business. However, the actual scope of housekeeping responsibilities may be different from those implied by the system description. For example, it is quite common for the responsibility of housekeeping to stop with the fabric of the building and not to extend to the grounds, gardens, car parks and garages of the property. Responsibility for these may lie with the maintenance department or, in the case of some large country house or resort properties, with a separate grounds staff. It would perhaps be unrealistic to expect housekeeping to be responsible for the upkeep of the greens on the hotel golf course, but it may not be unrealistic to extend the responsibility to the changing rooms of the hotel leisure complex. Indeed, if overall standards of cleanliness are to be maintained across the whole of a property, appointing one manager responsible for those standards may make good sense. Again, however, it is not unusual for housekeeping not to be responsible for cleanliness in other departments of a hotel, for example kitchens, restaurants and conference and banqueting. An example of a suggested distribution of responsibilities in a large hotel appears in Table 8.1.

The question of the boundaries of the housekeeping system is further complicated by the practice of contracting out certain housekeeping and other hotel

Area	Tasks	Responsibility
Guest rooms	including hallways, vending areas, stairways, floor pantries	Housekeeping
Public areas	including lobby areas, front desk, main entrance, corridors, toilets, lounges, shops	Housekeeping
Offices		Housekeeping
Employee areas	including locker rooms, toilets	Housekeeping
Linen and laundry room		Housekeeping
Housekeeping storage		Housekeeping
Recreation areas	swimming pools, tennis courts, etc.	Engineering and maintenance
	changing rooms, gym, sauna, etc.	Housekeeping
Grounds	including car parking, garages, gardens, landscaping, pathways	Engineering and maintenance
Maintenance shop		Engineering and maintenance
Food and beverage service	including restaurants, coffee shops, bars cocktail lounges	Engineering and maintenance
Kitchens		Engineering and maintenance
Banqueting	including ballrooms, conference and meeting rooms, exhibition halls	Conference and banqueting

Table 8.1 *Allocation of responsibilites in a large hotel* (adapted from Casado, 2000)

functions. For example, window cleaning, both internal and external, is frequently contracted out to an external specialist contractor, as may be the cleaning of chandeliers, polishing of marble floors or more generally 'night cleaning' – the intensive cleaning of public areas during the night. Although these particular activities may be carried out by outside agencies, it is still the responsibility of the housekeeping manager to ensure that they are conducted effectively and within cost parameters.

Interaction

The main linkages between the housekeeping system and other departments or activities are shown in Figure 8.2. The key elements of the housekeeping system – the housekeeping office, the rooms and the linen room – appear shaded. The laundry is shown as hatched, as the inclusion of a laundry is optional. It is unusual to find a large hotel in the UK that will operate its own laundry. Most either contract the service out or hire linen in. In the USA, however, it is very common for large, and not so large, hotels to operate their own on-site laundry and, in some cases, dry-cleaning facilities. Obviously, if there are no local businesses available to

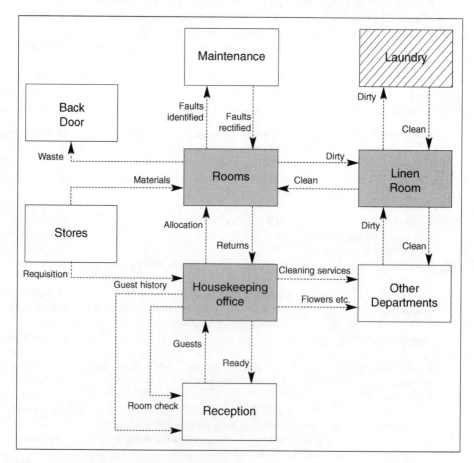

Figure 8.2 *Interactions with the housekeeping system*

provide laundry services, then it is an operation that the hotel must take responsibility for, even though it is a complex and specialist function.

Process choice

The issue of process choice for the housekeeping system poses some interesting problems. It is obvious that the rooms themselves, along with other areas that require cleaning, cannot be moved. Room attendants and cleaners must move from area to area taking their equipment and materials with them to complete their tasks. Most other examples of **fixed position** layouts, quoted in books on operations management, are of large-scale projects such as ship-building or construction, which are one-off long-term projects (as discussed in Chapter 2). Servicing rooms, on the other hand, is a small-scale operation carried out in a systematic way on a daily repetitive basis. This sort of high-volume repetitive operation would ideally be performed by some form of mass production technique. The servicing of bedrooms is, however, usually carried out by individuals or small teams working on an individual 'unit' at a time and so more closely related to a 'craft' or 'job shop' operation. It is difficult to see how this kind of distributed operation, rather like sending out field operatives to service calls, can benefit from mass production techniques and technology.

SYSTEM TYPES

The traditional view of the work of the housekeeping system is based on a clear hierarchy with a distributed workforce. A hotel room attendant or chambermaid would be allocated a number of rooms to service each morning by the housekeeping office. The number of rooms would probably be between 10 and 16 depending on the size and type of the room. The room attendant would clean and service the rooms on their own. A group of room attendants would be supervised by a floor or section housekeeper, who would check every room on completion against a checklist and either release the room to front office for allocation to incoming guests or ask the room attendant to revisit the room to correct any errors or omissions. This approach is clearly based on a domestic model that may be inappropriate to the process type discussed above. For this reason, a number of alternative approaches have emerged.

Individual v. team

An alternative approach is to group room attendants together into teams. A number of permutations are possible here. First, Casado (2000) suggests organizing the workforce into teams comprising five room attendants, one house porter and one supervisor. In this situation, the room attendants continue to clean the rooms on their own; the house porter provides supplies, removes rubbish, vacuums corridors and assists with any heavy moving; while the supervisor organizes the work of the team and carries out room checking. The benefit here is that keeping the team together generates a sense of group ownership for the rooms cleaned and allows workloads to be allocated across the team. A second approach recognizes that rooms can be cleaned more efficiently by pairs or sets of three working together rather than independently. The standard cleaning time for a Ritz Carlton corporate guest room is 20 minutes, but this is reduced to only eight minutes when doubling up in teams (Falbo, 1999). A third approach to teams is used by the Candlewood Hotel Company, which operates extended stay, all-suite properties in the USA.

CASE STUDY: CANDLEWOOD SUITES

Candlewood Hotels have revolutionized the way they clean rooms. When staff arrive at a Candlewood property in the morning, teams of housekeeping, front desk and management staff work together to strip all the beds, leave clean linen inside the room, put all dishes in the dishwasher and take out any rubbish. With this preparation complete, the housekeeping staff proceed to clean the bathrooms, make the beds and clean the rest of the room. The method has improved communications between management, front desk and housekeeping, raised commitment to the cleanliness of the whole hotel, increased cleaning speed and reduced any perceived imbalances in the workload between housekeepers.

(Adapted from Falbo, 1999)

The team approach has been advocated over a long period and it claims major gains in staff morale, commitment and efficiency. However, it is probably true to say that the majority of rooms are still cleaned by individuals and that changes to team approaches do meet with resistance, which may be difficult to overcome (see, for example, the team approach instituted by the Boulders Resort, p. 145)

Inspection v. self-checking

The traditional approach outlined above involves floor housekeepers or housekeeping supervisors inspecting every room once it has been cleaned against the hotel's standards. Many hotels have now passed the responsibility for checking to the room attendants themselves, giving them more control and responsibility for their own work. Housekeepers still carry out rigorous inspections against a detailed checklist but only on a sample basis.

CASE STUDY: GLENEAGLES HOTEL

The housekeeper's role has become less clear-cut as hotels have introduced empowerment and delayering by allowing maids to check their own work. The Gleneagles Hotel no longer uses the term 'maid' but prefers 'house assistant' and moved to self-checking many years ago. About 20 out of the total of 26 house assistants are now fully self-checking. In addition, to cover some 250 bedrooms at high occupancy requires only five floor housekeepers, two co-ordinators, an executive housekeeper and deputy. House assistants also take responsibility for stocking and checking mini-bars and tea and coffee facilities, as well as cleaning their sections of corridors. Housekeepers carry out spot-checks and each house assistant will have at least one room checked per day.

CASE STUDY: SHERATON PARK TOWER

At the Sheraton Park Tower in London, self-checking was introduced in 1991. The 140-room hotel needs about 11 room attendants per day to provide full cover and operates with eight permanent staff plus agency staff. Of the total – including agency and employees – 13 are trained to be self-checking. Some relish the responsibility, but others would prefer not to have the pressure of looking at their work from a housekeeper's point of view. Although the system needs two fewer floor housekeepers, the room attendants are paid extra for self-checking and receive a bonus if their spot-checked rooms reach consistently high standards.

(Adapted from Anon, 1995)

Success rates for this system are claimed to be very high and, as can be seen from the above examples, have been practised in the industry at the highest levels for many years, but there are still many hotels that continue to use the traditional approach very effectively. Some feeling persists that staff do not want the extra responsibility and that 'a second pair of eyes' should always check rooms.

Automation

Comparatively little automated technology has been introduced into the house-keeping system. The nature of the work involved and the variety of tasks to be completed in each room mean that introducing technology any more complex than a vacuum cleaner is very difficult. Accor have introduced self-cleaning bathrooms into their Formule 1 hotels that resemble the system used for public conveniences in major city centres. Formule 1 is a low-end budget chain offering very competitive room rates. The bathroom is shared between two rooms and this automated approach means that the room is always fresh for the next guest. Some automation has also been introduced into laundry operations for washing, drying and dry-cleaning, so reducing the level of expertise needed in individual in-hotel laundries.

KEY PROCESSES

Room servicing

According to a survey conducted by the American Automobile Association (AAA), cleanliness is the first thing that travellers look for when deciding where to stay. The top five factors that travellers in the USA and Canada look for in a hotel are: the room to be thoroughly cleaned and well maintained, with all equipment in working order, price, location, room amenities such as films, coffee-makers, hairdryers, etc, and professional friendly service (Anon, 2001). Given the guests' emphasis on cleanliness and maintenance, it is not surprising that the key focus of

Star grade	Accommodation requirement
*	Practical accommodation with a limited range of facilities and services, but a high standard of cleanliness throughout.
**	Good overnight accommodation with more comfortable, better equipped bedrooms – all with en-suite or private facilities and colour TV.
***	Possibly larger establishments, but all offering significantly greater quality and range of facilities and services, and usually more spacious public areas and bedrooms.
****	Accommodation offering superior comfort and quality; all bedrooms with en-suite bath, fitted overhead shower and WC.
*****	A spacious, luxurious establishment offering the highest international quality of accommodation, facilities, services and cuisine. It will have striking accommodation throughout, with a range of extra facilities.

Table 8.2 *Accommodation requirements for star grading*

the housekeeping system is on the efficient and effective servicing of the hotel rooms and their associated bathrooms and corridors.

The design of a hotel bedroom is critical not only in determining the type of product on offer to the customer but also in terms of how efficiently it can be cleaned. The English star grading scheme, as specified by the English Tourism Council, provides some simple guidelines regarding the level of accommodation that should be provided at different star grades (see Table 8.2).

This is only an extract from the complete guidelines, which can be downloaded from the English Tourism Council website (http://www.englishtourism.org.uk/downloads/Quality/HotelScheme.pdf). Even the complete guidelines, however, do not provide any detailed indication of room size, specifying only that 'all bedrooms and bathrooms should have sufficient space to allow guests freedom of movement', although they do provide a minimum size for the beds themselves. Room sizes do vary by grading, however. A study by Deloitte Touche Tohmatsu International (1992) looked at hotel construction in Europe and established the average bedroom sizes (see Table 8.3). Size will have a significant effect on the time taken to service the room as well as the variety and style of furniture and additional services that the room could hold.

The design of the room will also have to take account of the different activity areas (see Figure 8.3). This diagram shows the designated areas for six activities: access, storage, work, sleep, hygiene and leisure. While several of these activities will be essential for all guests, some will be more important to certain types of guests than

Hotel standard	Range in m²	Average in m²
Five star	23–43	31.0
Four star	23–36	28.1
Three star	23–33	27.6
Two star	19–21	20.5

Table 8.3 *Average bedroom size in Europe* (Deloitte Touche Tohmatsu, 1992)

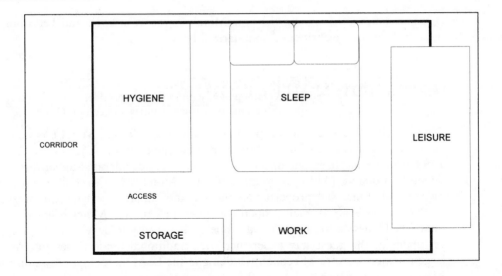

Figure 8.3 *Hotel room design*

others. For example, a business traveller staying for only one night may need room to work, with access to a telephone point to connect their laptop, but will bring very little luggage. A leisure traveller staying at a resort hotel for one or two weeks will need more storage space and areas in which to relax and enjoy their holiday.

The design of a hotel can have a significant effect on the bottom-line profitability of the property as a whole, as illustrated by the following report.

CASE STUDY: WIMBERLEY ALLISON TONG AND GOO

Using statistics collected by Smith Travel Research, WAT&G have calculated that the hotels they have designed show a consistent and quantifiable advantage over other hotels. Using standard industry benchmarks such as occupancy rates, room rate and revenue per available room (revpar), their hotels have outperformed competitors in all three areas over the seven-year period covered by the study. Having isolated several key variables such as location, management and time-frame, the remaining factor of who designed the hotel indicated a very strong statistically significant relationship between WAT&G's designs and hotel revenue. On average in the USA, hotels designed by WAT&G earn revpar $50 per night higher than a competitive set of hotels managed by the same operators over the same period.

(Adapted from Anon, 1998)

When designing a hotel bedroom, the effects of different design decisions on the servicing of the room should be borne in mind. The overall size of the room, the type and variety of floor surfaces, the location and make-up of the bed, the type of furnishing fabrics used, even down to whether the window has pelmets and sills, will have an effect on the room servicing processes. This is clearly illustrated in the decisions taken in designing the new Motel 6 prototype hotel and bedroom, as described on their website and summarized below.

CASE STUDY: MOTEL 6 PROTOTYPE 2001

Beginning in 1962 with one property in Southern California, Motel 6 is now the largest company-owned and operated lodging chain in the USA. Since August 1999, Motel 6 has been one of three proprietary brands operated under the Accor Economy Lodging (AEL) corporate umbrella. Motel 6 has over 800 company-owned and franchised properties in the US and Canada, providing more than 86,000 rooms – an average property features 115 rooms. Motel 6 has recently established a design for a new-build property that is easy to develop and maintain, yet upgrades the guest stay experience over traditional 'budget' designs. As the largest owner-operator of economy lodging in the USA, the design draws on their 35 years of experience and over 30 million guests annually.

Room size is one of the key features in hotel design. Each square foot of build has cost implications, but once built room size is almost impossible to change. Hotels therefore need good size rooms but must also offer efficient use of space. To maximize use of space, Motel 6 place the remote-controlled TV high over the wardrobe from where it can be seen in any part of the room without taking up important work surface space. The larger workspace has a convenient desktop-level phone jack and electrical outlet so that the phone can be moved from the bedside table, and the phone has a data port for modems.

Designs also need to be easy to clean, and to *keep* clean. The Motel 6 standard requires housekeepers to be able to clean a room thoroughly in 20 minutes; the room is designed to be easier to service. Flush windows have no sill where dust can gather. The light fixtures, with their flush surfaces, are easy to wipe clean. Rounded corners on the furniture also make cleaning easier.

Motel 6 believes an inexpensive room can still be functional and make the best use of space. With their purchasing power and long-term supplier relationships, they can secure favourable prices on custom-built items. They use a custom-designed desk/shelf combination and integrated valet/wardrobe that also serves as the TV stand. All furniture has a laminated finish for durability, sealed on all bottom edges to resist moisture absorption. The light 'beige wood' finish gives a modern, clean appearance and enhances the apparent size and openness of the room.

The open desk has a cantilevered top to allow a second chair to be used at one end. Shelves eliminate the maintenance problems of drawers, and reduce 'lost and found' problems after check-out. The wardrobe accommodates large hanging items and places the TV where it is visible throughout the room.

There are no sharp edges or recesses to hamper cleaning. Trim strips on the headboards, nightstands and other furniture are flush with the other surfaces. The vinyl chair upholstery looks like textured fabric, but resists stains. Bedspread and curtain fabrics co-ordinate, but the patterns do not match, to lessen the effect of differing replacement cycles and fading. The custom-made piece-dyed nylon carpet wears longer and reduces staining at a small incremental cost. Carpet cove base absorbs vacuum cleaner 'bumps' without harm. Long-life, energy-efficient fluorescent fixtures have no lampshades to deteriorate or require straightening. Textured paint wall finishes cost less and simplify maintenance. The entire room is designed with durability, long life and ease of cleaning in mind.

(Adapted from www.motel6.com/franchising/prototype.html)

Once the design of the hotel and the bedrooms has been determined to meet the requirements of the intended customers, the processes and procedures for servicing the room can be implemented. The processes for cleaning various types of rooms and for vacant, vacated and occupied rooms will differ, while following a similar approach. Branson and Lennox (1988) suggest a basic order of work sequence: open windows, remove litter and dirty crockery, strip bed, remove and replenish linen and towels, make bed, clean bathroom, dust, vacuum carpet and upholstery, spot-clean where necessary, replace room supplies, check. The actual order of work will depend on the particular approach adopted by the individual hotel and will vary according to service level and facilities within the room, such as tea- and coffee-making facilities, mini-bar, telephones, TV, balconies, and so on. This process involves a single room attendant working alone and entering the room once only.

CASE STUDY: BOULDERS RESORT, CAREFREE, ARIZONA

At a five-star resort, guests expect the utmost in service and cleanliness but can resent the housekeeping interruptions designed to ensure these high standards. Staff may well enter a guest room up to five times a day. The room attendant would come to clean the room, the houseman to clean fireplaces and patios, the supervisor to check the room, the mini-bar staff to check and restock the mini-bar, and the evening attendant to carry out the turndown service.

At Boulders Resort, by instituting a team approach, they have found a way to make the job more interesting, increase efficiency and reduce interruptions. The three-person teams take turns with all room duties, choose work areas, are responsible jointly for room quality and perform their own inspections. The approach was not an immediate success. At first, efficiency declined as staff got used to the new system. Some staff complained that they preferred to work alone. However, the team approach is now well thought of, giving more flexible scheduling and more employee control, faster room turn round and fewer intrusions for the guests.

(Adapted from Haussmann, 2000, and www.hotelinteractive.com/news, 10 April 2000)

Average cleaning times

Motel 6	20 minutes per room
Candlewood	18–22 minutes per suite
Atlanta Marriott Marquis	27 minutes per corporate guest room
Ritz Carlton	20 minutes per corporate guest room (8 minutes per room when doubling up in teams)

(Adapted from Falbo, 1999)

It might be expected that in what is a relatively simple repetitive process there would be one accepted way of doing things and that the average service times for rooms would be very similar between different hotels. The figures above show that this is not necessarily the case. Logically, it would take longer to service a larger and more elaborate 'up-market' hotel room (as offered by Marriott, for example), than the simple budget room offered by Motel 6. The difference, however, is a matter of seven minutes. It might come as a surprise that it could take less time to service an all-suite room (offered by Candlewood), including bedroom, bathroom, lounge and kitchen areas, than the same Motel 6 room. By changing the way that the room servicing process is organized, Candlewood have achieved a significant increase in productivity. This is further illustrated by the Ritz Carlton figures. Over an 18-month period, Ritz Carlton worked on their housekeeping process to reduce the time taken to complete the task and remove waste and errors from the system by going back to first principles and redesigning how they cleaned rooms. As a result, they reduced to 20 minutes the time taken for a single maid to clean a luxury room and bathroom – the same time as Motel 6. By using two maids working as a team, Ritz Carlton were able to reduce the time to only eight minutes!

Cleaning

The scale and complexity of maintaining the cleanliness of a large hotel should not be underestimated. Bally's Hotel in Las Vegas has 2,814 rooms and operates 24 hours a day. It is estimated that between 25,000 and 30,000 people walk through the hotel's lobby every day. The traffic volume, even on the guest floors, exerts heavier than normal wear and tear on floors and floor coverings and the materials, equipment and staff who clean them (Lerner, 2001). It is also important to remember that cleanliness comes high on most guests' list of priorities and they will judge the general standard and management of a property based on its cleanliness and general appearance.

The cleaning of public areas will follow a set programme of activity with different areas and different items receiving attention at different times of the day, night, week, month or year. While the carpets in hotel corridors will be hoovered at least once a day, those in the lounge areas may receive attention twice or three times a day. The marble floor in reception is difficult to clean during the busy times of the day and may therefore be cleaned overnight. The chandelier in the same area may need cleaning only every two months, but the finger marks on the glass entry doors may be polished off every hour. Similarly, public toilets need regular attention to ensure cleanliness and that supplies are replenished. These checks are commonly recorded in the area so that guests can see that they have been made.

The executive housekeeper will therefore have a complete schedule of cleaning activities, ranging from day-to-day cleaning tasks, through regular but less frequent cleaning of particular items, to deep cleaning or 'spring cleaning'.

The range of different wall and floor surfaces in a hotel, all of which may require slightly different treatments and cleaning regimes, amplifies the complexity of the cleaning task. Using the wrong chemical on the wrong surface may have a long-term harmful effect, and the control of these chemicals is therefore critical. These chemicals can also be potentially dangerous and their handling should comply with the relevant legislation, such as the Control of Substances Hazardous to Health Regulations 1999 (COSHH).

Many cleaning activities, such as carpet cleaning and hard surface polishing, involve the use of mechanical equipment. It is important that all relevant staff are fully trained in its use and maintenance to ensure that it is employed as safely and effectively as possible.

Asset protection

The housekeeping team also represents the front line in protecting the assets of the rooms department – in identifying any areas of wear and tear or damage that need repair and in maintaining vigilance over both the hotel's and the guests' property.

Although in large hotels there may well be a separate engineering department, which will have its own schedule of preventive maintenance, the housekeeping team are best placed to identify if any immediate repairs are necessary. While cleaning and checking the room, items such as faulty TVs, blocked shower roses or damaged curtain tracks, etc. will be identified. The maintenance team can then be notified of any defects and they can take corrective action. In smaller hotels, minor repairs, such as changing light bulbs etc., may well be undertaken by the house-keeping team directly. Ritz Carlton has taken this idea further by creating the Clean and Repair Everything (CARE) teams described below.

CASE STUDY: RITZ CARLTON CARE TEAMS

Introduced in 1996, Ritz Carlton Hotels Clean and Repair Everything (CARE) teams consist of a deep cleaner, an engineer and a painter who are charged with ensuring that rooms are immaculate. The team rotates around hotel rooms performing preventive maintenance at least four times a year and can tackle any maintenance, cleanliness or decor problem in the room immediately.

(Adapted from Wolff, 1997)

As well as overseeing the day-to-day care of all bedrooms and public areas, the housekeeping department is also involved in the longer-term refurbishment of these areas. This will need to be scheduled carefully into the work of the department to ensure minimum disruption both for the guest and for the operation. Scheduling major work for the lowest occupancy periods makes good business sense.

The housekeeping department is also closely involved in ensuring the safety and security of the building and the property within it. Key systems, as described in the previous chapter, make it easier to control access to guest rooms, and electronic systems will even keep an audit trail of who (based on their key identification) entered the room and at what time. This type of system can help to prevent theft from rooms by intruders and to some extent by staff, but will not stop guests from taking towels, bathrobes or even televisions from their own rooms. Close supervision by the housekeeping staff should be able to identify where theft of this nature has taken place and such cases can then be reported.

Room status

An important stage of the room sales process is for reception to know when rooms are available for occupation so that they can be allocated to arriving guests. Reception can provide housekeeping in advance with a list of rooms that are due to be vacated so that staff duties can be allocated accordingly. When the guest pays their bill and leaves the hotel, reception will know that the room is now unoccupied but dirty. Having serviced and checked the room, the housekeeping team can notify reception that the room is available for occupation. The way in which this communication takes place will depend on the scale and sophistication of the hotel.

In a small property, a simple list of departures can be drawn up, given to housekeeping in the morning and returned to reception once the rooms are ticked off as ready. In larger properties, where the turn round of rooms may be more critical, the 'return' of clean rooms may be done by telephone. The most efficient method, however, will utilize some form of computer-based property management system that electronically links the two departments.

Laundry and linen room

One notable difference between hotels in the UK and those in the USA is that very few UK hotels have their own in-house laundry operations, while this is quite common practice in the USA. The management and operation of a laundry operation involves a complex series of processes, which require specialist knowledge and are outside the scope of this text.

While a hotel linen room will function along the same principles as identified in Chapter 4 on storage, there are a number of special features that need to be taken into account. One difference in linen control is that the linen room has to process both dirty linen going out and clean linen coming in. Dirty linen from the bedrooms, and from other departments, will need to be sorted and counted before sending to the laundry. This can amount to a considerable task. If a double room generates a minimum of two sheets, four pillowcases, one bath mat, two bath towels and two hand towels a day, then a 100-bedroom hotel at full occupancy, assuming only double-bedded rooms, will produce 1,100 separate items of linen going out and a similar number coming in from the bedrooms alone. Add to that the linen that might be generated by the restaurants, conference and banqueting and room service, and the scale of this apparently simple task becomes apparent. In addition, hotels may also handle guest laundry and dry-cleaning through the linen room.

Another task that comes under the auspices of the linen room process is the management of staff uniforms. For those operations that provide uniforms for staff, their allocation, cleaning and repair can constitute a major task.

CURRENT TRENDS AND ISSUES AFFECTING SYSTEM

Staffing

It is clear from the previous discussions that the work of a housekeeping assistant is physically demanding and repetitive and has low status as an unskilled position. It is not surprising, therefore, that it is sometimes a difficult position to fill and one that suffers from high labour turnover. A range of approaches has been employed to make the job more attractive and to encourage a more motivated workforce.

The repetitive nature of the room servicing task lends itself to time and motion and method study approaches. Work study can be used to improve the process, to eliminate waste and to reduce cycle time (the time taken to clean one room). Ritz Carlton spent over a year looking at the housekeeping process in their hotels and reduced the time taken by restructuring the way the job was done and by introducing team working. As we saw earlier, this resulted in a cycle time of 20 minutes for a single maid and only eight minutes for a two-person team, without any reduction in the high level of service expected of a luxury hotel. As well as improving productivity, the new process is easier to complete and has allowed the company to increase wages significantly.

Incentives generally are seen as important in housekeeping. These incentives may be financial rewards for good performance or may be related to high job security, training or simply a supportive working environment. One approach adopted by the US Country Hospitality chain is to link pay to the number of rooms cleaned rather than the traditional approach of the number of hours worked. The company recorded an immediate improvement in productivity and a better link to demand patterns, as staff will volunteer to take on additional rooms and earn higher wages. They have also noticed a reduction in labour turnover and in the consequent costs of recruitment, but with a clear regime of inspection still in place, they have not suffered any diminution in standards (Kirwin, 1990).

The two scenarios described below are taken from real life examples of similar hotels within the same chain but highlighting a different emphasis in the mode of operation based on a different perceptions of the housekeepers' role and the prevailing local labour conditions.

CASE STUDY: THE AMBASSADOR

The Ambassador is a 250-bedroom four-star hotel appealing mainly to the business and conference market. Occupancy levels can vary considerably from week to week and day to day and are difficult to predict exactly.

The head housekeeper has worked in the hotel for ten years and has been in her present job for five. She has no vocational qualifications and has never worked in any other department. The aspects of her work that she likes the most are 'looking after her staff and dealing with staff problems'. She is less confident about the budgeting, control and paperwork aspects of her job.

All the chambermaids work full time. They are expected to clean 16 rooms each day and are paid per room. A supervisor, who is responsible for returning rooms to reception, checks each room. If the hotel is full or one or two maids ring in sick, supervisors have to clean rooms. On the other hand, if occupancy levels are lower than forecast and the department is overstaffed, the head housekeeper will try to meet the staffing budget by encouraging staff to take holidays or go on training courses. At these times, maids may only be required to clean 14 rooms, but even though this means losing money the maids don't seem to mind, as they find it extremely tiring to clean 16.

It is difficult to attract and retain maids, because the hotel is situated close to an airport where much better paid cleaning jobs are available. Staff working in other areas of the hotel are unwilling to help out if the department is short-staffed and, in any case, would not be sufficiently trained to do so, as it takes one month to train a maid to the required standard.

CASE STUDY: THE BERKELEY

The Berkeley Hotel is in the same chain as the Ambassador. It is slightly smaller but has a similar market profile. The head housekeeper, who is in her mid-20s, has vocational qualifications and an ambition to become a general manager.

Only eight of the chambermaids in the hotel are full time. The rest are part time – they are guaranteed two days work a week and agree to wait by the telephone on the other days up to 10 a.m. in case they are required. Labour turnover is low. Staff and supervisors do not mind changing jobs, and opportunities are provided for those interested in moving to other jobs in the hotel for variety and to improve their long-term job prospects.

As an experiment, the maids have been given more control and responsibility for their work. They now check their own rooms against the prescribed standard and return them to reception when ready. The full-time maids have been allocated a block of rooms on a particular floor as 'their' rooms. Supervisors now carry out rigorous inspections against a detailed checklist on a random sample basis. The current success rate is well over 90 per cent.

These examples show not only a different approach to flexibility of employment, enabling the Berkeley to match more closely the patterns of hotel demand, but also an increasing empowerment of the housekeeping assistants. This also introduces a change in the role and potentially the number of floor housekeepers, whose previous role in control is now replaced with scheduling and support.

Some hotels have indeed dispensed with the need for housekeepers altogether, as shown by this description of the budget hotel chain, Travelodge.

CASE STUDY: TRAVELODGE, UK

Housekeepers are not employed in the Travelodge chain. Instead, a room cleaner's work is checked by the receptionist, who fulfils various supervisory roles, and then spot-checked by the general manager. Traditional housekeepers are unnecessary because of the small size of the lodges, which average only 40 rooms. All the rooms are identical across the chain, which makes it much easier to standardize and to impose rigid quality controls. The group uses videos to train room cleaners and supplies them with photographic guides that show what rooms should look like. Overall standards are set and checked centrally for the group by the accommodation quality audit officer, who ensures that each lodge is spot-checked at least four times a year. This role fulfils the position of the executive housekeeper, but instead of a hotel with 20 floors this is a nationwide property with more than 4,000 rooms.

(Adapted from Anon, 1995)

Outsourcing

Having recognized the difficulty of finding appropriate staff for this area, many hotels have decided to outsource some or all of their housekeeping function to specialist companies. The scope of services contracted out can range from simply employing additional contract labour on a short-term basis through an agency or employing the services of a facilities management company that can take over the complete running of the housekeeping department. Between these two extremes, the housekeeping department may contract out specific services to specialists. These could include window cleaning, overnight cleaning of public areas, chandelier cleaning, deep cleansing of carpets or other floor surfaces.

The following extracts from the website of one of the largest UK hotel-servicing contractors provides a clear rationale for outsourcing, but these types of complete contracts are still limited to a comparatively small number of larger hotels.

CASE STUDY: PALL MALL

It is more than twenty years since Pall Mall entered the market, providing hotel-servicing contracts. One of the UK's top five cleaning and support services companies, Paul Mall now cleans more than one million hotel rooms every year in London alone, for some of the industry's biggest names, including Thistle, Millennium and Crowne Plaza, and recently Ibis hotels in the UK. Pall Mall only charge for rooms that have been occupied. This means that the hotelier can turn a fixed overhead into a variable trading cost and concentrate on its customers, leaving the housekeeping to Pall Mall. The service contract provides trained operatives and supervisory staff and Pall Mall account managers, who carry out regular audits and client reviews.

On their website (http://www.pallmall.co.uk/), the divisional director Nick Pipping is quoted as saying, 'Traditionally the hotel sector has employed its own staff but they're increasingly waking up to the benefits of our service ... they don't have to worry about losing control ... we commit to do everything on their behalf in partnership. We're a company that has the resources to do this. We handle staff shortages ... not only do our clients know these services will happen, they know they'll be carried out to a very high standard to meet their own bespoke requirements. They trust us to deliver high quality standards.'

Pall Mall's hotels outsourcing also offers other complementary services, including window cleaning, security, public area and kitchen cleaning.

(Adapted from www.pallmall.co.uk, 2002)

Technology

Since the basic processes of a housekeeping department are relatively simple, the application of technology has only had a limited impact. New and more effective equipment has been introduced for floor cleaning and polishing, while advances in cleaning materials have reduced the time and effort of cleaning to a certain extent, but there has been no large-scale automation of the processes. Nobody has yet invented the self-making bed and ideas such as rolls of disposable sheeting have never caught on.

It is computer technology that has made the greatest impact on the work of the housekeeping department, and even then as an information processing operation and not in the materials processing area. Property management systems have facilitated the communication between the housekeeping and reception departments – an area that in the past has caused some friction. Housekeeping managers can have access to immediate real-time information on the occupation status of all rooms to enable them to schedule efficiently. Room key access systems help to keep track of which rooms are being cleaned and by which housekeeping assistants. As soon as rooms have been approved as meeting the standards of the department, either by the housekeeping assistant or by a supervising housekeeper, they can be updated on the computer and become immediately available for resale. Any maintenance issues with any of the rooms can be logged on to the system and then tracked for completion. Computer systems also allow detailed records to be kept of inventories of linen, uniforms, cleaning materials and guest supplies, so improving security and ordering efficiency and helping to control costs. Computer-based staff scheduling systems can also be used to control labour costs.

An interesting development in computer technology described below allows users to scan a bar code in a room or on a piece of furniture with a hand-held terminal, which would then identify the appropriate cleaning and checking routine for that area and record any defects for immediate recovery.

CASE STUDY: OPEX

Introduced by Eurest Support Services, Opex is a bar code based system for monitoring and maintaining standards. Using a hand-held reader, the operator swipes a bar code in a particular area and a checklist of actions appears on the screen detailing the tasks to be checked and completed. Bar codes are usually sited in an appropriate room or fixed to a specific object. In checking the cleaning of a room for example, the bar code would be located in the room and when swiped, a series of monitoring questions would appear, such as 'are all ashtrays clean?' 'are all lights working?' or 'are the bathroom amenities correct?' If the response is unsatisfactory, the bar code reader will identify the action that needs to be taken to rectify the fault and who needs to take it. The data are then downloaded into a central system and the corrective action can be monitored. The area can then be rechecked to ensure the action has been taken.

(Adapted from Anon, 1999)

Environmental concerns (refer to Chapter 6)

There was a detailed discussion of environmental issues in Chapter 6, but the housekeeping area has been a particularly fruitful area for the introduction of 'green' policies to the benefit of both the hotel and the guest. These have included, for example:

- The introduction of recycling bins in hotel rooms to allow guests to sort their waste.

- The introduction of energy-saving devices such as low-energy light bulbs or lighting and heating, which are only activated when the room is occupied.

- The reuse of towels. Many hotels now ask guests if they wish their towels to be changed on a daily basis. The savings in energy for washing and drying towels that are changed only every other day is considerable.

- Some hotels have introduced bulk dispensers for shampoo and soaps in hotel bathrooms. The savings in bulk purchase and the removal of packaging is seen as beneficial. Some hotels will leave both individual and bulk items in the bathroom at the same time, so allowing the guest to choose their preferred option.

The HCIMA's Hospitable Climates initiative provides a wealth of interesting and useful information on their website (www.hospitableclimates.co.uk).

SUMMARY

Studies conducted of hotel and restaurant customers regularly report that cleanliness is one of the most important factors in both customer choice and satisfaction. It is the housekeeping department that is responsible for making sure that those customer expectations are met or exceeded.

The housekeeping process is deceptively simple, requiring the fairly straightforward execution of a series of routine and repetitive tasks. The tasks are not highly skilled but require considerable physical effort and a commitment to close attention to detail. These tasks are completed by a distributed workforce spread over a hotel, which may have little contact with each other and at a distance are difficult to supervise. Initiatives have therefore been introduced to improve the efficiency of the tasks themselves, making them easier to complete, perhaps by working in pairs or teams, and to allow housekeeping assistants to take greater control of their own work.

This should allow housekeeping managers more time to schedule and organize the operation to meet patterns of demand more closely and to train their staff in the best methods to ensure that high standards are consistently maintained. For a comparatively simple process, this is still a complex and difficult area to manage.

Further study

Read the following articles available on the internet about the hotel room of the future – including the first space resort – and compile your own view of what the room will be like. What are the implications for the housekeeping system in looking after this room?

- www.hotel-online.com/Neo/News/PressReleases1999_4th/Oct99_
  SpaceResort.html

153

- www.hotel-online.com/Neo/News/PressReleases1999_2nd/Apr99_
  FutureRoom.html

- www.hotel-online/Neo/News/PressReleases1999_3rd/Aug99_
  HyattGuestroom.html

- www.caterer.com/archive, 'Time travellers', 23 December 1999.

Prepare a chart to show the flow of information that would be required between housekeeping and reception and that should be included in a property management system.

Prepare a housekeeping organization chart and staffing schedule for a 25-bedroom two-star hotel and a 350-bedroom four-star hotel. What assumptions have you made about workloads?

Prepare a rota for the housekeeping assistants of the four-star hotel with the following percentage occupancy predictions: Sunday −65.7, Monday −90, Tuesday −92, Wednesday −100, Thursday −94.8, Friday −56, Saturday −68.

Bibliography

Adamo, A. P. (1999) 'Hotel engineering and maintenance', in Verginis, S. and Wood, R. (eds) *Accommodation Management: Perspectives for the International Hotel Industry*. London: Thomson Business Press.

Anon (1995) 'A checking career', www.caterer.com/archive, 22 June.

Anon (1998) 'Special report', www.hotel-online.com/Neo/News/PressReleases1998_4th/Oct98_WATG.html, October

Anon (1999) 'Coded successes', www.caterer.com/archive, 19 August.

Anon (2001) 'US drivers demand clean rooms', www.caterer.com/archive, 12 October.

Branson, J. C. and Lennox, M. (1988) *Hotel, Hostel and Hospital Housekeeping*, fifth edition. London: Edward Arnold.

Casado, M. A. (2000) *Housekeeping Management*. New York: John Wiley & Sons.

Deloitte Touche Tohmatsu (1992) *Hotel Construction in Europe*. London: Deloitte Touche Tohmatsu.

Falbo, B. (1999) 'Room cleanliness remains key to garnering repeat business', *Hotel and Motel Management*, 214(15), 60–1.

Hartline, M. D. and Jones, K. C. (1996) 'Employee performance cues in a hotel service environment: influence on perceived service quality, value and word of mouth', *Journal of Business Research*, 35, 207–15.

Haussmann, G. (2000) 'Heyman creates housekeeping efficiencies', www.hotelinteractive.com/news, 10 April.

Kirwin, P. (1990) 'A cost-saving approach to housekeeping', *Cornell Hotel and Restaurant Administration Quarterly*, November, 25–7.

Lerner, M. S. (2001) 'Clean sweep', *Hotels*, 35(5), May, 741–5.

Wolff, C. (1997) 'Raising the housekeeping bar', *Lodging Hospitality*, 53 (10), October, 26–8.

www.motel6.com/franchising/prototype.html

www.pallmall.co.uk, January 2002.

Recommended further reading

Verginis, S. and Wood, R. (eds) (1999) *Accommodation Management: Perspectives for the International Hotel Industry*. London: Thomson Business Press.

PART D

FOOD PRODUCTION SYSTEMS

In Part C we looked at the provision of accommodation services, some of which are carried out back-of-house (mainly in housekeeping) and some of which are front-of-house (mainly in the front office). This part of the book looks at the complex operations that occur back-of-house in any foodservice or catering operation. In the traditional catering operation, such a back-of-house system is commonly known as the 'kitchen'. However, as the two chapters in this part illustrate, food production may involve facilities, processes and equipment far more complex than the conventional kitchen. Moreover the scale may vary widely, from a small operation in a pub producing simple meals up to large-scale flight catering operations producing 30,000 'meals' a day.

The chapters in Part D explore the many different ways in which food may be prepared, processed, held and transported within the context of a wide range of alternative industrial contexts.

Food preparation and production[1]

After completing this chapter you will be able to:

- *explain the purpose and characteristics of the food production system*
- *apply principles of kitchen design*
- *explain systems of kitchen organization*
- *apply the principles of production planning and control and quality control*
- *evaluate the impact of recent developments in technology and consumer demand on the food production process.*

INTRODUCTION

'Line cooking done well is a beautiful thing to watch. It's a high speed collaboration resembling, at its best, ballet or modern dance. A properly organised, fully loaded line cook, one who works clean, and has "moves" – meaning economy of movement, nice technique, and, most important, speed – can perform his duties with Nijinsky-like grace' (Bourdain, 2001, p. 89). In this chapter we consider the food production system and how design and organization are essential to achieve the kind of work performance described by Bourdain.

PURPOSE OF SYSTEM

The purpose of a food preparation and production system is to take raw materials and put them through a series of transformations, to convert food into a ready-to-serve form. These processes are summarized in Table 9.1.

The efficiency and effectiveness of the system can be measured both in terms of simple input–output measures and also by service delivery criteria. The input–output measures cover:

- raw material efficiency (or waste)

1. This chapter is based on Chapters 3, 4 and 9 of Fuller and Kirk (1991).

Food preparation	Food production
Mechanical processes	Cooking
Size reduction	Boiling
Mixing and blending	Steaming
Peeling	Frying
Cutting	Grilling
Grinding	Roasting
Homogenizing	Baking
Measuring	
Shaping and forming	
Storing	Portioning
	Holding
	Serving

Table 9.1 *Food preparation and production processes*

- the ratio of the weight of prepared material compared to the weight of input material

- energy efficiency

- the energy input (kWh) per unit of food produced (kg)

- labour efficiency

- the labour input (staff hours) per unit of food (kg)

- service delivery criteria include the delivery of menu items at the time specified by the customer and of a quality and price they demand.

GENERIC SYSTEM CHARACTERISTICS

There are three key elements to a food production system. These are the catering policy, menu and kitchen design.

Catering policy

The food production and service concept starts with a catering policy, which specifies opening hours and the nature of the food offered during these hours. Market research will have determined the expected market for various times of the day in terms of numbers of customers and potential demand, and the menu planner should be able to answer such questions as:

- Is the market segment the same at lunch time and at dinner, or is there a need for a different menu and environment?

- Is the menu going to be the same throughout the day or will separate lunch, afternoon tea and dinner menus be needed?

- Is demand the same every day of the week or is there a need for low-cost fixed menus or specials on certain days or at certain times of the day?

The catering policy will also encompass a food policy. Seasonality of commodities such as vegetables, fruit, game and shellfish should be considered when planning the menu. While improved methods of distribution and preservation have extended the season of many commodities, high costs are associated with buying goods out of season. Over and above this consideration, however, is that of gastronomic appeal. The pattern of changing seasons forms an important aspect of lifestyle to many consumers. The wise menu-maker recognizes seasonal changes in menu-making for gastronomic and nutritional reasons, even when factors of cost and availability are no longer so acute.

The menu

Although we think of the menu as a simple *bill of fare*, to a catering operation it is much more than that. The working menu contains information about ingredients, portion sizes and yields. For a caterer the working menu arises from and expresses catering policy. For example, it determines equipment selection, kitchen layout and staffing needs (both numbers of staff and levels of skills). Many aspects of catering management and the day-to-day operation of the kitchen are determined by the menu. It also forms the basis of the *recipe specification*, which is a central component of the management control system. A typical working menu is shown in Table 9.2.

Composition of the menu

As part of a basic food operation plan, factors about the menu must be established ahead of any physical layout and equipment planning. These factors include:

- style and quality of menu
- whether à la carte, table d'hôte or a blend of both
- menu range related to number, variety and standard of dishes
- preparation and cooking of each dish in terms of recipes, portions, quantities and service styles
- speciality items to be featured (for advanced planning of appropriate equipment)
- extent of processed or convenience foods usage, i.e. types and quantities of foods to be produced and served determined so that requirements, in terms of processes and equipment, can be efficiently planned.

Another aim seeks to minimize the number of commodities that need to be purchased, received and stored, and this is helped by selecting food items that can have a multiple purpose. Convenience foods, especially pre-cut, high-cost protein items to close specifications, when effectively built into menus can affect production economies.

In some situations, another objective of the menu planner may be to limit the number of items on certain menus and to co-ordinate various menus used in any

Recipe number 101: Beef Stroganoff

Ingredients	Quantity	Purchase unit	Cost unit £	Cost
Fillet steak	1,000 g	kg	6.24	6.24
Chopped shallots	30 g	kg	1.80	0.05
Garlic	10 g	kg	2.80	0.03
Lemon juice	½ lemon	unit	0.09	0.05
Tarragon	5 g	100 g	2.75	0.14
Butter	120 g	kg	2.40	0.29
Double cream	125 ml	0.5 l	1.95	0.43
Salt	1 g	kg	1.25	0.01
Pepper	0.5 g	100 g	2.35	0.01
		Total costs		£7.25

Raw ingredients weight	1,336 g	Finish weight	1,179 g
Yield	88%		
Number of portions	4	Portion/size	250 g
Raw material cost/batch	£7.25		
Food cost per portion	£1.80		
Selling price	£7.40		
Food cost (%)	25.7%		
Preparation time	32 minutes		

Method

Cut fillet into julienne strips
Cook shallots and garlic to golden colour in third butter
Sauté beef in third butter
Drain and add shallots and garlic
Add cream and reduce
Add tarragon, lemon and remaining butter
Season

Table 9.2 *A working menu*

one operation. The co-ordination of menus for different rooms and functions can minimize production procedures and eliminate problems.

Types of menu

Today's menu can be one of several types or it may incorporate features from a number of types[2]. Terms in catering change, but there are basically six types of menu.

2. To get at proper feel for all the different types of menu, visit a few restaurant websites. For modern British and European cuisine try Conrans (www.conrans.co.uk). For authentic American style ethnic menus try Brinkers International (www.brinkers.com) or LettuceEntertain You (www.lettuceentertain you.com).

The **à la carte** menu offers a large selection of dishes, each independently priced, from which customers can compose their own meal by choosing from 'the card'. Naturally, à la carte selection may involve waiting a short time for some of the dishes, such as grills and sautés, while they are being cooked, unless the dishes have been chosen by the customer in advance. With the scaling down in size of the kitchen brigade, the number of items on an à la carte menu has been reduced. As an alternative to this, menu breadth may be maintained by the use of pre-prepared dishes, either prepared on site or bought in chilled or frozen form.

In some à la carte menus, items such as vegetables and side salads are costed into the selling price of the dish. In other cases, these items are described and costed separately. Many à la carte menus will also offer one or more daily specials. There are a number of ways in which information about specials can be conveyed to the customer. One method is to have a menu insert with a description of the specials, which is either loose or attached to the menu. Another method is to list the special dishes on a blackboard or lightboard. A third way is to get the waiting staff to describe the specials of the day.

The **table d'hôte** (literally the host's or hotelier's table) is a set menu at a fixed price with much less choice or even no choice at all. A restaurant may offer several table d'hôte menus, each at a different price, as in the popular French 'menu'. Another variation is to vary the price based upon the main protein item or to add an additional sum to the fixed price for certain selections.

The **selective menu plan** is a cross between table d'hôte and à la carte styles. It provides a limited number of choices within a fixed-price menu and with a fixed number of courses. A selective menu plan might be formulated from items along the following lines:

- four to six appetizers

- five to eight entrées

- three to six vegetables or salads

- four to eight puddings or desserts

If some of the selections involve high-cost items, they may necessitate the addition of a supplement to the basic fixed-cost menu.

Many restaurants, particularly in popular and fast-food catering, use a **static menu** that remains largely unchanged for long periods of time. This covers many speciality restaurants such as steak houses, carveries, pizzerias, hamburger restaurants and roadside restaurants. These restaurants are usually part of large chains where a consistent and well-known product is a part of their attraction.

Although unchanging, these menus gain through public familiarity and favour. The fixed menus allow national advertising of menu items in the press and on radio and television. The narrowness of the menu range enables the production and service teams to build up expertise. But, of course, review and change must still be applied even to static menus.

The **cyclic menu** is one which is 'rotated' or repeated in a predetermined pattern. A year is divided into quarters, normally coinciding with the seasons: spring, summer, autumn and winter. Within each quarter, a cycle's length and the number of times each cycle runs has to be decided by the menu-maker. However, it is wise not to have too long a cycle. Cycles often coincide with a fixed number of weeks, typically two, three or four. In this way, within any season, a cycle would consecutively run three to four times before the next seasonal cycle begins. Popular and non-seasonal items may be carried from one season's menu cycle to the next.

Cyclic menus require careful planning. The repetition of each dish or menu item in the same context with other dishes makes it easier to determine dish popularity. A menu-maker can therefore forecast more accurately how much of each item to prepare for the day's business. Sales history over a period of time allows accurate forecasting of sales and enables best-selling items to be used more often and less popular ones to be eliminated.

The planning of cyclic menus is particularly critical in the case of the captive consumer. The menu cycle must be long enough, and the dishes varied enough, to prevent menu fatigue. Additionally, the menus must be nutritionally balanced to provide macro- and micro-nutrients. In these situations, the computer can be of great value in calculating nutrient levels.

Market menus are those which are particularly responsive to season and availability. A new interest has been generated in market menus through the influence of chefs associated with la nouvelle cuisine. Market menus are therefore thought to have special application in so-called gourmet operations at all price levels, from modest chef proprietor to grand restaurants. Many restaurants with a fixed or other type of menu offer daily 'specials' based on the market menu principle.

Kitchen design

While the menu is the blueprint of a catering operation and is the starting point when designing kitchens, there are many constraints which make the kitchen planning process complex. These constraints include:

- availability of capital finance

- availability of space

- availability of staff

- skill levels of staff

- restrictions on building services.

In determining kitchen layout (as well as organizing subsequent work within it) certain fundamental intentions remain constant, whatever the operation. It is possible that traditional kitchen organization along sectional or partie (see page 176) lines may be compatible with achievement of the fundamental aims, but it is unwise to start with such an assumption. Planning must not be obscured by 'traditional' thinking, and when undertaking it, preconceived notions should give way to a logical approach. Principles applicable in designing any production or assembly plant can be applied to kitchens.

The conceptual plan

The conceptual plan begins with the marketing and merchandizing policy decisions concerning:

- the customer and the customer's specific needs in terms of time of day, acceptable price and food requirements

- the menu style: content and communication to the customer
- the service style: how the food is to be delivered to the customer
- the relationship between food production and food service.

Continuing cost inflation affects every industry. Catering involving labour, food and fuel is vulnerable to price escalation. Coupled with this, shortage of skilled staff and higher rates and rentals, particularly in city centre locations, spur the caterer to seek new answers to production problems. Trends stemming from today's economic problems include:

- greater mechanization
- simplified operations
- increased use of convenience foods
- use of new commodities
- development of new cooking appliances and methods
- reduced size of food production (kitchen) areas
- use of mechanical handling equipment, such as conveyors
- use of central kitchens supplying food to a number of service points
- use of computerized controls on equipment.

Luxury hotels and restaurants may appear to be least affected by these considerations: but even at this level there are adaptations in approach to kitchen planning designed to optimize the utilization of higher paid and scarcer staff and in the increased exploitation of pre-prepared commodities. Coffee shops, speciality restaurants, self-carving and self-help buffets are some manifestations of change. This is reflected in kitchen plans that involve fewer staff and more pre-prepared commodities, even at the highest level; in other areas of the industry these principles are long established.

The influence of marketing and merchandizing

Present trends in kitchen layout seem destined to lead to closer contact between actual points of foodservice and customers. This is seen in a number of ways, such as the greater involvement of customers in the service (and even cooking activities) and an increase in the exploitation of the 'theatrical' nature of cooking. These factors have an effect both on the type of equipment used and on the layout of facilities. Once holding and cooking equipment move into front-of-house areas, much more thought needs to be given to the aesthetics of their design and of their effect on the environment.

The other major influence on the marketing of the catering operation is the effect of location. It is beyond the scope of this book to discuss factors influencing the location of the restaurant, which is the chief factor in determining the position of the kitchen. The exception to this may be where a central kitchen, or commissary, is used to produce and supply foods to a number of catering outlets. Here, the decision about location of the central kitchen is determined by the pattern of distribution – the distance covered by delivery vehicles and the physical (geographical) relationship of the various end kitchens (Dilworth, 1989). This is discussed in greater detail in Chapter 10.

Information required

Before beginning kitchen planning, the following questions must be addressed:

- What type of meal will be offered?

- How many people will be served?

- When will these meals be required?

- How many sittings are there to be for each meal, or in the case of an all-day service, how long will each person be seated?

- What will be the extent of tea, coffee and foodservice for other areas in addition to the restaurant?

- Is allowance to be made for special functions?

- What area of floor space is available?

- What is the position of windows, ventilation, drainage, water supply?

- Are there any constraints on electricity, gas and other services?

- What type of service is proposed: self-service, cafeteria, waiter or waitress service?

This information can be used to determine the methods of preparation and production, the quantities of food required (average and peak), the processing stages, the timing of these stages and the equipment needs.

Area of the kitchen

While there are no hard and fast rules for determining the floor area required to produce and serve food for a specified number of customers, figures are available giving typical areas. These figures can be used as a rough guideline and to determine if special measures are required when there is too much or too little space. Kitchens are sometimes reduced in size in order to provide more space and increase seating in the restaurant. While this is sensible from a revenue generation point of view, this reduction does not necessarily increase the trading capacity of restaurants, as the kitchen, as much as the dining room, may determine the numbers that can be served during a service period. Reduction in kitchen size must, therefore, be planned to maintain (and even increase) productivity and still result in a satisfactory workplace for employees. Cramped kitchens lead to delays and faults in service, flaws that may ultimately deter customers.

In spite of these important reservations, the trend over the last thirty years has been to reduce the size of the kitchen. This has been possible because of the following factors:

- increased use of pre-prepared foods

- increased availability of mechanical preparation equipment

- increased productivity of new types of catering equipment

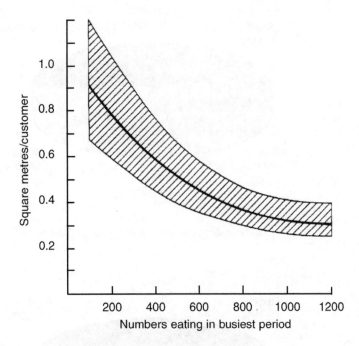

Figure 9.1 *Approximate indication of kitchen areas* (Fuller and Kirk, 1991)

- reduction in the size of menus

- changes in working practices within the kitchen.

These factors, among others, make the calculation of kitchen area difficult. Briefly stated, kitchen areas vary according to the type and number of meals provided and the method of production. There is an economy of scale in that, as the number of customers increases, so the kitchen area per customer decreases, as does the ratio between kitchen area and restaurant area. Figure 9.1 indicates traditional estimates of kitchen area requirements, but these can be reduced, using the techniques identified above. These figures include storage, preparation, cooking and holding areas, but do not include service areas, staff facilities or offices. Within the kitchen space, the approximate breakdown into functions is shown in Figure 9.2. The relationship between numbers of customers per service period and area is shown in Table 9.3.

Location of the kitchen

The location of the kitchen within the building is critical from an operational point of view, but even in new buildings it is not given sufficient attention. In order to provide the logical flow from deliveries to foodservice discussed below, the relationship between deliveries, kitchen and restaurant is vital. The kitchen requires good access for the delivery of food and for the removal of waste. These access points should be separated and well away from guest entrances and exits. Ideally, there should be five different entrances to the kitchen:

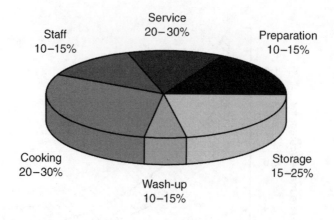

a) Main areas as a percentage of total area

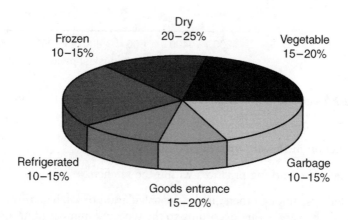

b) Stores areas as a percentage of allocated storage area

Figure 9.2 *Allocation of areas within the kitchen* (Fuller and Kirk, 1991)

- staff entrance to cloakroom
- goods entrance to stores
- garbage/refuse removal
- waiting/service staff to restaurant
- waiting/service staff from restaurant.

In practice, this level of sophistication is often not possible and some compromise has to be made. An important aspect of entrances to a kitchen is that of security. For this reason, the chef's or supervisor's office should have a good view of as many of these entrances as possible.

Kitchens should be located in a cool part of the building (facing north or north-east) and with good natural daylight. Windows should be located so that they do not cause sun glare or solar gain.

Space requirements for kitchens (m²)

Number of meals	400	600	800
Preparation	22	28	32
Cooking	40	47	52
Wash-up	18	22	26
Service	40	50	60
Storage	26	33	40
Staff facilities	16	18	20
Total	162	198	230

Table 9.3 *The relationship between meals and floor area* (based on Lawson, 1985)

The distance and ease of access between kitchen and dining areas(s) should be considered. Quality of food and speed of service depends, among other things, upon good communications and transport between these two areas. While the use of lifts and dumb waiters can overcome some of the problems of having kitchen and restaurant on different floors, these create operational problems and should be avoided if possible.

The importance of food hygiene and of the influence of kitchen design cannot be overstressed. From an ideal point of view, there should be a straight line flow from raw material to finished product, with no backtracking. The dirty (pre-cooking) activities should be separated from the clean (post-cooking) activities. This should include different staff or a change of uniforms. All materials and surfaces likely to come into contact with food should be easy to clean, including the sides, behind and underneath equipment. Any spaces which cannot be cleaned should be sealed to prevent build-up of food and to eliminate insects and rodents. There should be no cracks, joints or screw heads on equipment and smooth curves should be used rather than internal right angles.

One of the first tasks in developing a layout is to identify the **work centres** of a kitchen. The nature of these centres will vary according to the nature of the menu and production system (as discussed in Chapter 2). Techniques are available for determining relationships between work centres (Kirk, 1989). This involves:

- identifying all work centres

- identifying the approximate size of a work centre, based on staff and equipment needs

- determining the relationship between these work centres.

A common way of doing this is to classify relationships between any two work centres as either very important, important, slightly related, non-related or undesirable for close relationship. These relationships can be expressed in the form of a chart (see Figure 9.3). This information can then be used when organizing the relationships between work centres on the plan, as shown in Figure 9.4. When transposing this information to the plan, attention must be given both to the area of each work centre and the need for traffic lanes and work aisles. The information can be derived from flow process charts or from work study measurements of activity. The arrangement of work centres should also provide for the natural flow of food from raw material to finished produce, to minimize the risk of cross-contamination (see Figure 9.5).

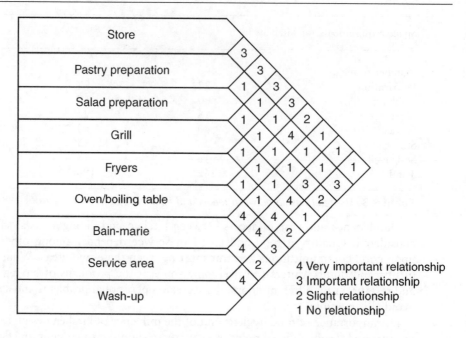

Figure 9.3 *Activity relationship chart* (Fuller and Kirk, 1991)

In practice, this type of exercise is often not required, because of the simplicity of relationships and because of the practices that are common to most kitchens. The difficulty comes in producing this logical flow within a particular building envelope. Layout becomes even more of a problem when the location of equipment is governed by existing constraints such as drainage and supporting pillars. The use of activity relationship charts is justified when planning large production kitchens, where there are multiple food outlets, and when designing kitchens for a chain of restaurants.

In a traditional kitchen, the work centres are often located in separate rooms. Today, this division is much less common, because it requires more space and introduces communication problems. Instead, use is made of half-height walls that physically divide an area but allow visual and verbal communication. This in turn has led to the development of multifunction open-plan preparation areas and the elimination of physical barriers.

Traffic lanes and work aisles

In order to ensure efficient flow through the kitchen, adequate and properly devised traffic lanes and work aisles are indispensable. A **traffic lane** represents the major route used by product as it passes through the process. It provides straight flow lines for the receipt, preparation, cooking and serving of product, together with the ancillary but important tasks of waste removal, dishwashing and pot-washing. Distances between key points such as goods entry, stores, preparation, cooking and servery should be as short as is practicable and compatible with the nature of traffic. For example, where the use of trolleys is envisaged, this information should be used when determining aisle widths.

Work aisles represent areas in the kitchen where staff carry out work. Ideally, the

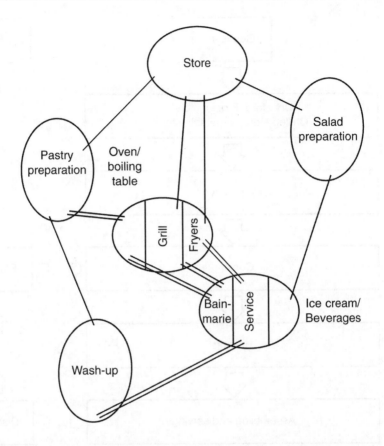

Figure 9.4 *Location of work centres based on activity relationship chart* (Fuller and Kirk, 1991)

main traffic flow should avoid work aisles, which, if possible, should be positioned at right angles to the main traffic routes.

The widths of traffic lanes and work aisles are governed by ergonomic factors. Typical values for the width of these spaces is given in Table 9.4

The basic layout of kitchens and work centres

Using the information provided so far in this chapter, it is now possible to create the basic layout. This is normally drawn at a scale of 1:50, which means that 1 mm on the plan is equivalent to 50 mm in real life. For people who are unsure about the use of scales, graph paper with 1 mm divisions can be useful.

A number of additional techniques are useful at this stage. Plastic templates (drawn to a scale of 1:50) can be used to draw furniture, bathroom fittings, WCs and hand-basins. Cut-out templates representing the size of pieces of catering equipment are also of value. For those who find it difficult to relate a two-dimensional plan to a three-dimensional outcome, the use of scale models can help. Alternatively, get the architects or catering consultants to produce three-dimensional drawings (isometric or perspective), which give a clearer indication of what the kitchen will look like.

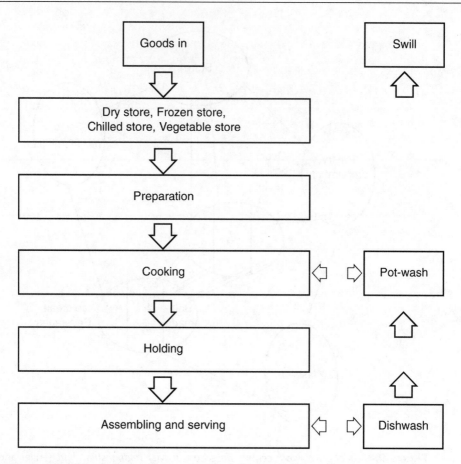

Figure 9.5 *Flow chart of kitchen activities* (Fuller and Kirk, 1991)

600	800 mm	Space for person working at preparation table, sink or for countertop cooking.
1,200	1,400 mm	Space in front of equipment with drop-down door and for tilting equipment.
750 mm		Minimum for work aisle.
1,500 mm		Minimum for main traffic lane.
1,000	1,500 mm	Allows two persons to pass.
1,500	1,800 mm	Allows trolley to pass one person.
1,500	1,800 mm	Allows trolley to pass between two persons working back to back.
900 mm		Minimum clearance between equipment and work tables (preparation area located opposite equipment)
1,000	1,200 mm	Minimum in front of cooking equipment to which food is conveyed by trolley.
800	900 mm	Person with tray.

Table 9.4 *Work aisles and traffic lanes*

Another useful tool is transparent overlays, which can show information such as food movement, staff movement, the layout of utilities (gas, water, electricity and drains), and so on. These are similar to the flow diagrams of Figure 9.5. The movement of staff and food can be ascertained through the use of flow process charts (as discussed in Chapter 2).

Storage space must be allocated for pots, pans and cooking utensils and for a number of other materials. For example, most kitchens carry a wide range of detergents and cleaning materials, which must be stored away from food materials. Dishwash requirements are discussed in Chapter 12.

Vegetable preparation area

The requirements of a vegetable preparation area depend upon the volume of vegetables and salads served and on the nature of the purchased commodity. For small operations and/or where large volumes of pre-prepared vegetables are used, a sink and preparation table will suffice, together with some way of handling waste and trimmings: this may be a bin, or the work centre may incorporate a waste-disposal machine. An electrically operated potato-peeling machine is usually justified. In addition, many kitchens now have vegetable preparation machines. The vegetable preparation area should be located close to cooking equipment used for vegetables – boiling tables, tilting kettles and steamers.

Preparation of fish, meat and poultry

Much of the meat, fish and poultry requirement is purchased in portion-controlled cuts. Breaded, ready-to-fry portions can further reduce preparation time and space. As a minimum, a sink and preparation table is required. Access to preparation equipment such as a mincer attachment on a mixer and a bowl chopper is useful. In larger kitchens, the meat preparation area may have its own equipment (preferable from a hygiene point of view), along with other specialized equipment such as sausage fillers and patty moulders, depending on the menu. A marble slab is often used for fish preparation.

Pastry and bakery preparation areas

In the smallest kitchen, and where much use is made of ready-to-bake and ready-to-serve pastry products, pastry and bakery areas may consist of preparation tables, a small mixing machine and access to oven space. Larger kitchens may have their own bakery or convection ovens located in this area. Where large amounts of pastry are being prepared, electrically operated pastry rollers may be of value, as can die stamping machines to produce pie bases. A marble slab is often required where there is a lot of hand pastry work. If bread or other dough-based products are to be made, a proving oven will be required and possibly other specialized equipment for portioning and moulding loaves and rolls.

Cooking areas

An analysis of the menu should reveal the type and capacity of cooking equipment required. This analysis should be summarized according to the different cooking processes, as follows:

- roasting and baking

- boiling

- grilling and toasting

- steaming

- deep frying

- shallow and griddle frying

- making of soups, stews and stocks

- hot water for culinary purposes.

An analysis of the menu should provide information about both the average and peak production requirements (kg/hour or litres/hour) for each of the above cooking methods. The exact appearance of this chart will depend upon the type of menu. A fixed menu will relate to specific dishes, while a cyclic menu will have main menu categories.

Having established these basic cooking methods and food quantities, this information can be translated into types and sizes of equipment. Cooking and serving high-quality food in large quantities, and to a strict time schedule, is an exacting task, even under the most favourable conditions. By the correct choice of cooking equipment, purely physical strain can be eased. Moreover, the favourable environment of an adequately equipped kitchen leaves greater scope for exercising skill, maintaining quality and controlling costs. In making decisions about the numbers of appliances to be used, multiple activity charts can be used to determine if there is any possibility of sharing equipment between menu items.

Economical cooking depends upon using appliances designed for a specific purpose, and deployed to meet average conditions. In a new kitchen it is important to guard against putting in too much equipment. The ideal is to prepare, cook and serve food with the minimum of appliances in active use. The effect of this 'menu justification' policy is to keep down capital outlay as well as to minimize running costs. Modern, high-capacity catering equipment is expensive but, provided that it is properly planned into the kitchen, its cost can be justified. There is a danger that a kitchen will be designed on traditional lines, with large amounts of conventional equipment, to which is then added some of the newer high-throughput equipment. This is an expensive solution, both in terms of capital and space. Confidence in tightly specified kitchens can be increased through the management of maintenance, repair and replacement contracts, as discussed in Chapter 5.

Decisions need to be made about whether to position all cooking equipment in a central line or island, or whether to locate equipment in separate work centres. In many situations a hybrid of the two provides the best arrangement. Thought must also be given to equipment disposition and to the degree of mobility in the kitchen. At its most basic level, some mobile equipment, such as mixers and food processors, may be mounted on castors to enable them to be shared between work centres. This is useful when a work centre cannot fully justify its own machine.

Some kitchens are now planned so that all equipment is mobile; this allows the disconnection and movement of equipment to simplify cleaning procedures. It also allows rearrangement of equipment to suit a particular menu or production plan. Location of equipment is often strongly influenced by the building and its services.

While in theory it is possible to use any piece of equipment anywhere in a building, in practice some locations are practically impossible (or very expensive) because of the need to lay new drains, install long ventilation ducts or bring in new energy services. For this reason, early discussion with the mechanical and electrical consultant is essential. However, it is important that the kitchen planning process is not compromised by these capital cost considerations. The effect of location on the efficiency of the kitchen during its life is equally important, and the catering consultant and representatives of the catering company need to be fully aware of this cost compromise.

Ventilation

Staff and kitchen efficiency are affected by heating and ventilation, factors that may either hamper or enhance productivity. Kitchen ventilation must meet three requirements:

- maintenance of comfortable working conditions

- prevention of condensation

- confining cooking smells to the kitchen.

We can differentiate between two types of ventilation: *background* and *localized*. Background ventilation relates to the movement of air in the total kitchen. It is normally provided using extractor fans together with vents that allow air to enter the kitchen. A typical kitchen requires 20 to 30 air changes per hour. However, some of this will be provided by the localized ventilation.

Localized ventilation may be provided in several ways but the most common method is to use a canopy. The canopy may be mounted on a wall or suspended from the ceiling. Localized canopies may be provided over individual appliances, such as dishwashers, or large canopies may be used over banks or lines of equipment. Typically, localized canopies extract air at the rate of 0.3 to 0.45 cu. m per second.

Whatever the location of a canopy, its edge should project beyond the cooking equipment by at least 45 mm on the side where oven doors open and 35 mm on the other sides. The canopy should be at a height of 2 m above floor level. The rate of extraction of air from the canopy and the balanced supply of make-up air requires the specialized knowledge of a mechanical consultant or a canopy supply company.

Canopies are usually made of one of three materials: metal, glass or plastic. Whatever the material, they should be functional, pleasing in appearance, easy to clean and should not introduce a fire hazard. They should be fitted with a small gutter around the bottom edge to deal with any condensation that accumulates before the canopy heats up. Normally, this condense gutter need not be connected to a drain, as evaporation is rapid. Canopies often incorporate a bulkhead light. Grease filters in canopies should be easy to clean, either by removal and washing in a sink or dishwasher, or by automatic 'in-place' wash-down systems. Many canopies are now fitted with fire detection and fire extinguishing systems.

Water supplies

Three types of water supply are required in a kitchen:

- cold, non-drinking water for staff rooms, toilets, showers, wash-up areas, pot-wash, wet bains-marie, hand washbasins and as a feed to the hot water system

- cold drinking water (mains water) for water fountains, food preparation and cooking areas

- hot water, at various temperatures, produced by a central boiler (possibly with a number of local calorifiers at different temperatures) for hand washbasins and preparation sinks.

In addition to the above, some specialized supplies may be required, such as softened water (for appliances like combination ovens) and high-pressure supplies (for pressure steamers and dishwashers). These supplies may be localized to one appliance if there is only a single requirement within the kitchen. Where mobile equipment requires a water supply, bayonet fittings can be used in conjunction with reinforced hoses.

Drainage

In addition to the need for plumbed waste connections to sinks, there may also be floor drains in the form of open gulleys (covered with a metal grille) or circular drains. These floor drains are useful in wet cooking areas and for floor washing. It is important that the floor is sloped to take water to these drains. Some appliances, such as steaming ovens, require a vented drain connection to prevent any danger of back-siphoning.

Drainage can be provided to mobile equipment, using a tun dish or screw-in sockets mounted in the floor. Kitchen drains are often fitted with a grease trap, which will retain fats and other solid material. These are normally located outside the kitchen and should be easily accessible for maintenance.

Flooring

Interesting developments in floor surfaces continue, but it is still hard to find the 'ideal' floor material. A floor material should have the following characteristics:

- ease of cleaning

- non-slip, particularly when wet and greasy

- non-tiring on the feet of employees

- attractive appearance.

The traditional floor consists of kiln-fired quarry or terrazzo tiling. This provides a good surface, but it is slippery when wet, and the grouting between the tiles can harbour dirt and bacteria. Carborundum particles may be added to improve its non-slip performance. Many of the new floor materials are laid as a continuous screed to eliminate joints. They can be made less slippery by the incorporation of carborundum chips, which stand proud of the surface. Where slipping is a problem with existing floors, it is possible to coat most types of surfaces with a rubber-based compound that will make it much less slippery. Skirtings and corners should be coved to facilitate cleaning and to eliminate joints that can harbour pests.

Walls

Kitchen walls should meet the following needs:

- easy to clean

- of attractive appearance

- able to reflect light.

There are many wall surfaces, including plastics and washable paints, that give good results in kitchens. Nevertheless, glazed ceramic wall tiles remain very popular, despite the fact that they tend to glaze, crack and reflect noise.

Alternatives to ceramic tiles, such as plastic sheet materials, overcome many of the problems associated with tiles and their use is increasing. The joints between the sheets of material are sealed with a silicone compound, avoiding the use of nails, screws or cover strips.

Lighting

Adequate lighting is necessary for many kitchen activities. Some kitchens are located in basements or semi-basements and, in any case, may not be sited to obtain the best natural light. Artificial lighting is almost invariably required. Kitchen lighting is important not only to support efficient operation but also in promoting cleanliness. It is not only the intensity of lighting that is important but also its direction (to prevent glare) and colour (to prevent distortion of food colours). Recommended lighting levels (ICMSF, 1988) are 540 lux for inspection, 220 lux for work rooms and 110 lux in other areas.

A planned fluorescent tube installation will provide uniform intensity, minimum shadows and low energy costs. The only drawback with fluorescent tubes is the possibility of colour distortion. Where this is a problem, colour corrected tubes can be used.

Ceilings

Specialist paints are available to treat kitchen ceilings to reduce moisture. Ceiling heights need no longer be excessive, for air change by artificial ventilation is a common means of promoting airy workplaces. However, very low ceilings should be avoided, both for reasons of air circulation and from a psychological point of view. A floor-to-ceiling height of not less than 3 m may be considered reasonable. Suspended ceilings incorporating washable ventilation panels are now available. These panels can be removed and passed through the dishwasher.

SYSTEM PROCESSES

The processes that need to be managed in a food production system relate to how to organize the staff, how to plan and control production, and how to assure quality.

Kitchen organization and management

There are two basic forms of organization the traditional system, which derives from the way the great French chef Escoffier organized his kitchen in the 1890s, and contemporary approaches that reflect new production systems in use today.

The partie system

The partie system, which evolved during the Edwardian era and particularly under the influence of Escoffier, revolutionized the way in which kitchen staff (or brigades) were organized. Many twentieth-century developments in the design and organization of the kitchen can be traced back to the partie system. The system developed because of changes in the menu and in cooking equipment. The demand for more freshly cooked food led to a change in the methods of operation, with a greater need for the pre-preparation of many items. In order to accomplish this, the work of the kitchen was subdivided into working groups, or parties.

Overall control of the kitchen was in the hands of the head chef or chef de cuisine, aided by one or more assistants (sous chefs). Each partie was under the control of a chef de partie, who functioned both as a supervisor as well as a craft specialist. Typical divisions might be:

- the storage of commodities, both perishable and non-perishable
- the preparation of meat, fish and poultry, etc. (larder work)
- the preparation and cooking of pastry and desserts (the pastry)
- the preparation of vegetables
- the general stove section at which prepared foods were assembled and cooked.

The partie system (or 'corner', as it is known in many British establishments), as perfected by Escoffier, was the result of analysing the work behind a collection of recipes and allocating tasks to the different specialists so as to produce even the most complex dishes regularly, efficiently and swiftly. This meant breaking down processes and allocating different tasks, even for one dish, to different sections, so that a veal escalope, for example, might initially be cut by the butcher, flattened and breadcrumbed by the larder cook, sautéed (shallow fried) and garnished by the sauce cook, using garnishes which might well have come from other corners of the kitchen.

In the kind of kitchen that Escoffier and his colleagues organized, the partie system reached the height of complexity, because the end products had to be of the highest quality and yet be completed to order in rapid sequence for a substantial number of customers.

In addition to the organizational hierarchy that the partie system introduced into the kitchen, the other important but related aspect was communication. With the need for fresh cooking and the prompt service of orders to tables, clear and accurate communication, both within the kitchen and between kitchen and restaurant, became essential. The servery became the focal point of this communication, where waiting staff placed orders and received cooked dishes. In the partie system, a member of the kitchen staff would stand at the hotplate and call out the requirements from the order chits left by the waiting staff. The appropriate partie(s) would then acknowledge this order. The chit would then be placed on a hook, where it would remain until the order had been collected by the waiter. At the end of the service period, the chits would act as a control of all the dishes that had been produced by the kitchen.

Contemporary kitchen organization

In many catering operations, such as hotel and restaurant kitchens, the methods of production have not changed greatly from those principles of production devised by Escoffier. In other areas, we are seeing the influences of mass production principles such as production-lining and batch processing (as discussed in Chapter 2). These changes are seen as a response to issues such as the lack of skilled staff, cost control, pressure on space and increased productivity.

In sectors such as fast food, which uses production-line principles, or large-scale, mass catering, where food is cooked in bulk, food production workers do not necessarily have the skills of a trained chef. This is because work has been broken down into simple tasks, as well as being mechanized or automated. In a fast-food restaurant, the small range of menu items requires only a limited number of cooking techniques – deep-fat frying for the French fries or chicken portions and grilling or frying of hamburgers. In addition, much food preparation, such as slicing tomatoes, shredding lettuce and chopping onions, is decoupled, so that these items are delivered in a prepared state. This means that fast-food workers can be 'multi-skilled' and deployed to any section of the kitchen, servery or dining area. Indeed, moving staff around the operation during a shift or working week is one way to reduce employee boredom and fatigue, since the actual tasks themselves are very straightforward and repetitive.

A similar organization exists in large-scale catering, such as central production units for local schools or hospitals, or flight kitchens. In this case, bulk equipment is used, such as boiling pans, bratt pans and baking ovens, etc. Work simplification here derives largely from the use of convenience products, so that soups, entrées and other dishes are prepared from dehydrated powders combined with raw ingredients and water.

Production planning and control

Food and beverage production planning (Davis *et al.*, 1998) is established around the systematic development of production plans, based on:

- projections of menu sales
- standard recipes
- standard yields
- standard portion sizes.

Control of production is based on an analysis of actual performance against the plan. It is possible to compare actual food consumed, production figures and sales volumes, and to produce variances from the plan. This information is used not only to control the operation but also to adjust future planning assumptions. The process of production planning and control is greatly simplified through the use of computer programs (see below). Information on the use of inventory, including estimates of food waste and pilfering, represent important management controls (Reynolds, 1999).

Alongside the planning and control of food production is the planning and control of revenue from food sales (Kimes *et al.*, 1999). Additionally, the analysis of stock consumption (in relation to sales volumes) is a key aspect of food production management. The value of inventory together with its rate of usage, stockholding costs, wastage and loss through pilfering is critical management information (Reynolds, 1999).

Labour scheduling in the kitchen forms an important aspect of both planning and control. Obtaining the correct mix of full-time, part-time and agency staff to suit shift patterns and work demand is a key aspect of food and beverage management (Thomson, 1999). After food, labour represents the second most expensive cost item.

Quality control

The *quality* of a service industry is much harder to define than is the case with production industries, and this is true of food production. We can define quality as the sum of all the attributes that make up a product or service and determine to what extent it measures up to the consumer's expectations. Dilworth (1989) considers quality in terms of:

- quality of design
- quality of conformance
- quality of performance or service.

Attitudes towards quality and the control of quality have changed in recent years, reflecting the influence of the Japanese 'just in time' manufacturing concept. The traditional view has always been of quality control as an external and monitoring function of production and service. Nowadays, it is realized that quality is the responsibility of everyone within the company and that it covers all functions, from interior design, menu planning, purchasing, stores, production, service, cleaning and maintenance. As such, it is difficult to separate the quality of food production from other aspects such as food service.

Another important feature is that every department is responsible for the quality of goods or service that it passes on to the next department; thus, every department should see the next department as its customer and should only pass on goods without defects. This means, for example, that stores should not send out low grade or deteriorating goods to the kitchen. Similarly, the kitchen should not hand over defective meals to the serving staff.

In a production industry the emphasis of quality control is on the establishment of numerical standards for a product and the checking of products against these standards, using statistical sampling techniques. These techniques are hard to apply in a service industry. We can, and should, define and measure quantifiable aspects such as portion sizes, service temperatures, maximum holding times and other conformance standards (Thorner and Manning, 1983), but we should also be able to measure the performance of the service element (Merricks and Jones, 1986). Here the danger is that we may concentrate on aspects of performance that we can measure, such as meals per minute. In doing this, we exclude large elements of the product, such as freshness, customization and appearance. Too often, complaints are used as an index of quality. This is not satisfactory for a number of reasons. First, for every customer who complains there will be many customers who will not, even though they are dissatisfied with some aspect of the product or service. Second, the nature of the complaint, as expressed by the customer, may not reflect the true problem area.

SYSTEM ADOPTION

Production kitchens range in size from small units, not too dissimilar from a domestic kitchen, up to very large units indeed that are reminiscent of a factory.

CASE STUDY: GRENDON AND SPRINGHILL PRISON STAFF KITCHEN[3]

About 360 staff work in Grendon and Springhill Prison and use the officers' mess, which is located in an old country house at the heart of the prison building complex. As well as meals for prison officers, the kitchen also provides buffets for meetings and functions. Meals are a combination of traditional dishes, including roast dinners, and fast food such as filled jacket potatoes and pizzas. On average, officers pay £2.50 for two courses.

The kitchen is operated by inmates, so staffing levels tend to be higher than normal. Generally, there are six or seven kitchen staff and on average they rotate every three months because of the length of their sentences. While working in the kitchens, some study for catering NVQs. About once a month, there are special themed lunches using the specialist knowledge of inmates from a variety of ethnic backgrounds, such as Turkish, Indian, Cypriot, Chinese and Italian.

The previous kitchen was old and some of the equipment was domestic. It did not have a proper servery – meals were served through a small hatch and officers had to queue down a corridor. In 2000, the kitchen was completely redesigned. The designer had several key priorities. Hygienic workflow was a must, along with plenty of space in the kitchen and separate work areas. Proper ventilation was a concern, as was hygienic cladding for the walls and non-slip flooring. Also, he was determined to have a servery, so that officers did not have to queue down the corridor. It was also decided to lower the height of the ceiling by 1.2 m and to install effective lighting.

The resulting design provides a main kitchen for general preparation and cooking and another room that is used for cold preparation, sandwich-making, storage and dishwashing. There is also a servery equipped with hot and cold counters, plus an office.

Equipment in the new kitchen comprises a range with a griddle and two fryers under a ventilation canopy. Ideally, the designer would have liked to install a

3. This case study is based on an article that appeared in the *Caterer & Hotelkeeper*, 27 September 2001.

combination oven, but it would have been difficult to plumb in. Instead, there is a potato-baking oven and a pizza oven. These are mounted above a fridge and freezer on a shelf with a gap under it to provide ventilation for the refrigeration. Also in the main kitchen is a table, counter and sink for general prep and a double fridge for vegetables and dairy produce. For beverages, there is a wall-mounted boiler. In the second room, there is an under-counter dishwasher and waste-disposal unit. There is also an assortment of fridges and freezers, a slicer, a mixer and a microwave oven.

CASE STUDY: ALPHA FLIGHT CATERING, HEATHROW[4]

Seven airlines, all offering different menus, are served from the Alpha Flight Services' kitchen. Each flight may comprise three or four different classes, each with different meals, and several meals and snacks may be served during long-haul flights. In addition, there might be requests for any of 15 special meal types, such as kosher, vegan or gluten-free.

Alpha's new kitchen cost £6 million to fit out and has a capacity of up to 25,000 meals a day. The operation replaces three separate kitchens that used to be operated at Heathrow. Its total area is 5,200 sq. m. which is located in three warehouse units rather than in a purpose-designed building. Having one large unit has created the opportunity to improve process flow. Food follows a horseshoe-shaped route from goods-in, to coldrooms, preparation, hot kitchen, blast chiller, tray assembly and dispatch chiller, before leaving from the loading bays alongside goods-in. Care has been taken to avoid backtracking – for example, the hot kitchen prep room has one door in from the food storage area and a second door out into the hot kitchen. The walls that separate the various areas are made from fridge panelling. As well as affording an easy-clean surface, this allows for good temperature control (for example, the assembly area is maintained at 14°C).

As well as producing Western food, the Alpha unit has a separate kitchen for Japanese food and a section of the main kitchen is dedicated to Oriental food. Where needed to produce authentic ethnic food, specialist equipment has been bought in from Japan, including a special grill and rice cooker. A presentation room has its own kitchen and holding fridge, so that test recipes and food for customer tastings do not have to be made in the main kitchen. And there is a separate kitchen to feed the 470 staff.

CASE STUDY: EST EST EST RESTAURANT, GATWICK[5]

The new Est Est Est at Gatwick Airport serves between 500 and 600 covers a day. It has a very compact kitchen, which is largely visible from the 112-seat restaurant. It has a row of cooking appliances with a pizza oven and counters in front of them, and occupies around 40 sq. m. Behind the scenes, there is a small prep area, a walk-

4. This case study is based on an article that appeared in the *Caterer & Hotelkeeper*, 14 December 2000.

5. This case study is based on an article that appeared in the *Caterer & Hotelkeeper*, 8 June 2000.

in coldroom, a blast chiller, plus a dishwash area that is shared with the outlet next door.

At the heart of the kitchen's design is an emphasis on fire safety. One of the main reasons the suite of electric equipment was chosen is that gas appliances are virtually banned from airports. The chargrill has electric elements which are hinged to allow thorough cleaning and there is a water bath under the elements to quench any sparks. The unit has also been modified so that fat spills are separated from the water. While all the high street Est Est Est restaurants have wood-burning pizza ovens, for safety reasons this was not possible at Gatwick. Instead, a twin-deck electric oven has been installed, together with a casing to make it look like a wood-burner. The emphasis on fire safety also affected the design of the extract canopy. Its stainless steel baffle filters can be cleaned in the dishwasher but may be removed only with the use of a key that is normally inserted in the control panel. As soon as the key is used to remove the filters, the system shuts down. In addition, the extract system is protected by an automatic Ansul fire extinguisher.

As the restaurant is located at an airport, it is open from 6 a.m. to 10 p.m. Breakfast accounts for 40 per cent of its business. So kitchen equipment has to be versatile. The electric range therefore doubles as a griddle and a solid-top hob. It has a highly polished surface so that eggs and other breakfast items can be cooked directly on it, and at lunch it is used with saucepans. Similarly, the boiler is used as a bain-marie at breakfast and as a pasta cooker at other times.

Staff are not organized in the traditional partie system, because this would not allow them to work fast enough. Instead, the six chefs under the head chef are all trained to work in every area of the kitchen so that they can help wherever they are needed.

CURRENT TRENDS AND ISSUES AFFECTING THE SYSTEM

Computerization

A computer may be used in a number of ways to assist in the menu planning process:

- to provide a recipe/menu database

- to generate menus

- to produce printed menus using word processors and desktop publishing

- to analyse sales of, and revenue from, each menu item (menu engineering).

A database represents an efficient and effective way of storing, recalling and editing information. A database is composed of two parts: a set of files and a database management program. The program is used to manipulate information in the files and to relate information from one file to another. A file is a collection of information about related items. It is made up of records, one per item. The records are indexed to facilitate the retrieval of information. For example, a menu database, may contain three files, as shown in Figure 9.6.

The database management program has options to add or edit ingredients, recipes and menus; to cost recipes and menus; and to calculate the nutritional value

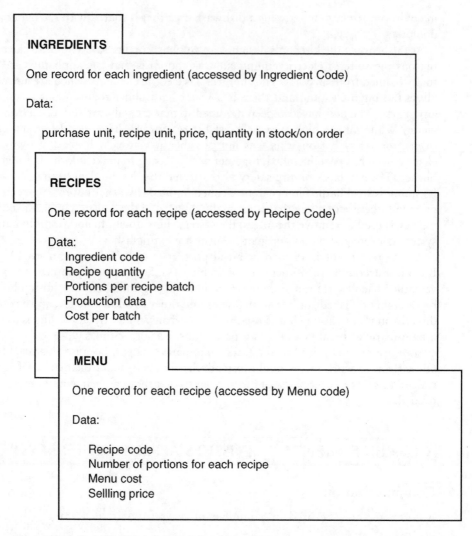

INGREDIENTS

One record for each ingredient (accessed by Ingredient Code)

Data:

purchase unit, recipe unit, price, quantity in stock/on order

RECIPES

One record for each recipe (accessed by Recipe Code)

Data:
Ingredient code
Recipe quantity
Portions per recipe batch
Production data
Cost per batch

MENU

One record for each recipe (accessed by Menu code)

Data:

Recipe code
Number of portions for each recipe
Menu cost
Sellling price

Figure 9.6 *Possible files in a recipe database* (Fuller and Kirk, 1991)

of recipes and menus. The value of a recipe/menu database is increased when it is used as part of a catering control system.

Word processors and desktop publishers can be used to produce more professional menus at a lower cost and they can be updated on a regular basis. In particular, the use of desktop publishing programs together with a laser printer can produce professional looking menus in a short period of time. This is particularly useful for market menus.

There are now many computer systems available for production planning and control within the catering industry. While these systems vary in their complexity, ease of use, storage capacity and number of users, they all perform similar functions. When considering the purchase of computer software for catering control, it is important to be clear about the objectives of the system.

The core of such a system is formed by a set of databases that stores information on suppliers, stock levels, recipes and menus. These are linked together by a database management program, (see Figure 9.7), which performs a number of functions (see Figure 9.8).

The fundamental part of a catering management information system is the ingredient file, which contains information about each stock item. Information held includes unit size, issue size, who supplies it, how much is in stock, how much is on order, how much is already committed and minimum stock levels. It also contains a price for each ingredient, which may be the average price paid for the stock or be based on the price of the latest delivery. Additionally, some systems allow the storing of a recipe price for dish-costing purposes. In many catering operations, the stock file may contain thousands of items.

Ingredients go to make up recipes that are held in a recipe file. The recipe is a list of ingredients and quantities required to make up a standard number of portions. The recipe file is likely to contain information about yields, cost prices and selling prices. The recipe may also contain information about method of preparation, preparation time and cooking time. The system must be able to handle a situation in which a recipe may itself be an ingredient. For example, we may have a recipe for brown stock, which is itself an ingredient in a number of dishes.

These recipes are linked to a menu file. In a cyclic menu, a database may be held for a periodic menu cycle of three, four or five weeks. These menus form the basis of the production planning process. The production plan consists of the menus for one meal, for one day, or for a period of time, together with estimated sales for each menu item and an explosion of ingredients programmed with information on the price of the dish. This information can also be linked into stock usage calculations and to accounting software. A further development has been the introduction of *hand-held* computer terminals, which are used by waiting staff for taking orders. This means that an order goes directly into the system at the moment the order is taken.

A number of systems are now available to ease the communication between kitchen and restaurant. The interface between kitchen staff and waiting staff is often problematic, as the pressures of service time can lead to friction between the two groups. Simple communication systems allow waiting staff to pass orders through to the kitchen at the same time as they are entering the order on to a point-of-sale terminal. The order may either be printed out on to one or more kitchen/bar printers or display terminals. When the order is ready, the waiting staff can be paged, so that they know when to come to the hotplate to collect their order. This paging may be done by discreetly placed monitors or printers, or by using personal pagers. This type of system can be linked into a food and beverage management system, to give total integration.

Another example of an application is the use of automated systems for recording patient menu choices in hospitals. In a hospital foodservice system that provides a plated service and patient choice, the collecting and recording of patient choices is a lengthy and costly process. This means that the process has to be carried out a long time ahead of production and service, which in turn leads to errors because of patient admissions and discharges. In order to speed up the process of collating patient information, a number of devices such as card readers and digitizers have been used to semi-automate the process. This means that the collation of information can take place much nearer to the time of production and service.

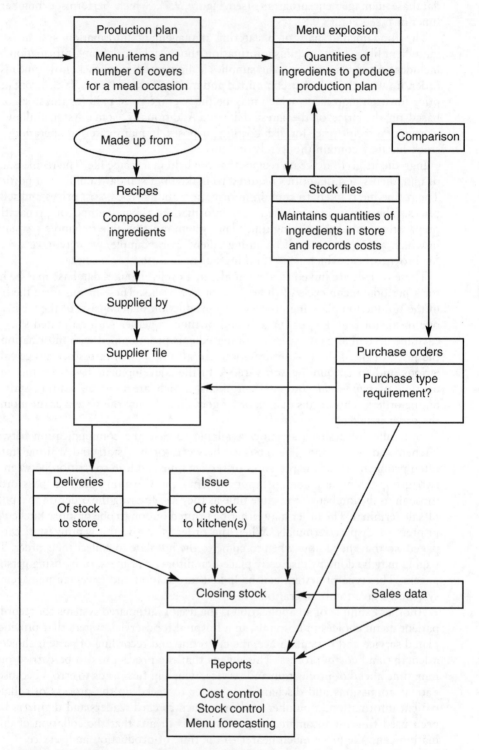

Figure 9.7 *Features of a production and control database management system* (Fuller and Kirk, 1991)

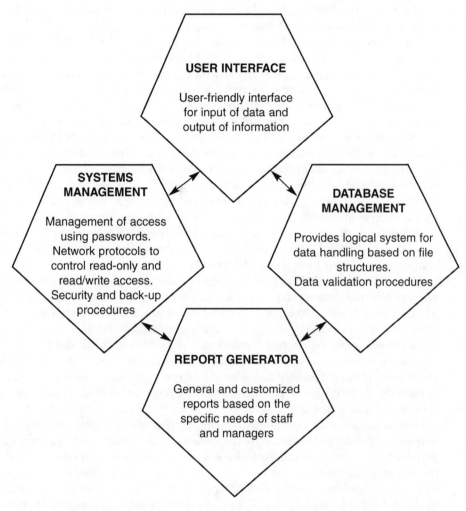

Figure 9.8 *Functions of a database management system* (Fuller and Kirk, 1991)

Outsourcing

A number of hotel groups are now turning to outsourcing as a means of managing their food and beverage operation. Generally speaking, the prime motivation for this has been financial. However, there are a number of quality-related issues. The key factor in successful outsourcing is the seamless operation of the franchised food and beverage operation within the overall environment of the hotel (Hemmington and King, 2000).

Demands from consumers

Consumer trends have undoubtedly affected both what is offered in the catering kitchen and how it is prepared. There has been a great increase in the awareness of foods, brought on by the influx of overseas travel, the increased variety of foods available for use in the home and the influence of the media. Food served in

185

restaurants is affected by a broad range of sociocultural, economic, political, legal, ecological and technological factors (Gillespie, 2001).

Travel has undoubtedly introduced the consumer to a broader range of food and beverage products. This has been supplemented by the growth of the ethnic restaurant, with increasing authenticity and sophistication. These trends have resulted in the development of a new international cuisine, based around a mix of ideas from across the globe – combinations of Asian, Oriental and South American dishes, often fused with traditional European menu concepts.

The media has also had a large influence on both customers, and their expectations of the food in restaurants, and the chefs themselves. The social values that are attached to food through its association with a sense of place, status and celebrity have had an impact on what restaurants offer to their customers (Randall, 2000). It is not only articles about food and restaurants but also the increased media interest in foreign travel that have emphasized the significance of food.

Other trends that have influenced food production include an interest in diet and health. Some of these trends are often short term, such as a decline in red meat consumption caused by fears of BSE in cattle.

As well as influencing what is produced in the kitchen, these trends have also affected how the food is produced. There has been a range of responses to the needs of consumers, such as the application of mass production techniques. In many chain operations food is produced centrally and distributed in a chilled or refrigerated form, with the kitchen reduced to a place for reheating and finishing. An alternative response has been that of mass customization, as seen in many fast-food operations. Here, a standardized selection of raw materials is used to produce an apparently wide range of products, with a degree of individual customization (Lockwood and Jones, 2000).

However, Taylor (2000) refers to a paradox that is apparent within the current developments of foods offered to the consumer in a restaurant. In spite of the perceived diversity of restaurants, there is actually a great uniformity in terms of the industrialization of services. Mass customization 'will allow restaurant organisations to continue to standardise their production processes and thus gain access to desired efficiencies, but this will be allied to an improved ability to meet the needs of individual customers'.

SUMMARY

In this chapter we have seen that, despite the many modern innovations, the principles of food production are basically those that were adopted during the development of restaurants at the turn of the century. The combined influences of better technology, a much more variable and reliable supply of food materials and sophisticated consumer demands have resulted in many changes to the product that emerges from the kitchen. The variety of menu format and the choice of food available have increased alongside a dramatic rise in the number of meals consumed away from home.

These trends will continue into the future under the joint influences of the push of technology and the pull of consumer demand. It is important that, when judging the impact of these changes, the starting point should be the satisfaction of consumer demand and not the blind application of technology. Technological solutions have been very prevalent in institutional foodservice. There is a danger that the decision to go for a technological solution is based much more on issues of production processes than consumer satisfaction (Reeve *et al.*, 1999).

Further study

Visit the kitchens of a range of catering operations, including hotels, ethnic restaurants and hospital catering departments. Identify the common components and the differences in the food production systems. How do these relate to the nature of demand (both in terms of service times and service volumes) within the kitchen?

With the aid of examples, discuss the way the menu influences the design and equipping of the food production system. What other factors may influence the design?

Go to the website of the magazine *Chain Leader* (www.chainleader.com), an American publication about hospitality chains. Click on 'Issue Archive' and conduct a search for the key words 'kitchen design'. This will take you to over 150 stories about restaurant kitchens that usually include plans of these kitchens, along with a description and photographs of the food production area.

Bibliography

Bourdain, A. (2001) *Kitchen Confidential: Adventures in the Culinary Underbelly*. London: Bloomsbury.

Davis, B., Lockwood, A. and Stone, S. (1998) *Food and Beverage Management*, third edition. Oxford: Butterworth-Heinemann, 184–96.

Dilworth, J. B. (1989) *Production and Operations Management: Manufacturing and Non-Manufacturing*. New York: Random House, 549–75.

Fuller, J. and Kirk, D. (1991) *Kitchen Planning and Management*. Oxford: Butterworth-Heinemann.

Gillespie, C. (2001) *European Gastronomy into the 21st Century*. Oxford: Butterworth-Heinemann, 157–79.

Hemmington, N. and King, C. (2000). 'Key dimensions of outsourcing hotel food and beverage service', *International Journal of Contemporary Hospitality Management*, **12** (4), 256–61.

ICMSF (1988) 'Hygienic design of food operating areas', in *The Hazard Analysis and Critical Control Point System to Ensure Microbiological Safety and Quality*. Oxford: Blackwell, 62–80.

Kimes, S. E., Barrash, D. T. and Alexander, J. E. (1999) 'Developing a restaurant revenue management strategy', *Cornell Hotel and Restaurant Administration Quarterly*, **40** (5), 18–29.

Kirk, D. (1989) 'Layout planning', in Pine, R. (ed.) *Catering Equipment Management*. London: Hutchinson, 63–72.

Kirk, D. (1994) 'Design and layout', in Davis, B. and Lockwood, A. (eds) *Food and Beverage Management: a Selection of Readings*. Oxford: Butterworth-Heinemann, 145–58.

Lawson, F. (1985) 'Catering design', in Tutt, P. and Adler, D. (eds) *New Metric Handbook: Planning and Design Data*. London: Architectural Press, 164–73.

Lockwood, A. and Jones, P. (2000) 'Managing hospitality operations', in Lashley, C. and Morrison, A. (eds) *In Search of Hospitality*. Oxford: Butterworth-Heinemann, 158–76.

Merricks, P. and Jones, P. (1986) *Management of Catering Operations*. Eastbourne: Holt, Rinehart & Winston, 74–91.

Randall, S. (2000). 'How does the media influence public taste for food and beverage?', in Wood, R. C. (ed.) *Strategic Questions in Food and Beverage Management*. Oxford: Butterworth-Heinemann, 81–93.

Reeve, W. G., Creed, P. G. and Pierson, B. J. (1999) 'Institutional food service systems: does technical innovation work against consumer satisfaction?', *International Journal of Contemporary Hospitality Management*, 11(1), 51–3.

Reynolds, D. (1999) 'Inventory turnover analysis', *Cornell Hotel and Restaurant Administration Quarterly*, 40(2), 54–8.

Taylor, S. (2000) 'Is McDonaldization inevitable? Standardization and differentiation in food and beverage organizations', in Wood, R. C. (ed.) *Strategic Questions in Food and Beverage Management*. Oxford: Butterworth-Heinemann, 48–64.

Thomson, G. M. (1999) 'Labor scheduling part 4: controlling workforce schedules in real time', *Cornell Hotel and Restaurant Administration Quarterly*, 40(3), 85–96.

Thorner, M. E. and Manning, P. P. (1983) *Quality Control in Foodservice*, Westport, CT: AVI.

Recommended further reading

Davis, B., Lockwood, A. and Stone, S. (1998) *Food and Beverage Management*, third edition: Oxford: Butterworth-Heinemann.

Gillespie, C. (2001) *European Gastronomy into the 21st Century*, Oxford: Butterworth-Heinemann.

Wood R. C. (2000) (ed.) *Strategic Questions in Food and Beverage Management*, Oxford: Butterworth-Heinemann.

CHAPTER 10

Holding, transportation and regeneration

After completing this chapter you will be able to:

- *identify and explain the relationship between holding, transportation and regeneration*

- *describe alternative approaches to holding, transportation and regeneration*

- *explain key processes in these systems*

- *identify current trends in these systems.*

INTRODUCTION

In Chapter 2, we identified decoupling as a major trend in the development of operations. This chapter focuses on foodservice operations in which the back-of-house (i.e. kitchen) has been separated from the front-of-house. **Food holding systems** are found within the food production areas of most hospitality operations. However, this food holding procedure may vary in length from holding food for a few minutes, between production and before service, to a long-term storage of cooked foods, using refrigerated or sub-zero centigrade temperatures. Under the latter conditions, it is possible to transport the food between the point of production and the point(s) of service, introducing the need for a **transportation system**. Following on from the holding stage (and any transportation, if required), it is necessary to process the foods so that they are ready for service. This conversion process is known as **regeneration**.

This chapter explores the benefits to be gained from introducing a holding stage in the process and goes on to look at some of the common food production systems based around holding procedures and the associated transportation and regeneration stages.

PURPOSE OF SYSTEM

Within any system, a **holding** function is there as a means of introducing a buffer stage between two closely linked systems or subsystems. Why should we want to introduce an extra stage between subsystems, since it is an additional step in the process that adds cost and does not appear to add value to the product?

The purpose of a holding stage is to act as a means of decoupling individual processes or stages that are directly linked, in the sense that the output of one process is the direct input of a second process. Thus, by introducing a holding phase, we provide a level of buffer stock between two subsystems or processes. This increases their independence. Rather than the output of one process forming the direct input to a second process, a proportion of the output is held in store, to be drawn on by the second process as required. This means that the first process can continue to produce output, without necessarily having to wait until the second process is free to take that output. Similarly, it means that the second process is less likely to have to wait for input materials from the first process. This is what we mean by **decoupling**, in which the direct link between any two processes is separated by a buffer stock.

Decoupling may be used to separate the two processes in time, place, or both. By locating holding stock between two subsystems, these two subsystems can be separated in time, allowing each process to be optimized. For example, it may be that one process is best operated as a batch process and the other as a continuous process. Where there are peaks and troughs in the demand for input from one system, buffer stock can be used to smooth out the relationship with the system providing that input. This would be difficult without buffer stock. It also means that different types of operations (see Chapter 2) can be used for individual stages. For example, a very large catering operation (such as a large hospital) might organize production using assembly lines and service using batch processing.

The separation also means that the two processes, with the addition of a transport stage, can occur in different places. It also means that the output of one system may be used to provide input to a number of other systems. This allows centralization of some processes and decentralization of others.

The purpose of a transportation system is to move materials from one physical location to another. At a basic level, we can see that many separate transportation processes are required to move food from the goods reception area through to the restaurant. In this chapter, we are more concerned with systems where a formal transportation stage is introduced as a subsystem so that, for example, production can take place at a location some distance away from service.

In process terms, transportation does not add any value to the product and should therefore be minimized as much as possible. However, in some situations, transportation is an essential stage in the process. An example of this would be in a hospital catering operation, where a central kitchen produces food for several wards and staff restaurants. Similarly, a contract caterer may use a centralized kitchen to produce foods for a number of foodservice outlets.

After long-term storage (be it chilled or frozen), it may be necessary to process the food to convert it to a 'ready-to-eat' state. This is referred to as **regeneration**.

The performance of a holding, transportation and regeneration system is measured in terms of:

- minimized food waste between production and service

- smoothing of the food production cycle

- optimized quantity and quality of food at the point of service

- additional costs of transportation and storage more than balanced by higher productivity and lower food waste levels.

GENERIC SYSTEM CHARACTERISTICS

From the above definition, we can see that the holding stage takes place at a system boundary. A boundary is designed to control the flow of materials, information, people or money from one system (or subsystem) to the environment (or to another subsystem). In designing and operating a system, one particular concern relates to the management of movement across these boundaries. In some situations, the boundary processes introduce constraints on the two subsystems on either side of the boundary. In other words, in order to satisfy boundary requirements, it may be necessary to operate subsystems at less than their optimal level.

As an example, we might consider the relationship between the kitchen and restaurant in a commercial catering operation. The kitchen is involved in what is essentially a production process, where raw materials are converted into finished menu items. On the other hand, the restaurant is a service process, in which meals are delivered at a time and place ordered by the customer. If the kitchen and restaurant are directly coupled, the initiation of production in the kitchen will be triggered by the placing of a customer order in the restaurant. In other words, the production processes in the kitchen will be directly controlled by the service demands in the restaurant. In practice, of course, the kitchen staff anticipate demand ahead of the order being placed and commence production accordingly. Additionally, staff may build a limited buffer stock of partially or fully prepared menu items in anticipation of demand.

We have seen then that, in order to manage the relationship between the conflicting demands of these two subsystems, it is often desirable to introduce a holding stage. This may involve the introduction of a simple buffer stock to manage short-term fluctuations in supply (production) and demand (service). Alternatively, the time and place of production may be separated entirely from that of service, in which case significant volumes of long-term buffer stock may be required.

In a holding system, materials that have been produced can be held for a defined period of time, with no deterioration in quality and at minimal cost, until required by the next stage in the process. In this way, holding allows individual processes to be optimized by introducing a buffer stock to balance the flow of materials between the two processes. In a close-coupled system, production must be scheduled to match the demands of service. In many forms of catering, food is produced in advance of service and held in short-term storage ready for the service period. In a fully decoupled system, production can take place over the full working day, even though service is concentrated during one or two periods in the day.

When we apply these principles to a catering operation, there is an added complexity, because food materials are particularly difficult to store without deterioration in quality and without the introduction of a microbiological hazard. Therefore, in the case of food materials, it is useful to differentiate between short-term holding (of up to one hour, where quality loss and microbiological hazards are minimized) and longer-term storage (where quality and safety issues become paramount).

At the end of the holding process (and after transportation, if required), it is necessary to convert the food into a ready-to-serve form. The precise nature of this stage will depend upon three factors. First, there is the holding temperature (refrigerated or frozen). Second, there is the necessary serving temperature (frozen, chilled, ambient or hot) based on sensory and safety factors. This regeneration or reheating process is required to convert the food safely, and with minimum deterioration in quality. Third, there is the issue of pack size. Foods may be held in bulk containers or packs and portioned just before or immediately after regeneration. Alternatively, the food may be held in individual portion packs. Therefore, at the time that the system is designed, integrated decisions must be taken about issues such as holding temperature, holding time, pack size, method of transportation and method of regeneration.

SYSTEM TYPES

If we analyse trends in the hospitality industry over the last twenty years, we can see a dramatic change in the nature of the three processes discussed in this chapter. Traditionally, most foods have been cooked and held at warm temperatures in servery areas. However, greater scientific knowledge has shown that warm holding causes a significant loss of nutrients and there is a risk of the growth of pathogenic bacteria. Additionally, the flavour and colour of the food deteriorates during periods of warm holding. Thus, warm holding is normally restricted to 60 minutes. The need to achieve economies of scale, by producing food in bulk, as well as hygiene factors has therefore led to the development of chilling and freezing as holding methods. In addition to chilling or freezing, individual meals may also be vacuum-packed, the so-called sous-vide system.

Holding

We can differentiate types of holding systems in a number of ways. One obvious way to describe a food storage system is in terms of its temperature, where we can utilize hot holding (above 70°C),[1] ambient (room temperature), chilled (below 8°C)[2] or frozen temperatures. Closely related to the service temperature is the maximum shelf-life of the stored food. The shelf-life determines the maximum duration of foods held within the holding system. Typically, hot foods can be kept for one or two hours, although in some industries (such as fast food) maximum holding times are limited to a few minutes. In the case of chilled foods, these can be

1. In most countries, the actual minimum temperature is controlled by legislation. This temperature is related to that required to destroy the vegetative cells of pathogenic bacteria.
2. As with hot holding, legislation covers the maximum temperature for chilled storage.

held for a maximum of five days, from chilling to consumption. Frozen foods have a longer shelf-life, which can be measured in months.

Warm holding

If we look at the physical facilities involved in the production of food, we can identify two main physical subsystems: the *kitchen* and the *restaurant*. However, in order to manage the transactions between the two, and to introduce short-term buffer stock into the system, a *servery* is juxtaposed between them. Throughout the history of the commercial kitchen, use has been made of short-term storage, to allow materials to be partially prepared ahead of service. In fact, it is so commonplace that it has its own term – *mise en place*. These materials, once prepared, are kept, either in refrigerated storage (cabinet or walk-in), in hot cupboards (dry heat) or in bains-marie (wet heat). The choice of dry heat or wet heat is largely based on the control of moisture loss or gain by the food.

We can consider the movement of the following across these boundaries:

- material: food; dirty crockery, cutlery, etc.

- people: kitchen staff to the servery area; servery staff into the restaurant; customers into the restaurant area

- information: details of menu to customers; customer orders to the kitchen; food-ready information to waiting staff; request for more food to the kitchen from the servery.

The relationship between kitchen, servery and restaurant is different in each sector of the hospitality industry. These differences can be described in terms of the nature of the boundary between the following three physical areas:

A **silver service restaurant** includes the following characteristics:

- The hotplate forms a physical boundary between the kitchen and servery.

- There is no vision or sound barrier between the kitchen and the servery.

- There is usually a physical and environmental boundary between the restaurant and the servery to control the flow of noise and smells.

- The flow of food is usually undertaken by waiting staff, who carry the food from the servery to the restaurant.

- The flow of dirties and waste is performed by waiters, who carry these materials from the restaurant to the kitchen dishwash area.

- There is a formal communication of information based on the menu.

- Written orders are communicated to the kitchen using the waiter and the waiter's pad.

- Verbal communication between the kitchen and the restaurant centres on the servery.

- Electronic systems sometimes replace written and verbal communication between the kitchen, the servery and the restaurant.

In a **self-service restaurant** the kitchen, servery, restaurant interface is as follows:

- There is often a physical barrier between the kitchen and the servery, but no physical or visual barrier between the servery and the restaurant.

- Written communication to customer is by a point-of-sale display in the servery.

- Other communication to customer is by visual selection of food on display in the servery.

- Communication to the kitchen by the servery is undertaken by staff, who predict how long stocks are going to last.

- Today, electronic systems sometimes replace written and verbal communication between the servery and the kitchen.

The **fast-food outlet** has a very different interface:

- There is no physical barrier between the kitchen, servery and restaurant.

- Extraction systems are used to provide an environmental barrier, to prevent heat and fumes from the kitchen entering the restaurant.

- Written communication to customers is by point-of-sale displays at the servery.

- Communication to the kitchen is based on maintaining a buffer stock in the servery and/or electronic communication.

In all of these operations, buffer stock is kept to a minimum, in order to reduce waste, improve quality and diminish the threat from microbiological hazards. For example, in developments such as fast food and call order service, food is produced for a specific customer order and storage times are short or non-existent.

Chilled or frozen holding

Where a greater degree of separation between production and service is required, the complete *decoupling* of production and service by the interaction of a buffer stock with a longer shelf-life must be introduced. Decoupled systems have three elements – a method of extending product shelf-life (usually chilling or freezing), a method of transporting food items, and a method of regenerating them to service temperatures. This is sometimes referred to as **interrupted catering** and is based on a process that will rapidly reduce the temperature of cooked foods to a safe level. This normally requires specifically designed refrigeration plant to extract the heat. Typical guidelines are that the food must be reduced from its post-cooking temperature down to +5°C (in the case of cook-chill) or −5°C (in the case of cook-freeze) in less than 90 minutes.

The normal method of reducing the food temperature is to use high-velocity air (5 m/s) that is circulated over containers of food. The thickness of the layers of food must not exceed 30 mm in order to achieve the required chilling or freezing times. Alternative refrigeration systems, based on liquid carbon dioxide, liquid nitrogen and baths of chilled water, are also used.

An important aspect in reducing materials handling is the standardization of container sizes, and, wherever possible, using the same container for more than one purpose. For example, it should not be necessary to move food from one container to another when transferring it from a cooking appliance to a blast-chiller. To make this possible, containers of uniformly standard size are available that can be used for storage, cooking and service.

As large-scale cooking and meal production has become more systematic, multipurpose containers to aid in rationalizing operations are being increasingly introduced. These containers mean that food can be stored, cooked, frozen, chilled, reheated and held, all in the same sized compact modular container. The dimensions of these containers are based on the *gastronorm* modular dimension of 530 mm by 325 mm. This is now the basis of both BSI and European standards, although it is not yet an international standard. Obviously, one container size cannot suit all purposes and therefore a number of variations are possible:

- multiple and fractional container sizes allow greater or smaller amounts of food to be stored

- container depths are available from 20 mm up to 150 mm to suit different types of foods and processes

- containers are available with solid or perforated bases.

Transportation

We have seen that food must be maintained at its correct temperature during transportation. In fact, in most cases, it is seen as an extension of the holding stage, with little or no change in temperature. Transport systems can be classified according to three factors:

- the temperature of the food

- the volume of food

- the distance to be travelled and the difficulty of the journey.

With regards to temperature, there is the transportation of frozen, chilled, ambient or hot foods. In terms of volume, this may be by individual portions, plated meals or bulk distribution. In addition to the distance of travel, specific features of the journey must be taken into account. Is the transportation all within a building, or is there a need to travel between buildings? Is there a requirement for lifts or ramps to allow for changes in level and gradient? If there is transportation between buildings, is this all within a single site, or does it require road transport?

Regeneration

From the above, it is clear that any regeneration system should be designed to match the characteristics of the holding/transport systems. This may involve bulk regeneration, the regeneration of individual plated meals or tray systems. Regeneration normally consists of a heating process. This can be based on microwaves, steam, water baths, convection heating, infrared or a combination of processes. The choice of process is related to the physical characteristics of the food (i.e. is it dry/crisp in texture or soft/moist?), the numbers to be served, the space available and the time available.

KEY PROCESSES

Having identified the key elements of the system, we shall now consider the three stages in process terms.

Holding

In areas of the hospitality industry such as school meals and hospitals, production and service were carried out in different physical locations, thus introducing the requirement for a distribution stage. For example, many local authorities operated a central kitchen where food was prepared early in the morning, packed in insulated bulk containers and distributed to schools. At the school the food would be transferred to storage units in the servery area (hot cupboards and bains-marie) prior to service. A similar system was used in hospitals, where bulk containers containing hot food were transported to ward level and plated ready for service. However, this system introduced high levels of food waste, and the foods suffered a loss in quality and nutritional value.

In order to overcome some of these problems, alternative systems have been used. For example, in hospitals systems were developed that facilitated the plating of meals in the kitchen. These plated meals were then distributed to the ward. The system components for a plated meal service are:

- individual menu choices entered onto a menu card by patients

- menu choices collated (usually by a card reader) and compiled into production schedules for the kitchen

- patients meals plated according to the choices on the menu card

- plated meals placed in a trolley system for distribution to the ward.

A number of patented distribution systems have been designed to maintain food temperature during the distribution phase. These include heated pellets placed under hot items and insulated trays that segregate and maintain the temperature of hot and cold items. A common feature of a tray distribution system is a meal assembly belt, consisting of a conveyor system in which the tray passes along the assembly line and at each station components are added (food, crockery, cutlery, condiments), based on the individual menu card.

In an interrupted catering system, the operation is designed around a managed holding system, which separates production from service, but does so in a controlled manner. Depending on the extent of the buffer required, measured in terms of the number of days of storage needed and distance of travel, a holding system is designed to manage the quality and safety of food (Department of Health, 1989). Rather than keeping it warm or at ambient temperatures, the food is rapidly chilled or frozen to a temperature that controls the growth of pathogenic bacteria and maintains food quality (Harrigan and Park, 1991). There are two main approaches:

- A **cook-chill** system. This uses a mix of all forms of raw material and production is planned on the basis of the schedule of a standard menu cycle, with demand based on requirements for up to the next five days. Food is cooked in

Cabinet	5–35 kg
Roll-in cabinets	75–150 kg
Modular cabinets	70–280 kg

Table 10.1 *Freezing/chilling capacities (per batch)*

batches, packaged into containers (disposable or reusable aluminium, steel or polymer) and rapidly chilled, either as individual plated meals or in bulk. The food is then stored under refrigeration (−1 to +3°C) for up to five days. There may be a distribution stage from central kitchen to satellite kitchen, where reheating takes place.

- A **cook-freeze** system is similar to the above, except that the production schedule is based on the requirements for the next month or so. Once cooked, food is rapidly frozen and held at temperatures below −20°C.

In order to process foods rapidly, either a blast-chiller (for cook-chill) or a blast-freezer (for cook-freeze) is required. The capacity required is based on the maximum volume of food to be processed (see Table 10.1). Typically, it is possible to process 20 kg of food per cubic metre of chiller or freezer. A single batch takes up to 90 minutes. The normal chilling medium is high-velocity air (up to 7 m/s) cooled to −40°C. Alternatives to the use of air are liquid carbon dioxide (−70°C) and liquid nitrogen (−196°C).

Large units are semi-continuous, arranged as a push-through tunnel, in which trolleys of unprocessed food are pushed in from one side and trolleys of processed food removed from the other side. Even larger units operate as continuous tunnels and are arranged so that the air flow moves in the opposite direction to the food flow.

As an alternative to blast-chillers, some forms of cook-chill use refrigerated water baths to chill food products that have been vacuum-packed in plastic bags. In the **sous-vide** system, foods are subjected to a pasteurizing heat process after vacuum-packing in a polymer bag. They are then chilled using air or a refrigerated water bath. This allows an extended shelf-life, compared to conventional cook-chill foods (Johns *et al.*, 1992). The absence of air from the pack maintains the flavour of the food and prevents aerobic bacteria from growing.

Closely associated with any holding system is the packaging process. Packaging provides an important aspect of any holding process. It must be chosen in relation to:

- containment
- protection
- information.

The type of material used for any packaging is critical. It must be able to withstand processing conditions (highest temperature, lowest temperature and humidity). It must maintain the quality of the food, by acting as a moisture barrier and a microbiological barrier. It must be made from a material that is safe to use in contact with food (i.e. the food must not absorb any metals, plasticizers, inks or other contaminants).

The size of the pack is important in relation to further processing. It is now

Meals per day	Cook-chill (five-day storage)	Cook-chill (one month storage)
	Store capacity (m³)	
100	0.25	1.5
500	1.25	7.5
1,000	2.5	15.0

Table 10.2 *Storage capacity for food holding*

common practice to use standardized containers that can be moved from storage to processing equipment, into transportation devices and holding and on to regeneration, without the need to transfer the material from one container to another.

Decisions must also be made about how the food will be packed. Should the food be in individual or bulk packs? Should the food be solid or free-flow? For medium to long-term holding, the packaging should incorporate product information, such as its content, the packing date, the use-by date, storage conditions and regeneration instructions.

The basic principles of operating stores were outlined in Chapter 4. These principles apply to any holding stages introduced into the processing and service of food. Storage capacity is based on the number of meals to be stored. One cu. m of storage can be used to hold approximately 2,000 meals. However, the actual capacity is at least twice or three times this, to allow for shelving, racking circulation space and trolleys. Typical store capacities are shown in Table 10.2.

The location of any medium to long-term storage is critical to any interrupted catering system. We need to decide the right mix of central v. end-user or satellite storage. It is normal practice to hold materials centrally and to deliver to satellite stores from 12 to 24 hours before use. This obviously depends upon the volume of material to be transported and the distance over which goods must be moved. The logistics of distribution are critical to the cost-effectiveness of an interrupted system.

In the case of cook-chill and cook-freeze, the design of temperature-controlled stores has a major impact on the effectiveness of the system. For low-volume operations, cabinet store units may be sufficient, but usually walk-in stores are required. For larger operations, a through-flow of materials is desirable with separate in and out doors.

Packaged foodstuffs may be stored on shelves, trolleys or pallets. This choice will be dictated by the volume of goods moving through the system. High-volume operations require efficiently designed stores, to minimize materials handling and to simplify good practice such as first-in first-out (FIFO). Storage on trolleys is more expensive than shelves but can simplify the movement of materials. Palletized systems are only used in the largest of operations. Live storage is also a possibility, where the food packs are placed on conveyorized rollers.

Transport

Transport may involve the use of:

- trolleys

- conveyor systems, using belts or rollers

- electric or motorized vehicles, such as fork-lift trucks, tractor and trailer units, road vehicles.

The choice of system depends upon the volume of food to be moved and the distance of travel. Mechanized systems (including conveyors) reduce labour content and running costs, but are expensive to install and so require high utilization if they are to be considered as a sound investment. Conveyors can be used to transport items over relatively short distances and under ambient conditions. Although conveyors work best on the level, with only small inclines or declines, it is possible to introduce lifting and lowering sections into the systems, but this increases the costs. Conveyors are normally used under ambient conditions (because of the high cost of temperature-controlled conveyor systems), although the choice of packaging or container may be chosen to include insulation, to minimize temperature changes.

Trolleys may be ambient, chilled, frozen or heated. They may be passive (that is, using the temperature of the food at the point of loading), relying on high levels of insulation, or they may contain refrigeration or heating units. Passive units can hold temperatures for short periods of time (measured in minutes), but for longer periods heated or chilled trolleys are required.

In the case of chilled or frozen food, and where large volumes and long distances are involved, an alternative is to use refrigerated vehicles. Where long-distance transportation is required, great care is needed in selecting a method of operation. Typically, a critical decision is whether to rent, lease or buy transportation. This decision will depend on a careful financial analysis, taking into account vehicle full-life costing, together with the utilization of both vehicles and associated staff.

Transportation of hot, chilled and ambient foods over rough surfaces (be they in food trolleys or road vehicles) can result in spillage. This is one of the benefits of frozen foods where, because of the solid nature of frozen foods, spillage is not an issue.

Once a method of transport has been decided, great care is needed in planning distribution logistics. In particular, where a single production kitchen is supplying food to a number of outlets, a planned distribution network will be necessary (Fawcett *et al.*, 1992), based on:

- distance from origin to delivery zones

- number of 'drops'

- vehicle capacity

- average volume of each 'drop'

- frequency of drops

- loading and unloading times

- drivers' hours

- load planning

- inventory management.

Regeneration

The choice of a regeneration system is based around a number of factors associated with the food:

- initial temperature of the food

- final temperature of the food

- volume of food to be heated at a time

- nature of the pack (single or multi-portion)

- texture (liquid, solid/moist, solid/crisp)

- food safety factors (susceptibility of the food to the presence and growth of harmful bacteria).

Microwave ovens are normally used for individual meals, although there are examples of large-volume regeneration systems using microwave tunnel ovens. More typically, microwaves are used in low-volume operations or as a back-up to other forms of regeneration, where they have the benefit of relatively rapid heating for small volumes of food. Microwaves are most suited to moist foods with high water content.

The regeneration of frozen foods can be difficult in microwave ovens, because of the problem of uniform thawing. There is always the danger that some parts of the food will thaw first and then heat rapidly to boiling point, while other parts remain frozen.

Infrared heating is used in some makes of chilled food regeneration trolleys. Infrared heating provides rapid heating with minimum changes to the quality of the food. It is limited to the heating of thin layers of food (up to a maximum of 25 mm). The infrared device may be built into a specially designed trolley, or in batch or conveyor ovens. The texture of the food can, to some extent, be controlled by heating with the lid on or off. Leaving the lid on results in moisture retention and limited drying out, best suited to steamed, boiled and casserole dishes. Heating with the lid off produces a drier and crisper surface for grilled, fried and baked foods.

Convection ovens use forced air convection to heat foods rapidly. They can be used in batch ovens or with trolley-based systems, which allow integration of the holding, transport and regeneration systems. Alternatively, in large-scale operations continuous ovens may be used. Forced air convection can cause drying and browning of foods, which is more acceptable for fried, roasted and baked products. As in the case of infrared ovens, lids may be used to control the amount of drying out that takes place. Alternatively, for moist foods, water (in the form of a spray) may be introduced into the oven cavity to control drying.

Steaming ovens use forced convection steam. This overcomes any problems associated with drying out, crisping or browning. They are most suitable for moist products such as casseroles and vegetables. Steaming ovens have the benefit that moist air heats more quickly than dry air. Steaming ovens may hold the food on shelves or trolleys.

Combination ovens provide a mixture of both convection and steam, allowing greater flexibility of use. The user can manipulate the mixture of hot air and steam to control the both the rate of heating and texture change within the food. Most combination ovens can be programmed to control the time and conditions for regeneration. They can also be used to reheat chilled foods that have been vacuum-packed in polymer-based packaging, often as part of a sous-vide system.

Water baths are also used to reheat sous-vide pouches. The water (which is held at or just below boiling point) can provide rapid heating of individual portions of food and is used with what are often referred to as *boil-in-the-bag* packs.

Thawing cabinets are used to thaw frozen foods quickly and safely. They work on the same principles as a blast-chiller. Air at 10°C is circulated over the containers of frozen foods. This removes any danger of parts of the food heating to the point where bacterial growth can start, before the coldest part of the pack has thawed.

SYSTEM ADOPTION

The provision of meals to airline passengers has always involved holding, transportation and regeneration (see case study in Chapter 1). In the 1970s, many caterers based in the institutional sector (hospitals, school meals, industrial catering, the prison service) and in popular catering (such as roadside restaurants) adopted cook-freeze as a means of organizing food production in a more systematic manner. Food production could be centralized in a kitchen designed around batch or continuous processing, resulting in lower unit food costs and providing food of a higher nutritional value than had been the case with hot-holding systems. The prepared materials were held in frozen storage allowing long-term production cycles. Foods were distributed to the service unit (known as satellite, end or finishing kitchens), where they were stored for short periods prior to reheating (or regenerating) ready for service.

Although the systems were widely adopted, they have been criticized on a number of grounds:

- freezing changes the characteristics of the food (texture, colour and flavour)

- not all food products can be handled by the system

- long-term storage of frozen foods adds an additional cost element.

Although cook-freeze is still used, cook-chill came to be recognized as a more effective system. Although chilling gives a much more restricted shelf-life, it does not cause such large changes to the food materials and a wider range of food items, such as salads and sandwiches, can be included within the system. In addition to institutional and popular catering, cook-chill is seen as an ideal system for the banqueting departments of hotels and for in-flight catering. However, many cook-chill systems installed in the 1980s have been replaced by conventional systems, because of problems over quality and cost (Walker, 1989).

CASE STUDY: VOLKSWAGEN, GERMANY

An example of a cook-chill application in a large industrial complex is the Volkswagen Autostadt complex in Germany. The factory has six foodservice outlets, with a total of 1,300 seats. The outlets cover many forms of speciality restaurants and a range of service levels. Here a centralized production kitchen supplies a number of service outlets, including an automobile theme park, the 100,000 factory workforce, together with a number of other contract catering sites. The last are supplied on a commercial basis. The factory requires 24-hour food-service, because of the working pattern. Between 60 and 70 per cent of all food goes through the cook-chill system, and the production kitchen uses cook-chill technology. The kitchen has an area of 3,000 sq. m and provides an output of up to 32,000 meals per day. These meals normally have a shelf-life of three to five days, except when they are vacuum-packed, when the shelf-life can be extended up to a maximum of 12 days. The production kitchen has six roll-in blast-chillers, allowing the processing of 2,700 kg of food per cycle.

CASE STUDY: VELINDRE HOSPITAL[1]

In 2000, Velindre Hospital NHS Trust, Cardiff, introduced a system whereby frozen meals were regenerated and served at ward level, replacing a system whereby the food was cooked and plated at a nearby hospital and transported hot to Velindre.

In the new system, frozen multi-portion meals are delivered twice a week to a central walk-in deep freeze. Menus for main meals are on a two-week rotation. The choice is from two hot meals, such as lasagne or chicken supreme, salad, sand-wiches or omelette and two desserts, which always include a milky pudding (popular with ill people!).

Each day the meals are called up to the ward kitchen. This comprises a large upright fridge, deep freeze, dishwasher, two-ring electric hob, microwave and a hostess trolley. The trolley regenerates the food in 90 minutes. In addition, with an overhead gantry, the trolley also serves as a display trolley, which is very important in allowing patients to see the food.

CASE STUDY: HOTEL BANQUETING

In 1995, the *Caterer & Hotelkeeper* reported a revolution in the way banqueting was being carried out. 'A number of banquet venues are switching to plated service – thus speeding up delivery, reducing the numbers of waiting staff and allowing chefs rather than waiters to do the final presentation' (*Caterer & Hotelkeeper*, 10 August 1995). Two alternative approaches were identified, one based on warm holding the other on cook-chill.

At the Regent Hotel, London, the approach has been to cook food immediately before service rather than cook-chill. A special system has been installed to keep food really hot from the time it is cooked, during plating and through to service. Food is cooked in the main kitchen, then transported in cabinets to the finishing

1. This case study is based on an article in *Caterer & Hotelkeeper*, 13 April 2000.

kitchen. Temperatures are controlled precisely in the cabinets. Plating up in the finishing kitchen is carried out under strips of heated lights. Waiting staff operate in teams of five, each carrying two plates, so they can serve an entire table at once. 'They use a specially choreographed routine when placing the plates on the table which has been known to draw a round of applause from guests.'

Cook-chill is also being used more frequently. According to the article, 'equipment suppliers have noticed these changing practices and are beginning to put together banqueting packages, typically including combination ovens with compatible blast-chillers and trolleys that fit both'.

The Novotel in Hammersmith, London, has installed such a system. It can now prepare food on Thursday or Friday for service at a Saturday night function. Rather than being served from multi-portion containers by silver service waiting staff, food is now individually plated. Central to the system are a blast-chiller and three combination ovens that are used for virtually all cooking tasks – from vegetable steaming to meat roasting. They are also used for regenerating the chilled plated meals, a process that takes about five minutes for a full load of 80 plates. Eight trolleys are used for both transport and cooking, together with thermal insulation hoods that keep food hot until service.

The hotel has identified a number of advantages with the new system. Food is served hot, because the plates retain the heat from regeneration. More attention can be paid to presentation too, because chefs have time to work on it in advance. The kitchen workforce can be scheduled more easily so that banqueting production takes place during quiet times. Quality is more consistent, as more time can be taken over presentation. The system does away with silver service skills, so there are savings on waiting staff too.

CURRENT TRENDS AND ISSUES AFFECTING THE SYSTEM

Food hygiene

One of the major impacts on food holding systems has been the development of food quality management systems, such as Hazard Analysis and Critical Control Points (HACCP). The storage of food will always introduce a food-poisoning hazard, because of the potential for the growth of bacteria. Recognizing this risk, HACCP procedures always require the strict control of time and temperature during food storage (Johns, 1995).

These practices are resulting in a number of changes to food production and service systems, including:

- better labelling of foods to indicate date of production

- closer temperature control of refrigerated and frozen storage

- data loggers to monitor the performance of refrigerated and frozen storage

- stricter policies on shelf-life management

- higher levels of training of food operatives.

Just-in-time manufacturing

A principle of 'just-in-time' manufacturing is the minimization of stock levels. Organizations adopting these principles have been forced to look at all storage and holding stages in order to reduce stock levels to the minimum. These principles raise issues about the real benefits of the longer-term storage of frozen foods.

Outsourcing

Another major trend has been the removal of some or all of the preparation and cooking stages away from the hospitality premises to the premises of a food manufacturer. The hospitality premises then become concerned only with the reheating, assembling and garnishing of meals. In this way, the business can concentrate on the *service* aspect of the business, leaving the production aspect to another organization. Some hospitality organizations have set up their own manufacturing units. In other situations, food manufacturers produce food to the specification of the caterer.

SUMMARY

In this chapter, we have seen how a holding stage can be used to decouple production and service. This separation of the two processes introduces a number of benefits. First, production can be optimized as a process when it is separated from service. Second, one production kitchen can be used to produce foods for a number of service points. Third, a distribution system can be introduced, so that production does not have to be carried out at the same geographical location as the service.

Further study

Read through current issues of trade journals (such as *Caterer & Hotelkeeper* or *Hospitality*) and identify articles or news stories about catering systems based around interrupted catering, holding, transportation and regeneration. Analyse the articles or stories in order to:

- classify the system in terms of process and technology

- comment on the benefits or disadvantages of the system

- comment on food quality, food safety or management control.

Bibliography

Department of Health (1989) *Chilled and Frozen: Guidelines on Cook-Chill and Cook-Freeze Catering Systems*. London: HMSO.

Fawcett, P., McLeish, R. and Ogden, I. (1992) *Logistics Management*. Harlow: Prentice Hall.

Fuller, J. and Kirk, D. (1991) *Kitchen Planning and Management*. Oxford: Butterworth-Heinemann.

Harrigan, W. F. and Park, R. W. A. (1991) *Making Food Safe*. London: Academic Press, 27–35.

Johns, N., Wheeler, K. and Cowe, P. (1992) 'Productivity angles on sous vide production', in Teare, R. (ed.) *Managing Projects in Hospitality Organisations*. London: Cassell, 146–68.

Johns, N. (1995) *Managing Food Hygiene*. Basingstoke: Macmillan.

Recommended further reading

Sutton, A. (1990) 'Hospital catering counts the cost', *Hospitality*, September, 11–15.

Hemmington, M. (1996) 'Welfare catering', in Jones, P. *Introduction to Hospitality Operations*. London: Cassell, 209–33.

Walker, A. (1989) *Success or Failure in Cook-Chill Catering: An Investigation in Technology Transfer*. Bradford: Horton.

PART E

FOOD AND DRINK SERVICE SYSTEMS

Dining out of the home in civilized societies originated at least as far back as ancient Greek and Roman times. Along their roads the Romans built inns, known as *mansiones* and *divorsia*, to provide the traveller with refreshment and sustenance, while in the towns they had taverns or *tabernae*, which emerged as a rendezvous for the local community for hospitality and eating rather than for drinking. The food served consisted of a simple meal and was usually plated and taken to customers, who ate it seated on stools around a communal table and often in a hall. Before the eighteenth century, prepared food for consumption outside the home was mainly only available from such establishments and the food was regarded, like a bed, as a convenience. Only around the turn of the eighteenth century 'was the idea conceived of serving fine food at a low price in rooms devoted to that purpose – in fact, of splitting the rich man's manorial table among the many' (Sansom, 1961).

The public dining room that came ultimately to be known as the restaurant originated in France. The first restaurant is believed to have been opened in France in 1765 by A. Boulanger. Although inns, taverns and hostelries often served paying guests meals from the host's table or table d'hôte, Boulanger's restaurant was, according to Lang (1997), probably the first public place where any diner might order a meal from a menu offering a choice of dishes. Since then many nations have contributed to the development of the restaurant and today dining takes a variety of forms and occurs in a variety of different contexts, drawing upon a range of different foodservice systems. Each of these systems has different characteristics.

Put simply, dining is about eating a meal, but in reality dining out has been regarded as a complex activity involving a number of variables. Sansom (1961), for example, maintained, 'Dining is not eating, nor even eating well. Dining is a confluence of many pleasures – of good company, elegant service, tranquillity and good health – i.e. extreme care of all the senses.'

In this part of the book we look at those systems associated with the service of customers – foodservice and dining systems, bars and clearing systems.

In particular, this section focuses on customer processing operations, in contrast with previous chapters, where the focus has largely been on materials and information processing.

Bibliography

Lang, G. (ed.) (1997) 'Restaurants', in *New Encyclopaedia Britannica*, 15th edition, **9**, 1042–4.

Sansom, W. (1961) 'Luncheon at La Bonne Auberge', in *Blue Skies, Brown Studies*. London: The Hogarth Press.

CHAPTER 11

Foodservice and dining

OBJECTIVES

After completing this chapter you will be able to:

- *identify the purpose of foodservice and dining systems*

- *describe the characteristics of these systems*

- *identify and describe the different types of system*

- *explain key processes*

- *identify current trends in foodservice and dining.*

INTRODUCTION

This chapter considers the foodservice and dining systems of hospitality operations. Service is an essential feature of hospitality operations. Indeed, many people consider that the primary reason for the existence of hospitality operations is to serve customers and to satisfy their service requirements. The use of the word 'customer' here conceals a number of nuances. These are discussed later, but for ease 'customer' is used in this chapter to cover all contexts and circumstances.

Many customers of hospitality operations seek the service of food, whether as a snack or as a meal. For some operations, such as stand-alone restaurants, fast-food outlets and cafés, foodservice is the core service offered, while in others, foodservice is ancillary. In hotels, foodservice is probably ancillary to accommodation service; in hospitals, foodservice is an ancillary service of medical treatment; on an aeroplane, foodservice is secondary to the flight itself. All hospitality operations have foodservice systems, since these are the means by which customers are provided with meals. This may occur either on the premises of the hospitality establishment or elsewhere in decoupled operations such as hospital wards, on aeroplanes or at home as take-aways or home-delivered meals. If consumption takes place on site, the hospitality operation would also have some form of dining system. The dining systems considered in this chapter are designed and in the control of the hospitality operation, i.e. on site. In view of the involvement/presence of the customer in both service and dining and the particular closeness between these two stages, they are considered together.

PURPOSE OF SYSTEM

Foodservice systems

Foodservice has been defined as that part of the operational system wholly concerned with the presentation of food to the customer (Davis and Stone, 1991). Essentially this means that foodservice is concerned with how food reaches, or is served to, the customers of hospitality operations. However, ideally, this food also needs to be served at the time when the customer requires it and in the place they choose. For these reasons the functions of foodservice systems are as follows:

- To serve food to the customer when they require it.

- To serve food where they require it. This embraces locational and atmospheric aspects. Customers may want food to be served to them on site in an appropriate service setting that supports and reflects the foodservice being offered.

- To serve food in a manner that takes account of the customer's requirements and the resources and policies of the hospitality operation. This relates to both the technical aspects of foodservice (i.e. the methods of service) and the interpersonal aspects of the service encounter between employees and customers (e.g. social skills).

The intention should be to serve the customer with the right food (attractive and of good quality) at the right temperature, in the right quantity (according to operational standards), at the right place and time and at the right price (as advertised) to ensure customer acceptability.

While the emphasis upon foodservice may permeate all the way through a hospitality operation, especially a foodservice operation, the actual act of and system of foodservice is conventionally associated with the part of the operation that is directly experienced and visible to the customer, i.e. the front-of-house area. This is where the foodservice is open to public scrutiny. In this situation the foodservice system involves the interaction between the hospitality organization, its staff and the customer. Normally front-of-house is located on site, but when food is delivered to the customer's home or place of work (e.g. 'meals on wheels' or pizza home delivery), an element of the service system may be off site.

Dining systems

Dining systems are concerned with facilitating the dining experience and, from an operational or technical perspective, are concerned with how dining areas are laid out in terms of the nature and spatial arrangement of furniture and facilities. The dining area is, usually, the context in which foodservice takes place. Exceptions to this are take-away or 'off-site' or 'home' delivery operations.

GENERIC SYSTEM CHARACTERISTICS

The mission of a restaurant, café, take-away and foodservice activity in any other type of hospitality operation is not to prepare meals, it is to serve meals to cus-

Context: e.g. restaurant dining area, take-away retail area, pub lounge, hospital ward		
Inputs	Transformation process	Output

Transforming resources: $\longrightarrow$
  Materials – utilities
  Furniture and equipment
  China, crockery, cutlery
	Deliver and serve prepared food and provide supplementary information to the customer for consumption and socio-psychological elements	Used serving equipment, utensils

Service employees (hospitality or other staff) Information – marketing, operating	$\longrightarrow$	Expended employee, time, skill
Transformed resources $\longrightarrow$ Materials – prepared food		Customer served with food, information etc.
Information – orders Customers		

Figure 11.1 *Foodservice system*

tomers. Indeed, the delivery of foodservice cannot take place without the customer – it is not possible to serve a meal unless a customer has placed an order (Nevan Wright, 1999), whether they be on or off site. All foodservice systems therefore have customers as inputs (see Figure 11.1).

The use of the word 'customer' conceals a number of different interpretations that are largely a consequence of consideration of the person buying the service, the person receiving the service, the person consuming the service and/or the context in which this occurs. First, customers are normally regarded as the purchaser. While the recipient of a service in a hospitality operation may be the purchaser of the service, they may have the service purchased for them (e.g. a child with his parents, or a person receiving hospitality from a host). Second, the purchaser may be someone who does not personally receive and consume a particular hospitality service (e.g. an employer paying for subsistence for an employee travelling on business, or the state paying for a patient in a hospital). Third, in certain contexts different terminology may be used. For instance on a cruise liner the 'customer' may be called the 'passenger', in a university a 'student', in a hotel a 'guest' or perhaps in a private hospital a 'patient'. Thus, 'customer', while used herein, hides a number of complexities.

Since customers flow through the system, they may be thought of as a transformed resource, as they are acted upon within the foodservice system. The transforming of customers sounds rather technical or mechanical, focusing mainly on satisfying physiological needs, namely hunger and thirst. Indeed, this may be identified as the main task by certain operations such as employee cafeterias and fast-food chains. But the transforming or satisfying of customers in other operations may be more complicated and involve providing for social and psychological needs as well. Customers are a key input to the foodservice system and often create uncertainties for the hospitality operation, as it cannot always be certain what the customer requires or what to expect from the customer. Foodservice system customers may want to satisfy one or a number of needs. These may be physiological, economic, social or psychological. Thus, customers may require food for their physical and mental well-being; value for money; and social and psychological stimulation from the atmosphere generated by the service environment and contact with the service personnel. In an early study of the so-called 'meal experience', Campbell-Smith (1967) identified 43 different reasons why people may choose to eat out. Furthermore, customers may also seek additional services, such as hot water for baby food, doggie bags for leftovers, information related to the ordering and consumption of the food, and facilities such as a cloakroom, lavatories, etc. Many of these are predictable and can be prepared for. Others are less so and may affect the ability of the hospitality operation to create and deliver an effective service.

CASE STUDY: ROADSIDE RESTAURANT FACILITIES

The former managing director of one of the UK's largest roadside restaurant chains recalls the first time he commissioned some market research. At that time there were two major chains competing with each other and the research was designed to investigate why customers preferred to use one brand rather than the other. Naturally enough, the first question on the survey was 'Why did you stop at this roadside restaurant?' The MD was shocked to find that over a half of the respondents replied that they stopped to use the toilet facilities. He recalls, 'I had been in the roadside restaurant business for 15 years before I realized I was actually in the toilet business.' This knowledge made him rethink the design and operation of toilets in his restaurants. Rather than locate them at the rear of the premises, all new restaurants sited them near the entrance to make it easier for people to access them. They were also increased in size and the equipment in them upgraded to a higher standard. For instance, the female toilets had larger mirrors and better lighting. New cleaning routines were adopted to make sure that the facilities were kept very clean and checked on an hourly basis.

Other transformed resources, which are shown in Figure 11.1, include the stored prepared food that is waiting to be served and information inputs such as details about the customer's order, which the system processes both for its benefit (customer sales records) and the customer's benefit (the bill). Foodservice systems also employ transforming resources that act upon the transformed resources. These include physical inputs – equipment, utilities, staff (hospitality staff or staff providing a hospitality function, e.g ward staff, airline flight attendant) and information inputs (e.g. staff operating instructions and menus). Customers might also be considered a transforming resource if they replace staff in the service of food (e.g. in self-service systems).

These inputs are then combined and converted so that prepared food in the form of a snack or a complete meal is delivered and served to the customer for consumption. In addition, supplementary information (for instance, regarding the order and socio-psychological elements of the hospitality package) are also provided. This is the transformation process, which predominantly involves food materials and customer processing with some information processing.

The key output of the foodservice system is the served customer, but there are others, as Figure 11.1 shows. This whole foodservice process takes place within a context which might be a restaurant dining area, take-away retail area, pub lounge, hospital ward, etc.

SYSTEM TYPES

In theory, hospitality operations have choices concerning foodservice and dining systems, but in practice these may be restricted. The selection of the most appropriate foodservice and dining system will be determined by a number of inter-related factors. These factors have been variously referred to by different authors, including Davis and Stone (1991), Kinton *et al.* (1992), Lawson (1987) and Lillicrap and Cousins (1994), and relate to the operation, the customer, the food and the pattern of demand. They include:

- business policy and financial objectives associated with the hospitality operation and the mode of operation – availability and skills of staff and the technology available

- the size (capacity), location and design of the premises

- the target market – the type of customer to be served and any circumstances influencing their choice (e.g. time and money available to eat)

- the type of menu and the cost of the food served

- the pattern of demand – volume of customers, complexity of orders, turnover of customers.

Foodservice systems

Foodservice system types have developed, and continue to develop, as a result of social and economic changes, altered business practices, consumer trends, the internationalization of cuisines and new developments in technology. Generally the system types have been equated with service methods. Sometimes these methods have been simply listed (e.g. Jones, 1986; Kinton *et al.*, 1992). Others (e.g. Lawson, 1987) outline the basic methods of foodservice, as follows:

- waited service at the table

- self-service selection from a counter or display

- counter service with meals consumed at, or served, at the counter

- assembled meal service.

They then identify and discuss the main types associated with these basic methods. Lawson, for instance, groups self-service facilities into cafeteria systems, free-flow systems, mechanical systems, automatic systems and self-help systems. This might be regarded as a simple classification of foodservice types. Few classifications of foodservice systems exist. Jones and Huelin (1990) classify catering systems into three levels of analysis. Level 1 comprises the generic systems, which in this case

Level 1	Level 2	Level 3
Service	Waiter/ess	Plated, semi-plated silver service and guéridon
	Assisted waiter	Buffet, family and carvery
	Counter	Fast food, free-flow, echelon, blister, etc.
	Self-service	Vending

Figure 11.2 *An analysis of foodservice systems* (Jones and Huelin, 1990)

would be foodservice; Level 2 incorporates the subsystems and Level 3 shows the variations. Figure 11.2 is an adaptation of this model for foodservice, incorporating additional insertions in Level 3.

Another attempt to classify food (and beverage) service systems has been undertaken by Lillicrap and Cousins (1994), who identify five service methods available to the food and beverage operator and then categorize them according to five elements of the food and beverage process, namely: the food and beverage service area, the method of selecting/ordering food, who undertakes the service, where dining/consumption occurs and who clears. Figure 11.3 shows an analysis of these service methods.

The choice of service method has many implications for the operation. These include the layout of premises, the space required, the nature and arrangement of fixtures, fittings and furniture, the numbers and required skills of staff, the prices charged and the behaviour of customers.

The layout of foodservice areas should be considered with the overall objectives of facilitating efficient operations and satisfying customer service. In foodservice systems the physical flow of people is key, and consequently the optimization of movement, congestion reduction and the maximum utilization of space need to be addressed in layout design. Foodservice systems may adopt different layouts (see also Chapter 2).

Fast-food systems (without seating) and cafeteria line systems adopt a **product layout**, where the customer moves from facility to facility. Here the process tends to be continuous and the sequence of customer food requirements is generally common to all customers. Floor space may be minimized and layout will aid customer flow. Lawson (1978) identifies eight different counter layouts for cafeterias based around variations of the straight-line counter:

- single line

- divergent flow

- convergent flow

- multiple outlets

- parallel flow

- bypassing

- free-flow with counters in line

- free-flow with counters in perimeter.

SERVICE METHOD	ORDERING/ SELECTION	SERVICE	PLACE OF CONSUMPTION
Table service	From menu	By staff to customer	At laid cover
'Service to customers at a laid cover'			

Waiter a Silver/English
        b Family
        c Plate/American
        d Butler/French
        e Russian
        f Guéridon
Bar counter			

Assisted service	From menu, buffet or passed trays	Both staff and customer	Usually at laid cover
'Combination of table service and self-service'			
Assisted a Carvery b Buffet			
Self-service	Customer selects own tray	Customer carries	Dining area or take-away

Cafeteria a Counter
           b Free-flow
           c Echelon
           d Supermarket			

Single point service	Ordered at single point	Customer carries	Dining area or take-away
Take-away Vending Kiosks Food court Bar			
Specialized or in situ service	From menu or predetermined	Brought to customer	Where served
'Service to customers in areas not primarily designed for foodservice' Tray Trolley Home delivery Lounge Room Drive-in			

Figure 11. 3 *An analysis of foodservice methods and elements of the service process* (Lillicrap and Cousins, 1994)

Since then, other forms of counter have been developed, including the hollow square, echelon and carousel (Jones, 1986).

Traditional table service systems, in contrast, have **fixed position layouts**, where the food is delivered to the customer. This does not mean that the dining system (i.e. tables and chairs) are fixed. In some cases they may be, either for safety reasons, such as on ships and aeroplanes, or in mass catering, such as large cafeterias and fast food. In other cases, both tables and chairs will be movable, allowing the operator to adjust their customer space flexibly to accommodate parties of different sizes.

Buffets are often arranged in **cell-like layouts** with each area having all the processes (dishes) required to serve customers according to their needs. In some operations all three layouts may exist.

It follows, therefore, that different types of operation will require a different space in which to serve customers, as illustrated in Table 11.1.

Dining systems

Even fewer attempts have been made to analyse dining systems. Jones and Huelin's (1990) analysis (Figure 11.4) is one. Fixed furniture has some advantages over loose furniture. First of all, it remains neat and tidy. This is especially important when customers are carrying their own food around the dining area. It helps to ensure that they do not trip over a stray chair or get knocked by someone shifting back their chair. It also helps with cleaning, as some table sets are designed to minimize the number of legs supporting them, making it easier to clean the floor. Finally, as Table 11.1 illustrates, more customers can be fitted into a space if the seating is fixed, especially if the tables are relatively large.

Type of foodservice system	Area per diner sq. ft.	sq. m.	
Commercial restaurants			
Table service			
Loose furniture	11–18	1.0–1.7	
Fixed tables and chairs	8–11	0.7–1.0	(arranged in booths)
Counter service	15–20	1.4–1.9	
Cafeteria service	15–19	1.4–1.8	(includes service area)
Banquet service			
Long tables	10–14	0.9–1.3	
Industrial canteens			
Cafeteria service			
Tables of 4 to 6	14–19	1.3–1.9	(includes service area and
Table of 8 or more	12–17	1.1–1.6	trolley lanes)
School dining rooms			
Primary schools			
Counter service	8	0.74	
Family service	9	0.83	
Secondary schools	10	0.9	
Further Education colleges	12	1.1	

Table 11.1 *Space allocation for different types of foodservice and dining systems*

Level 1	Level 2	Level 3
Dining systems	Standing	Customer in single position or in various positions, e.g. stand-up buffet
	Seating	Loose tables and seating
		Fixed tables and seating
		Mixed seating and tables

Figure 11.4 *An analysis of dining systems*

SYSTEM PROCESSES

There are two main processes associated with running a restaurant or cafeteria – laying up (or *mise en place*) and service itself. Lay-up refers to the process of preparing the room ready for service. For all operations, this will include cleaning. In some cases this may be done overnight or between shifts by specialist staff, or in other cases foodservice employees will clean the dining area.

Mise en place

After cleaning, in table service operations *mise en place* involves laying the table with whatever equipment the service concept requires. In a smart, traditional restaurant this might comprise a linen table cloth, silver cutlery, crystal glassware, china side plate, cruet set and possibly flower vase, whereas in a bistro-style café stainless steel cutlery may be laid on the table top itself or on a paper place mat. As well as laying the tables, staff will also prepare materials and equipment in other areas. Most table service restaurants will have sideboards, which will be stocked with spare tableware, glassware, specialist equipment and linen. Restaurant staff also normally prepare the servery area (see Chapter 10), which usually includes a 'still room' in which butter is prepared for service and stored in a refrigerator, bread baskets are set up and hot beverages served from.

For counter service operations, lay-up involves preparing the counter area itself, as well as the station from which customers collect trays, cutlery, serviettes and salt, pepper and sauces (often in individual sachets). In cafeterias, food is typically displayed in hot counters or chilled units. Hot counters may either keep food hot by heating the food dish from underneath, on from above by heat lamps, or a combination of both. Counters should have transparent 'sneeze guards' designed to prevent airborne food contamination by customers.

Service

As for *mise en place*, service processes vary between table and counter service. In essence, this difference is based on the general principle that in the former everything is done for the customer by members of the restaurant staff, whereas in the latter the customer serves him or herself. In practice, this is not always the case. For instance, in family service, food items are brought to the table but customers help themselves from the dishes placed on the table. Likewise in cafeterias, customers self-serve from chilled units but are served hot items by service staff. Figure 11.3 explains many of these nuances between different styles of service.

SYSTEM ADOPTION

The following cases of foodservice and dining systems illustrate how different operations employ different foodservice methods, namely: table service, assisted service, self-service and single point service (take-away).

CASE STUDY: TEA TERRACE, REID'S PALACE HOTEL, FUNCHAL, MADEIRA

Reid's Palace Hotel was founded in 1891 by Scotsman William Reid and for over a hundred years has been recognized as one of the foremost luxury hotels in the world. The hotel prides itself on individual attention to the requirements of its guests. This is reflected in the varied selection of restaurants, which includes The Dining Room, Pool Terrace, Brisa do Mar, Les Faunes and the Trattoria Villa Cliff. Reid's classic Tea Terrace, overlooking the 10 acres of sub-tropical gardens surrounding the hotel, epitomizes the relaxed yet distinguished style and system of foodservice in the hotel. Afternoon tea is served on the terrace from three to six in the afternoon, and guests enter the marble-floored terrace through French windows. They are greeted by one of the four on-duty waiters, elegantly clad in white jackets and wearing bow ties, and seated at one of the tables either adjacent to the dark green railings at the edge of the terrace or next to the French windows. Each table has cushioned wicker chairs that are movable and is laid up with Wedgwood china on starched linen cloths. Small accompanying tables abut the dining table to accommodate a three-tiered cake stand containing a selection of delicate sandwiches, cakes and confitures and cream. These are served by the waiters from the cake trolley on view at the end of the terrace and brought to the table. In addition, scones are silver-served and guests can choose between six teas. Service is relaxed and the waiters are attentive to the guests' every need.

CASE STUDY: PARK HOUSE, TOBY CARVERY, SUTTON COLDFIELD

The Park House is a listed building in Sutton Park and operates as a Toby Carvery and Inn. This is one of the chain of 127 carving room restaurants operated by Six Continents Retail. The restaurant is open for lunch and dinner and comprises a main dining area and conservatory with a seating capacity for approximately 70. Seating is mainly loose, with some fixed bench seats. Customers are greeted in an adjoining bar area and when ready are escorted to their table. Customers choose their meal from the menu and are served their first course, dessert and coffee at their table. The main course includes a varied selection of roasts and vegetables, and for this customers visit the counter, where they are served by the chef. Customers can also serve themselves from the counter with some items. Alternatively, some items are cooked to order, plated and served at the table. Service in the restaurant is fairly relaxed, while food is priced mid-range. On receipt of the bill, customers normally pay at the cash desk on their way out. Tables are cleared during and at the end of service by service staff.

CASE STUDY: THE GRANARY, WELCOME BREAK, LEICESTER FOREST EAST SERVICES

This is one of 23 motorway service areas operated by Welcome Break. Open around the clock, it includes a Red Hen restaurant, a Burger King and a KFC food service outlet. It also has The Granary on the bridge above the motorway. This is a bright, friendly, self-service restaurant with a full range of hot and cold food. The area is divided into two parts: the self-service area and the dining area. The self-service area has counters around the edge of the service area. After collecting a tray, customers move to the counter section/s, from where they help themselves to food and drink. Hot food and drinks are normally served by staff positioned behind the counter. Customers then proceed to one of the two cash points to pay for their purchases and then move through to the adjacent dining area. Here seating and tabling is movable and is shared with customers who use the adjacent Burger King and KFC outlets. Floor staff are on hand in this area to clear tables after customers have finished.

CASE STUDY: McDONALD'S, HUDDERSFIELD

This is one of over 1,000 McDonald's restaurants in the UK. It occupies a prime corner site on a busy junction in the centre of Huddersfield. Open all day, it has high pedestrian flows, especially during the daytime, facilitating large throughput and high sales volume. Like all McDonald's restaurants this is designed around a system of foodservice that resembles a manufacturing production line, in which the design and layout, the scheduling and procedures of work are systematically planned to produce consistently standardized products. This is a counter service operation, with the 10 m counter placed at the rear of the restaurant on the ground floor, adjacent to the production area and directly opposite the door. Careful design and layout allows best use to be made of the available space on the two floors of the restaurant, and the traffic flow is manipulated to minimize congestion and maximize exposure to the menu range. Menus are simple and limited in length and composition, which makes the service of food and beverages simple, quick and efficient. Standardized customer service also exists. In this particular restaurant, customers have the choice of eating on the premises (there are 30 fixed seats downstairs and 100 upstairs around fixed tables) or taking food away. Orders are taken at one of ten counter cash points, bills paid for and the ordered food and drink delivered in disposable packaging to the customer waiting in front of the counter. If eating on site, customers either self-clear their table on completion of their meal or, more likely, floor crew clear away to clearing stations positioned in the dining area. Staffing numbers vary throughout the day according to the expected volume of business. At 3 p.m. on a weekday there are typically ten counter crew, ten production crew and one member of staff clearing on each floor.

CURRENT TRENDS AND ISSUES AFFECTING SYSTEM

Foodservice and dining systems have been, and continue to, be influenced by a range of demand and supply factors.

Demand factors

Successful foodservice is tied to customer needs, wants and behaviour. Customers decide when they require food, what they want, where they require it and how they want it served. Customers therefore influence foodservice systems and dining systems. Operations ignoring this do so at their peril. If foodservice operations are aware and understand the who, what, where, why, when, and how of customer behaviour related to the service of food, then the probability of success will increase. The difficulty for operators is that customer demands, expectations and behaviour are always changing. The challenge is to keep abreast of these changes.

A number of contemporary trends in demand, often working in combination, have influenced foodservice and dining systems. These include the following factors:

- Greater average real personal disposable incomes, which have enabled people to eat out more often.

- Less formal eating patterns and more casual eating – 'eating on the run' or 'grazing', as it is sometimes called – have increased. This has resulted in an increase in take-away and home delivery systems.

- Better access to transport and increased travel and by a wider range of methods has had many consequences, e.g. desire for foreign foodservice concepts, facilities in many more locations, food system designs that cater for large volumes, foodservice and dining systems on aeroplanes, drive-thru and other travel-thru systems (e.g helicopter and ski-thru fast-food systems) have been reported in the trade press.

- The increasingly informal nature of society, which has resulted in a decrease in traditional foodservice, e.g. silver service.

- More hurried people encouraging faster service and dining.

- An increased awareness of food safety, which has led consumers to expect high standards of cleanliness and food hygiene.

- Higher expectations of the public with regard to the range of restaurants, the variety of product range, service standards and value for money. Food courts have developed partly as a consequence of customers' desire for choice and quick, value for money meals when at leisure.

Supply factors

A host of supply factors impact on the design and operation of foodservice and dining systems. Many of these are generated outside the organization, for example:

- Strategies of operations (partly a response to above), e.g. more space for consumers in café-bars, free-flow systems to enable greater volumes to be satisfied.

- Legislation – the relaxing of licensing laws means that foodservice may be required at different times, lending itself to certain systems, while the deregulation of motorway services has influenced the location of service systems.

- Internationalization – the import of overseas systems, e.g. Benihana, sushi.

- The influence of technological developments on foodservice systems, e.g. hand-held computerized meal ordering systems, cash point technology, internet booking/ordering, enhancements in insulated packaging for take-aways and home delivery.

- Cost pressures/labour shortages, which have resulted in measures to use the customer more as an input in foodservice and dining systems, e.g. hot drink trays and mini-bars in hotel rooms, carvery and buffet-style operations, vending systems. Increased consumer participation through self-selection, self-service and self-clearing is being designed increasingly into foodservice systems.

The foodservice industry has experienced tremendous changes during the last forty years. One key global trend has been the growth in fast-food systems. While such systems have the same constituents as other foodservice systems, the characteristics of their input–process–output constituents differ. This has raised many issues. For instance, the use of disposable materials rather than traditional plates, cutlery, etc. has proved controversial to environmentalists and others. Fast food has de-skilled its tasks and hence its workforce is universally unskilled. Fast-food service staff do not require basic technical waiting skills and therefore the labour market for recruitment to fast-food operations has widened. Concerns over the nature of the fast-food workforce, i.e. dependency on young casual staff, and whether, because of this and the unskilled nature of the work, fast-food jobs are real jobs, have been expressed in some quarters. Some might even argue that the decline in the number of people with traditional service skills has been a factor in encouraging the development of fast food! The skill and knowledge requirements of foodservice staff in fast-food and other developing food-service sectors have been a key issue for hospitality educators, leading them to reflect on the nature of their provision and the design and operation of course curricula.

For some foodservice customers the movement towards fast food has been regarded with horror as traditional operations have closed and time-honoured service has been eroded. In Italy some have tried to halt what they consider the inexorable slide to fast food by promoting a 'slow-food movement'. However, change is inevitable and ultimately consumer demand will determine whether fast-food or slow-food systems prevail.

Another issue that has emerged from the increase in self-service and single point foodservice systems has been associated with the increased use of technology and in some cases the replacement of staff by technology. As Ball (1994) suggests:

If technology is to increase productivity and realize other benefits and not be resisted, rejected, bypassed or overcome by workers or customers, then consideration should be given to how workers (and possibly customers) use the technology, the environment in which it is to be used and the workers' and customers' attitudes towards the technology.

SUMMARY

Foodservice systems are involved with the service of meals or snacks to customers. Usually consumption takes place out of the home, but some systems may involve delivering food to the home and some commercial operations even provide dinner parties in the home. Thus, the dining/consumption context of this snack or meal could take place on hospitality premises, in a hospitality operation on other premises (e.g. in a factory or on a hospital ward) or in some other location (e.g. at home as a take-away meal). The foodservice server could be a hospitality member of staff, staff providing a hospitality function (e.g. ward staff, airline flight attendant) or the customer. Sometimes staff and customers share the service.

Dining systems are concerned with facilitating the dining experience. In technical terms they are concerned with the layout of dining areas, which relates to the presence, nature and spatial arrangement of furniture and facilities.

Foodservice systems and dining systems are usually integrated. A number of factors might be considered when choosing the most appropriate systems. These relate to the operation, the customer, the food and the pattern of demand.

A range of different groups and types of foodservice methods can be identified. The groups comprise: table service, assisted service, self-service, single point service and specialized service. The staff skills and tasks associated with each of these groups vary in complexity. The fixtures, fittings, furniture, serving and other equipment will be appropriate to each foodservice system and may differ between systems. A sequence of foodservice steps or tasks can be applied to each foodservice systems. Again this sequence and the steps may differ between systems.

Foodservice systems have changed, and will continue to change, as a consequence of a range of social, technological and other factors. These factors raise issues and offer opportunities and challenges to foodservice operators, facility and equipment designers, equipment manufacturers, foodservice staff and others. Ultimately the success of a foodservice or dining system will largely be determined by the customer, for without the customer foodservice and dining would not occur.

Further study

Select a job which you have held in the front-of-house in a foodservice operation (or observe someone else's job in this context). Sketch the layout of the front-of-house and describe the foodservice and dining systems, outlining the effects of the systems, both positive and negative, upon you, the manager, customers (or workers if you have not held such a job) and the organization.

Draw up a flow process chart (refer to Chapter 2) for the front-of-house operations in a fast-food restaurant (dine in and take away), a home delivery operation, a cafeteria operation and a self-service buffet.

Under what circumstances should a foodservice operation use the customer for foodservice and what operational and marketing steps might be used to facilitate this?

Go to the website of the magazine *Chain Leader* (www.chainleader.com), an American publication about hospitality chains. Click on 'Issue Archive' and conduct a search for the key words 'restaurant design'. This will take you to over 150 stories about restaurants that usually include plans of these units, along with a description and photographs of the service area.

Bibliography

Ball, S. (1994) 'Improving labour productivity', in Jones, P. and Merricks, P. *The Management of Foodservice Operations*. London: Cassell, 201.

Campbell-Smith, G. (1967) *Marketing the Meal Experience*. Guildford: University of Surrey.

Davis, B. and Stone, S. (1991) *Food and Beverage Management*. Oxford: Butterworth-Heinemann, second edition.

Jones, P. and Huelin, A. (1990) 'Thinking about catering systems', *International Journal of Operations and Production Management*, 10(8), 36–46.

Jones, U. (1986) *Catering: Food Preparation and Service*. London: Edward Arnold, 163–88.

Kinton, R., Ceserani, V. and Foskett, D. (1992) *The Theory of Catering*. London: Hodder & Stoughton.

Lawson, F. (1978) *Principles of Catering Design*. London: The Architectural Press.

Lawson, F. (1987) *Restaurants, Clubs and Bars: Planning, Design and Investment*. London: The Architectural Press.

Lillicrap, D. R. and Cousins, J. A. (1994) *Food and Beverage Service*, London: Hodder & Stoughton, fourth edition.

Nevan Wright, J. (1999) *The Management of Service Operations*. London: Cassell.

Further reading

Anderson, C. and Blakemore, D. (1991) *Modern Food Service*. Oxford: Butterworth-Heinemann.

Axler, B. H. (1979) *Foodservice: A Managerial Approach*. Chichester: John Wiley & Sons.

École Technique Hôtelière Tsuji (1991) *Professional Restaurant Service*. Chichester: John Wiley & Sons.

Fuller, J. (1992) *Advanced Food Systems*. Cheltenham: Stanley Thornes.

Johns, N. (1994) 'Foodservice layout and design', in Jones, P. and Merricks, P. *The Management of Foodservice Operations*. London: Cassell, 59–77.

CHAPTER 12

Clearing and dishwash

After completing this chapter you will be able to:

- *identify the purpose of clearing and dishwash systems*
- *describe the characteristics of these systems*
- *identify and describe the different types of system*
- *explain key processes*
- *identify current trends in clearing and dishwash.*

INTRODUCTION

Clearing and dishwashing comprise the last two stages of the foodservice system. Clearing and washing-up are emotive terms. They are often regarded as unpleasant, time-consuming, tedious, dirty activities that lack any scope for creativity. Dishwashing has been described as 'Cinderella work, given to the lowliest and sometimes, least trained staff in the industry' (Anon, 1996). Both clearing and dishwashing are invariably forgotten or ignored parts of foodservice and are rarely considered in the academic literature. One can only speculate why this may be. It may be that the foodservice process is considered finished when the customer has been served, or it may simply be that they are regarded as unimportant or disagreeable activities. Whatever the reason, clearing and dishwashing are necessary parts of foodservice operations systems, and have important planning, operational and managerial implications. Clearing and dishwashing are also important because of the impact they can have on the customer experience. A clean and shining table setting can heighten anticipation of an enjoyable meal just as much as a well-constructed menu, while removing unwanted dishes from a table can contribute to an enhanced meal experience. Satisfactory methods of clearing and dishwashing are also vital to hygienic foodservice and the economy of the operation.

Hyam suggests that dishwashing has important considerations for 'the health of customers, the morale of staff who provide for customers, and the economic use of energy' (quoted in Whitehall, date unknown).

This chapter considers both clearing and dishwashing and includes an overview of the dishwash function, along with an explanation of alternative dishwash systems, such as the flight conveyor. Also considered are the often overlooked but related areas of glass-washing and pot-washing. The need for pot-washing results from food production but may also result from foodservice (e.g. trays from counter systems).

PURPOSE OF SYSTEM

Clearing involves collecting and removing crockery, glasses, silverware (cutlery), linen, etc., when they are no longer required by the customer, from the point of food and drink consumption in the hospitality operation. Post-meal debris is cleared to make room for the next diner. Clearing normally occurs at the dining table and the removed items may have been used or remain unused. Clearing may take place either while the customer is eating or drinking in the hospitality operation or when they have left. It is normally undertaken by waiters or other foodservice staff, but in some instances it may be the customer who clears (e.g. fast-food operations). When staff clear, it should be undertaken carefully, to avoid any breakages, spillages or accidents, efficiently and unobtrusively, creating the minimum of inconvenience for the customer. Clearly, this is especially important if the customer is still at the table.

Dishwashing is concerned with washing dishes in hot water and detergent so that they become free of any food particles and are rendered hygienically safe. Scriven and Stevens (1989, p. 199) observe that 'dishwashing, whether manual or mechanical, can be defined as using nothing more than some hot water, detergent and a lot of motion to clean tableware'. Glass-washing and pot-washing should realize similar outcomes. Dishes, glasses and pots, however, need to be transported to and from the site where the actual washing occurs and handled before and after the cleaning process. Therefore dishwashing can be viewed in wider terms than merely the washing function.

The purpose of clearing and dishwashing systems is to remove soiled dishes, silverware, glassware and any other used items or debris from the dining area to the dishwash area and then, in the case of cleaned items, transferring them back to the appropriate storage area ready for service. Dishes therefore travel in a cycle and ideally they should be routed from the dining area, according to Kotschevar and Terrell (1961, p. 229), 'in a manner to create the least noise, confusion and unsightliness'. The manner in which clearing and dishwashing is undertaken differs between operations.

GENERIC SYSTEM CHARACTERISTICS

Clearing

Figure 12.1 illustrates the main components of a generic clearing system. The inputs comprise those items to be cleared, whether they be clean or soiled: e.g. items of crockery, glass, silverware, linen, etc. Prescribed procedures for clearing may be followed, such as those described in Lillicrap and Cousins (1994, pp. 292–8), which are concerned with the clearing of plates from restaurant tables. A clearer is also required. Traditionally the clearer has been a waiter or another member of

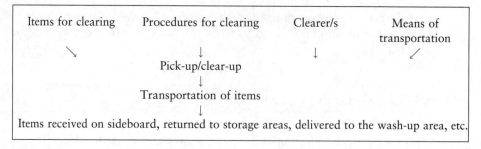

Figure 12.1 *A generic clearing system*

the food and beverage service staff. However, increasingly, and often for productivity gains, the customer is being requested to clear (e.g. in a quick-service outlet, where the customer is required to self-clear their table). In certain circumstances clearing is undertaken by both customers and staff (e.g. in tray service cafeterias, where customers are asked to put all crockery etc. back on to the meal tray used to carry the meal to the table and then to deposit this on a trolley or at a clearing section near the exit or wash-up area. Staff then take over and transport/ prepare the soiled dishes and crockery for washing.

Clearing staff perform effectively when they are alert to customer needs and circumstances and when clearing is timed appropriately according to the stage of meal consumption. When items are cleared by staff from tables the use of a clearing technique could be beneficial. According to Lillicrap and Cousins (1994, p. 292), for a restaurant: 'The correct clearing techniques allow more to be cleared, in less time and in fewer journeys between sideboard and table. In the long term, this speeds up the eating process and allows for greater seat turnover.'

Finally a means of transporting the items away from the customer/table to the wash-up area or back to storage is required. This may simply be manual carriage by the waiter, or it may also involve a trolley or an automated system such as a conveyor belt.

The second stage of a clearing system is the act of picking up items and transporting them elsewhere, e.g. to a sideboard or the dishwash area. The collecting of items may form part of a set service procedure laid down in an organization's operating guidelines/manual. For example, traditionally, it has always been prescribed that dirty plates should be cleared from the right-hand side of the guest. Catering students are taught and practise such procedures, while foodservice employees are either employed with such knowledge or are trained to use the employing organization's procedures. The amount of items to be cleared will vary in proportion to the volume of diners, the number of meal courses, the amount of cutlery and crockery used and the type of food and beverage service adopted.

Dishwashing

Irrespective of the system of delivery to the wash-up area, the sequence of events for the washing of dishes will be generally the same thereafter for both manual or machine washing (see Figure 12.2).

As can be seen from Figure 12.2, dishwashing systems comprise three main elements or subsystems:

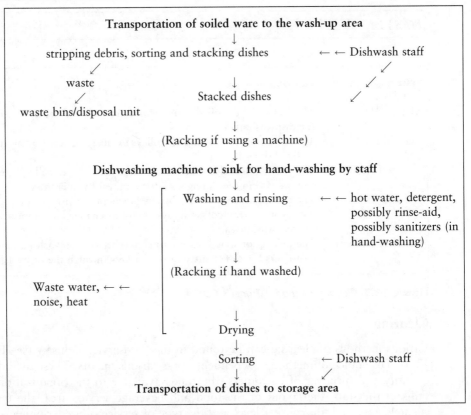

Figure 12.2 *A generic dishwashing system*

- transportation and handling prior to dishwashing

- dishwashing by hand or machine

- handling and transportation after dishwashing.

When planning for dishwashing, decisions associated with the washing sub-system itself, e.g. how items will be washed and which, if any, machine will be used, are important and often tend to dominate. Some of the issues related to this will be considered in the next section. However, there are a number of other considerations that should be taken into account relating to handling before and after dishwashing. These include:

- Amount of ware to be moved, time taken to return soiled ware to the dishwash area, which is influenced by staff availability, physical distance, interfloor transfer, provision of conveyors/trolleys and amount of space for gathering soiled and clean ware.

- Waste disposal arrangements prior to washing, which are influenced by staff availability, the potential for self-scrapping by customers and the use of disposal equipment, space for/removal of waste.

There is no standard formula for the design and provision of a rational, economic and effective overall dishwashing system. Every case is different and therefore has to be treated according to its own circumstances.

SYSTEM TYPES

System	Description
Manual (1)	The collection of soiled ware by waiting staff and transportation to the dishwash area
Manual (2)	The collection and sorting to trolleys by operators for transportation to the dishwash area
Semi-self-clear	The placing of soiled ware by customers on strategically placed trolleys within the dining area for removal by operators
Self-clear	The placing of soiled ware by customers on a conveyor or conveyorized tray-collecting system for mechanical transportation to the dishwash area
Self-clear and strip	The placing of soiled ware into conveyorized dishwash baskets by customers for direct entry of the baskets through the dishwash

Figure 12.3 *Clearing methods (Croner's Catering)*

Clearing

Various methods of clearing can be found in the foodservice industry (see Figure 12.3). The choice of method is dependent upon various factors. These include the quantity and turnover of customers, the funds available to the organization, the skills of the staff, the layout of the food and beverage service area, the type of clientele expected, the market level and the type of service offered. Some clearing methods tend to be more typically found alongside particular foodservice methods (see Figure 12.4).

Dishwashing

Dishwashing systems can be divided into two groups: those that include manual (hand) washing or those that employ machine washing. (These wash systems are described in Table 12.1). Both systems usually commence with the removal of left-over food debris, followed by a preliminary rinse in hot water. In the case of manual washing, this preserves the cleanliness of the wash water. Whichever sys-

Service method	Clearing
Table service 'Service to customers at a laid cover'	By staff
Assisted service 'Combination of table service and self-service'	By staff
Self-service	Various
Single point service	Various
Specialized or in situ 'In areas not primarily designed for foodservice'	By staff or customer clearing

Figure 12.4 *An analysis of clearing related to foodservice methods* (Lillicrap and Cousins, 1994)

Method	Form	Description
Manual		Soiled ware is washed by hand or brush machine.
Machine	Single tank	Soiled ware is loaded manually into a dishwashing machine, where all washing and rinsing takes place in one tank. This compact arrangement is employed on both front-loading and larger pass-through machines.
	Multi-tank	Soiled ware is loaded in baskets and processed by conveyor, or loaded on to pegs mounted on the conveyor, and processed progressively through two or more tanks, where washing and rinsing processes are separate. Machines tend to be either flight or rack-type dishwashers.

Table 12.1 *Dishwashing systems*

tem is employed, the following basic factors are required that will determine the effectiveness of the system:

- hot water for washing and rinsing (this can be hotter for machine washing)
- chemical action to break down food debris and staining
- mechanical action from brushes or a cloth for physical cleaning
- contact time of soiled ware with water or chemical solution.

Many catering premises, often small operations, only use manual methods. They may use either single or double sinks for washing. Single sink washing is not regarded as 'effective or hygienic as either the double sink or the dishwasher' (Sprenger, 1998, p. 200). Machine washing is generally preferable to, and often more economical than, manual washing. However, factors of cost or space may prevent the use of a machine. For smaller throughputs, the cost of a machine may not be justified in terms of savings in labour costs. The general sequence of events is described in Figure 12.5.

Dishwashing machines in larger establishments may be economic but even where they are not, they will improve poor working conditions for staff. According to Whitehall, machines take two basic forms: single tank or multi-tank.

An alternative classification of dishwashing machines is illustrated in Kinton *et al.* (1992), who classify dishwashing machines according to the type of machine, rather than the number of tanks they possess. Such an analysis is useful, as it gives an insight into the way the machines clean dishes. There are three main types of machine in this classification:

Spray types. In these, the dishes are placed in racks/baskets or on conveyor-mounted pegs and then travel into the machines, where they are subjected to a spray of hot detergent water at 60°C from above and below. The dishes then move on to the next section, where they are rinsed by a fresh hot shower (82–85°C). At this temperature they are sterilized, and when they exit the machine they quickly dry off in the air.

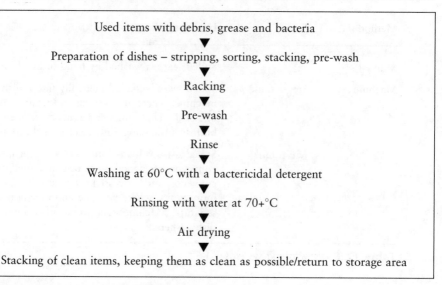

Used items with debris, grease and bacteria
▼
Preparation of dishes – stripping, sorting, stacking, pre-wash
▼
Racking
▼
Pre-wash
▼
Rinse
▼
Washing at 60°C with a bactericidal detergent
▼
Rinsing with water at 70+°C
▼
Air drying
▼
Stacking of clean items, keeping them as clean as possible/return to storage area

Figure 12.5 *Functional stages of the dishwash process*

Brush-type machines. These use revolving brushes for the scrubbing of each item in hot detergent water. The items are then rinsed and sterilized in another compartment.

Agitator water machines. Baskets of dishes are immersed in tanks of hot detergent water and cleaned by means of the mechanical agitation of the water. A sterilization rinse then takes place in another compartment.

Dishwashing machine systems generally incorporate all or some of the sequential functions shown in Figure 12.5. A detailed description of these functions can be found in Pine (1989).

Many larger establishments have dishwashing machines because they are labour saving, replace an arduous job and can cope with a high turnover rate of dishes. If maintained and working properly, they also ensure that a good supply of clean, sterilized crockery is available. Table 12.2 provides an analysis of general features and suitability of dishwashers. The machine throughput is a key element in determining the appropriate size and type of dishwasher for an establishment.

Throughput embraces volume and the length of time the washing process takes. Table 12.3 shows the typical throughput for specific sized dinner plates and racks through different machines. Flight machines are fitted with continuous runs of rubber, plastic or composition pegs or 'fingers' that hold the dishes in place, so racks are not required. For this reason Table 12.3 only shows throughputs for plates for flight machines.

In addition to the throughput of the machine, the choice of machine is dependent upon the following factors:

- the type (and amount) of washing-up to be completed

- the capabilities of the staff who will use the machine

- the frequency with which the machine will be used

Dishwasher type	Typical throughout	Cycle	Suitability (covers)	Rating (kW)	Dimensions (mm)
Single tank					
Compact or Under-counter	up to 200 plates/hour	variable from 180 secs	up to 60	3–5	600×600×850
Front-loaders	200+ plates/hour	90–210 secs	up to 200	6–8	610×640×950
Hinged or round hood	up to 300 plates/hour	60–180 secs	70–300	7–10	710–800×710–620×1,190–1,330
Vertical hood or door type, semi-automatics	300 + plates/hour	variable from 90 secs	150–400	7.6–11	600×700×2,000 (hood raised)
Multi-tank					
Automatic rack conveyor	1,080–5,000 mixed pieces/hour	continuous	large catering operations	12 plus 12–30 rinse heating	1,000–3,600×650×1,500
Flight	1,300–10,000 mixed pieces/hour	continuous	large catering operations	16–45 plus 18–54 rinse heating	3,000–8,830×700×2,000+
Single rack					
Under-counter and vertical hood	400 + plates/hour	120 secs	150–400	2.4	600×700×2,000
Twin rack	800+ plates/hour	120 secs	400+	4.8	1,010×700×2,000

Table 12.2 *Characteristics and applicability of dishwashers* (CaterElectric, date unknown)

	Dinner plates/hour	Racks/hour
Single tank		
Under-counter	400	25
Pass-through single rack	560	35
Pass-through two rack	1,120	70
Multi-tank		
Rack type, 1,000 mm long	1,600	100
Rack type, 3,000 mm long	3,520	220
Flight, 4,500 mm long	2,500	–
Flight, 7,000 mm long	5,500	–

Table 12.3 *Typical machine throughputs of dinner (10½ in) plates per hour* (Whitehall, date unknown)

- the space available for the installation of the machine.

Dishwashers have environmental impacts. Specific technical details about water and energy consumption threshold levels and best practice criteria related to the usage, recycling and performance of dishwashers for qualification for an eco-label are cited in the *Official Journal of the European Communities* (1993). They can also be found on the web.

Pots and pans used in food production or in foodservice also need to be cleaned effectively. This is often carried out in an area separate from the dishwashing area due to the greasy nature of the items. The pots and pans are often cleaned by hand but mechanical brushes may also be utilized. A method for undertaking pot-washing is described in Kinton *et al.* (1992, p. 469). Pot-washing cabinet machines are available and operate similarly to front-loading dishwashers but have greater internal measurements, a higher pressure spray action and longer wash cycle. Often pre-washing is required for difficult stains.

In public houses and bars, glass-washing equipment is frequently used, although many still wash glasses manually. Glass-washing is often carried out beneath or behind the bar, and equipment ranges from smaller models that rely on revolving brushes to larger cabinet models that use water jets and appropriate bactericidal detergent and incorporate a rinse cycle. Most glass-washing machines are front-loading cabinets, similar in design to cabinet dishwashers. Specialized conveyorized machines may be found in high-volume situations. The size of glass-washer is dependent on the number and type of glasses and the time needed to wash glasses at peak time.

The wash-up area is one of the main service areas behind the scenes in a hotel, restaurant, cafeteria or catering department. The layout and position of this area is important to ensure an even flow of work, safe and appropriate working conditions for the staff and that it is conveniently situated in relation to the foodservice area, kitchen, crockery etc. storage areas and exits for rubbish removal. It has been shown that the design and layout of foodservice operations affects employee productivity and staff motivation. The dishwash area is no exception. Mill (1989, pp. 47–52) demonstrates this with reference to the Bank of England. He describes a situation where there was a washing machine on each of six floors. The catering facilities were outdated and highly labour intensive, while equipment was obsolete and energy intensive. As a consequence of modernization and change, there was a

reliance on customers to clear tables themselves, allowing a single centralised washing area [to be] developed for china, crockery, and glassware. All washing up of tableware then was centralised on a single floor in the building, using conveyor belts to move used trays to a central point, and mobile carts to move glassware from the bars; this permitted the closing of five separate washing areas and enabled five staff members to take care of all the washing-up and clearing operations...

The main features of the washing areas included:

- daylight for washing-up staff

- ceramic tiles of various colours

- open storage of machinery and detergents, in place of storage cupboards

- air conditioning

- full heat recovery on automatic dishwashing machines

- removal of waste bins in favour of waste-disposal units

- introduction of labour-saving devices such as automatic removal of cutlery from trays.

Mill concluded: 'These changes enabled the company to recruit and hold a number of key staff in an area that traditionally has a high turnover.'

SYSTEM ADOPTION

As previously mentioned, the type of dishwashing system adopted within an operation is partly a function of the expected/actual throughput of dishes. The following case studies contrast two different systems and illustrate the impact of volume on the type of system and its operation.

CASE STUDY: POPPA PICCOLINOS, HOLMFIRTH

Stephanie and Derek Atkinson have owned and managed the only Italian pizza restaurant in Holmfirth, a small town in West Yorkshire popularized by the television programme *Last of the Summer Wine*, for eight years. The restaurant has two floors and offers table d'hôte and à la carte menus. It is open every evening and also at lunch times at the weekend. Most of the clientete are locals, who over the years have come to enjoy the service, but some are tourists. There are number of other restaurants and wine bars in the town, but these have not had a detrimental effect on the restaurant. The weekly turnover of the restaurant is typically about £10,000. Saturday evening is the busiest daypart of the week with 200 covers being usual from two sittings: 6.30–8.30 and 8.30–10.00 p.m. To cope with this level of business, the restaurant has a Hoonved ED 650 dishwashing machine positioned to the side of the kitchen, which is located on the ground floor of the restaurant. This is a roll-in/pull-out single-rack, single-tank system with a wash/rinse/sterilization cycle. On a Friday and Saturday night there would be two dishwash operators. All pans, tableware and cutlery pass through the machine in a rack. The cutlery is pre-soaked and pans are power-washed before entering the machine. According to the owners, they purchased this machine because of the number of covers expected, their particular needs and its price. It was selected following discussions with suppliers. The machine, although a little slow, otherwise performs well and is user-friendly.

CASE STUDY: PARK LANE HOTEL, HONG KONG

The Park Lane Hotel is a luxury hotel located in Causeway Bay with 804 bedrooms and multiple food and beverage outlets. The 27 Restaurant & Bar enjoys spectacular views over Victoria Park and the harbour. It is served by an adjacent kitchen and dishwash area, which is one of four in the hotel. This area also serves a function room on the same floor. On a typically busy night, such as a Friday, there may be 50 covers in the restaurant and 200 plus covers in the function room. In addition, there may also be 30 to 40 kitchen staff on this floor making both the front-of-house and back-of-house areas busy. This floor is serviced by a Hobart C24 dishwashing machine, which is housed in an area about 8 sq. m. This machine utilizes a conveyor belt system, onto which are loaded racks of cutlery and tableware. Again there is a power wash available for use prior to the racks going on to the conveyor. On a Friday night there may be one full-time dishwasher and four casual staff. In contrast, on a quiet night there would be only one staff member on duty. The pot-wash area is separate and has one full-time operative. There is a dishwashing supervisor who oversees all the dishwash areas in the hotel. The chemicals used in the dishwasher are checked every month by the chemical supplier. The dishwashing machine performs adequately for the throughput and the hotel is satisfied with it. The only problem encountered during the previous twelve months was a malfunctioning motor pump. Also, some congestion occurs when the crockery/cutlery from a single course of a function is bussed into the dishwash area.

CURRENT TRENDS AND ISSUES AFFECTING SYSTEM

The clearing and dishwashing activities are a function of the numbers of meals served. The amount of china, tableware and glassware per meal served will also have an influence on the amount and nature of these activities. Previously (i.e. before approximately 1970 and the introduction of modern fast food), it could generally be said that the more meals served in catering operations, excluding takeaways, the more clearing and dishwashing would be generated. This was especially true if the average amount of crockery etc. used per meal served remained the same. However, this cannot be said today, as the prevalence of fast-food, take-away and home delivery establishments, automatic vending and outdoor catering has resulted in the significant growth in the use of 'disposables'. The growth of these products has been a response to changing lifestyles, including more leisure time and a greater disposable income, with more and more people eating away from home.

Specific figures for the consumption of meals using china, glassware and tableware or disposable ware are unavailable. However, an indication of the trends in the amounts of clearing and dishwashing can be gained from analysis of movements in the market and a knowledge of the type of service and clearing methods employed in different sectors.

Between 1995 and 1999 the number of meals served in the UK catering industry increased from about 8,500 million to nearly 9,000 million (British Hospitality Association, 2000). This suggests more clearing activity on catering premises, particularly as the number of cafés and take-away meals served during this period declined. Fast food has been one of the sectors that has experienced the largest increases over the period. Approximately 70 million of the 500 million increase in meals served occurred in this sector, which, although not having implications for dishwashing, given the use of disposable ware, does lead to more clearing and waste packaging. Fast-food organizations often try to encourage customer clearing to save on staff clearing and staff costs, but this has had mixed results due to customer attitudes and apathy. As a consequence, staff clearing continues in fast-food operations. Much of the increase in the meals served between 1995 and 1999 has occurred in sectors where china etc. is predominantly used (e.g. in hotels, restaurants and pubs). This would mean not only an increase in staff clearing but also more dishwashing in these sectors, if one assumes no decrease in the average amount of china etc. per meal.

Forecasts suggest that the general upwards trend in meals served will continue and therefore it is likely that clearing, whether by staff or customers, will rise. Furthermore, while the continuing growth in the use of disposables is expected, a further increase in dishwashing activity is also likely in particular sectors.

The need for sound catering practices in response to tighter hygiene legislation, and a greater public awareness of the standards required, has caused caterers to consider their dishwashing methods. Manual washing is both labour intensive and uncontrolled and has, as a consequence, led to the view that the dishwashing machine is the only effective way of achieving consistent standards of cleanliness (Jack, 1990). Some have opted for disposables to improve the standard of hygiene on their premises. This has been a key element in their increased use (Walford, 1990). Hygiene will continue to impact upon dishwashing methods and be a factor in the choice between disposable and non-disposable.

Energy utilization is another key issue impacting upon the choice of dishwashing method and machine and whether to use crockery or not. With their heavy dependence on large quantities of heated water, dishwashing machines are major consumers of energy. Moreover, energy usage can be, and often is, greater than it needs to be through inefficient use (e.g. leaving them turned on all day, washing half-full trays of soiled dishes). Energy monitoring and targeting improvements may help. Basic operational practices, such as the correct loading of racks, are important to energy saving, but equipment efficiencies can also be achieved from heat recovery, automatic cut-outs, improved insulation, using hot rinse water twice, chemical sanitization and other energy-saving devices. These can reduce both running and environmental costs. Other areas to target savings, reduce wastage and provide environmental benefits relate to chemical and water usage. Machines are continually being designed to save water and chemicals.

Certainly the development of dish/pot/glass-wash machines will continue apace as manufacturers seek to satisfy the demands of their customers, to meet all current and planned EU safety and hygiene regulations and to improve machine performance related to energy utilization, speed, safety, noise pollution and cleaning performance.

A further issue concerns the difficult conditions in which dishwash staff often work. Dishwashing areas can be cramped, dirty, steamy and dangerous places. This has led many businesses to improve training and working practices, to look at the layout of areas, to think about job design, working times, multifunctioning etc., and either to replace manual with automated systems or use disposables.

In their attempts to improve productivity, hospitality organizations have considered the adoption, and have even tried, self-clearing systems. This may have been encouraged by the efforts of existing customers to clear items themselves. It may also have appeared attractive as it would prevent staff from undertaking what might be perceived as boring and repetitive tasks. However, for self-clearing to be successful, it will have to be marketed positively to alter customer expectations and behaviour.

SUMMARY

This chapter has examined clearing and dishwash systems, both vital elements of foodservice systems. Clearing is important, as it enhances the customer experience by creating table space and removing soiled crockery, utensils and any other debris. Dish and glass-washing are important both aesthetically, in the presentation of food and drink and the appearance of cutlery, crockery and laid-up dining areas, and to safeguard health.

While procedures and methods vary between different operations, it is possible to identify a number of generic clearing and dishwashing systems. The choice of clearing and dishwashing methods will be influenced by a range of operational, financial, marketing and human resource factors. Key factors involved with the design of a dishwashing system for each facility are the space available, the volume of business, the layout, the traffic flow, the amount and type of food soil and the length of time it will remain on the dishes, and the hardness of the water.

Clearing systems can be divided into staff clearing and customer (self) clearing systems. Dishwashing systems can be divided into two groups: those that include manual (hand) washing or those that use machine washing. Dishwashing machines can be categorized as either single-tank or multi-tank machines, spray type, brush type or agitator machines.

Finally, a number of issues confront the choice and use of clearing and dishwash systems. Some of these are common to both and relate to:

- automation of work and labour-saving measures – the replacement of dishwash staff by machines and the use of customers and machines in clearing

- safety and hygiene

- staff working conditions

- environmental impacts.

Others are more specific. For example, energy utilization and compliance with legislation are more applicable to dishwashing.

Further study

Draw up a checklist of points to consider when purchasing a dishwashing machine and a glass-washing machine.

Visit a catering exhibition and record all those exhibitors displaying dishwashing and glass-washing systems, along with the names of the dishwasher and glass-washer suppliers. Try to determine the criteria that some of the suppliers are using to sell their dishwashing and glass-washing machines. Is there a difference of emphasis between those points you identified in the first task? Why do you think this is?

Arrange a visit to a local restaurant or hotel and find out the following:

- the types of dishwasher/glass-washer

- the reasons for purchasing these machines
- the number and type of dishwash staff and supervisors
- the performance strengths and weaknesses of the machines
- the maintenance arrangements
- layout of the wash-up area
- any operating issues, e.g. related to safety, hygiene, the environment, congestion, efficiency, staffing, workflow, space allocation, energy utilization, installation.

One way of improving labour productivity is to replace labour inputs with customer inputs. To what extent is this feasible for clearing in a foodservice operation and how can self-clearing by customers be made to work in such operations?

Bibliography

Anon (1996) 'Making the right choice', *Scottish Caterer*, September, 36–7.

Anon (1999) 'What to buy?' *Catering Update*, August, 39–42.

British Hospitality Association (2000) *Trends and Statistics, 2000*. London: British Hospitality Association.

CaterElectric (date unknown) 'Dishwashing'.

Jack, A. (1990) 'The mechanics of hygiene', *The Hotel Catering and Institutional Management Association Reference Book 1990/91*. London: Sterling Publications, 255, 257.

Kinton, R., Ceserani, V. and Foskett, D. (1992) *The Theory of Catering*. London: Hodder & Stoughton, 336.

Kotschevar, L. H. and Terrell, M. E. (1961) *Food Service Planning, Layout and Equipment*. London: John Wiley & Sons.

Lillicrap, D. R. and Cousins, J. A. (1994) *Food and Beverage Service*. London: Hodder & Stoughton, fourth edition.

Mill R. C. (1989) *Managing for Productivity in the Hospitality Industry*. New York: Van Nostrand Reinhold, 47–52.

Official Journal of the European Communities (7 August 1993), L 198/39.

Pine, R. (1989) *Catering Equipment Management*, London: Hutchinson, 40–50.

Scriven, C. R. and Stevens, J. W. (1989) *Manual of Equipment and Design for the Food Service Industry*, New York: Van Nostrand Reinhold.

Sprenger, R. A. (1998) *Hygiene for Management*. Doncaster: Highfield Publications, eighth edition.

Walford, A. (1990) 'Disposables and the environment', *The Hotel Catering and Institutional Management Association Reference Book 1990/91*. London: Sterling Publications, 301–2.

Whitehall, B. (date unknown) 'The Winterhalter Guide to dish and glass washing', *Caterer and Hotelkeeper*. London.

Recommended further reading

Weblinks: http://www.ecosite.co.uk/depart/eubkinfo/dishwash.htm

CHAPTER 13

Bars

After completing this chapter you will be able to:

- *identify the main purposes of a bar system*
- *describe different types of bar*
- *describe the design and layout of bars*
- *explain key processes in operating a bar*
- *identify current trends in these systems.*

INTRODUCTION

The word 'bar' can have different meanings. In Ireland and the USA, a bar is a place where people go to have drink. But in England such places are typically known as public houses or pubs, in which there may be one or more 'bars' – or rooms – in which alcoholic drink is dispensed. The traditional public house would have a 'public bar', which was relatively plainly furnished, and a 'saloon bar', which had better decor and furnishings. Furthermore, the word 'bar' also describes the area from which, or the counter over which, such drinks are dispensed. From a systems perspective, it is clear that each of these definitions of a bar draws different boundaries around the 'system' – ranging from a specific part of a building in which alcohol is dispensed to an entire building designed for that purpose. For the purposes of this book we are interested in how a bar system operates, so we consider not only how drinks are dispensed but also the environment in which customers consume them. Our definition is therefore based on the traditional English use of the word.

From this discussion it is clear that bars may be dedicated systems, designed solely for the sale of alcohol, or integrated with other systems, such as restaurants or hotels.

PURPOSE OF SYSTEM

As we shall see there are several types of bar, but generally we define a bar as a system designed for the purpose of dispensing and consuming alcoholic and non-alcoholic beverages. This sounds relatively straightforward, but unlike other systems discussed in this book, bars are subject to specific legislation related to the sale of alcohol. All bars selling alcohol in the UK must be licensed. This is why the pub sector is sometimes referred to as the 'licensed trade'.

Such regulation is a good example of the concept of 'multiple systems containment', as discussed in Chapter 1. Pubs are clearly part of a locale's social system, where people go to meet, drink and be merry, but they are also part of the country's legal system, which imposes regulations in order to control public drunkenness and unruly behaviour. Licensing has very little impact on the design and technical operation of bar, but it does regulate operational aspects relating to opening hours, the sale of specific types of alcohol, the selling of alcohol to specific categories of person, and the general conduct of the premises.

Under this legislation, a bar is defined as 'any place exclusively or mainly used for the sale and consumption of intoxicating liquor'. This definition is especially important with respect to whether or not children are permitted into all or part of the premises. Children under 14 are not allowed into a bar, while those aged from 14 to 17 are allowed in but cannot buy or consume alcohol. The difficulty arises in interpreting 'exclusively or mainly' when premises serve meals as well as drinks, since children are allowed into dining areas, and over the age of five may even consume alcohol with their meal. Sargeant and Lyle (1998) state 'the interpretation and definition of a "bar" may vary widely from one licensing district or one police area to another, so what is acceptable in one area is not acceptable in the other'.

A second feature of bar operations in the UK is the way in which the licensed trade developed over the last two hundred years. In the 1700s beer was sold on the same premises as it was brewed. Indeed a feature of the contemporary bar scene is the re-emergence of pubs with their own 'micro-breweries'. Over time, however, due to the considerable economies of scale associated with brewing, regional brewers developed. Such brewers invested their profits in pubs in order to secure outlets for their product. This is known as 'vertical integration'. They leased their properties to tenants for very low rents, in return for an exclusive right to supply the pub with their own beers. This is know as the 'tied-house system', because pubs were 'tied' to one brewery. From the 1960s onwards, there were significant mergers between brewers, especially with the advent of keg beers. By the 1990s six major companies dominated the sector, between them owning 25,000 pubs, nearly half of the UK total. This was deemed to be anti-competitive by the Monopolies and Mergers Commission (MMC), so legislation was enacted requiring these large firms to limit the number of pubs they could own. This has led to the emergence of national pub companies, who run pubs but do not brew beer, such as Pubmaster and the Grand Pub Company, as well as the growth of regional brewers as pub operators, such as Greene King and Vaux. A feature of this change has also been a shift by the bigger companies away from tenancies towards directly managing the outlets. Throughout this time there have always been independently operated pubs without a tie to a brewer known as 'free houses'. This has led to pubs being owned and operated in six different ways, as follows:

- managed houses

- brewery-tied tenancies

- brewery-tied leases

- independent pub company-tied premises

- free leases

- freehold free houses.

While most customers would not be aware of who owns and operates their pub, there may be some slight operational differences. Certainly most free houses will stock and serve a wider range of products than tied houses.

GENERIC SYSTEM CHARACTERISTICS

The bar systems inputs comprise the different beverages for sale typically divided into spirits, wines, beers and soft drinks. The transforming inputs are the premises themselves in which customers consume these drinks. The processes associated with this system are concerned with stocking of the bar, dispensing and selling drinks, entertaining the customers and clearing and cleaning. The desired outputs are satisfied customers, conformance with all legislation and regulation, and profits. To achieve this there are two main areas – the bar counter or serving area and the customer seating area. The ratio of space for different types of customer is shown in Table 13.1. The exact amount of space allocated to standing, seated and dining customers will depend very much on the market. Bars with standing room only are typically found where large numbers of customers have limited times in which to drink, such as sport stadia and theatres. Current retail thinking suggests that every square foot of space should generate revenue, so getting this mix right is essential.

Bar counter layout and design

The service area has two key elements – the storage and display area behind the bar counter, known as the 'backfitting', and the counter itself. Both the counter top and working surface of the backfitting should be a convenient working height, between 1 to 1.15 m (3 ft 3 in to 3 ft 9 in). The space between these should be at least 0.9 m (3 ft), and preferably 1.2 m (4 ft), especially if more than one person is working the bar. The counter width is typically 0.6 m (2 ft), but the counter top should be less than this – 0.45 m or 1 ft 6 in – to allow access by the bar server to the work surface and sink located below the counter top. This under-counter area is typically 0.3 m (12 in) below the counter, so that glasses and equipment can be stored or handled

Type of customer	Floor area (sq. ft)
Customers standing at bar	5
Customers seated drinking only	10
Seated customers drinking and dining	15

Table 13.1 Floor area per customer

there. The beer taps or pumps for dispensing draught beers are mounted on the counter top.

Both the counter and backfitting have shelving 0.3 m (12 in) apart, allowing for three shelves, mainly for bottled beers and soft drinks. These may be stored at ambient temperature, but more often are stored chilled whether on chiller trays or in glass-doored, refrigerated cabinets. Above the counter of the backfitting there are narrower storage and display shelves for bottles of spirits and fortified wines. The most frequently used drinks may be mounted on optic dispensers, typically at a height of 1.5 to 1.6 m (5 ft to 5 ft 4 in) above the floor. The wall behind this shelving is often mirrored. This is not just for appearance sake, but allows the bar server to observe the counter area even when their back is turned to the customer. Some bars, especially in pubs, may also have shelving over the bar counter suspended from the ceiling at a minimum height of 1.8 m (5 ft 11 in).

The efficient operation of a bar greatly depends on how the backfitting and counter are stocked with products. The stock held should reflect the sales mix of the bar, with not only more of the highest selling items being stocked, but also placed at the most convenient height and location along the bar. In this sense, each bar should be thought of as a work station or series of work stations for one or more servers. Such a station would have everything the server requires for service – a full range of bottled drinks, appropriate glassware, beer pumps, optics, ice, garnishes, bottle skip (for empty bottles), till and glass-washing facility. In larger bars, there would be a number of such stations, with certain items such as the low demand spirits, till and sink being shared between two stations. In some cases the glass-wash facility is located not in the bar area but in the rear as a separate operation (see also Chapter 12).

Seating layout and design

Different types of bar have different layouts and types of seating. As in food service these may be loose or fixed tables and chairs (see Chapter 11). The main difference between restaurant and bar furniture is the size of the table. Bar tables may be much smaller than dining tables. This is why many pubs that have increased their hot food sales have either designated a separate part of the bar as a dining area or have had to change their tabling to accommodate place settings.

In certain types of bar, lounge furniture – 'coffee table', sofas and armchairs – is also found. Traditionally, this would be the case in lounge bars in hotels, but modern bar concepts such as All Bar One also adopt this style of seating.

SYSTEM TYPES

It is difficult to categorize bars into types, as there is a range of criteria that might be applied. In the trade itself, differentiation is often based on market segmentation. However, we are more interested in the operational and technical aspects of the system, so we present the classification shown in Figure 13.1.

The types of bar shown in Figure 13.1 are basically of three kinds. The first type is essentially a retail operation, since drinks are 'sold' by the bottle or can. Off-licences sell drinks directly to customers, and in large hotels and restaurants bottles

Bar	No consumption of alcohol on premises			Dispense bar Off-licence
	Consumption of alcohol on premises	Narrow product range		Ale house Wine bar Champagne bar
		Wide product range	Drink-led	Traditional pub Branded pubs, e.g. sports bar Cocktail bar Club
			Food-led	Traditional inn Contemporary bar/restaurant

Figure 13.1 *Types of bar*

of wine are 'sold' or *dispensed* to wine servers from a dispense bar. In effect, the dispense is an interim store between the cellar and the dining room.

The second type of bar is a highly specialized operation purveying a very narrow range of products. In some cases this may be simply because the premises are only licensed to sell certain types of alcohol. This is typically the case with regards to old, traditional ale houses. In many cases, however, it is because the bar concept is to specialize in particular types of alcohol. The emergence of wine bars in the 1980s is a good example of this, although specialist bars have always existed, notably champagne bars at racecourses. More champagne is drunk at UK racecourses than in any other type of venue. The trend in the 1990s has been to develop non-alcoholic refreshment 'bars' based around coffee (such as Starbucks), fruit juices (Orange Julius) or other specialist drinks, such as smoothies. From a systems perspective, these types of operation are categorized as 'bars' because they too are essentially in the business of dispensing beverages.

The third type of bar is the archetypal operation purveying the full range of beverages – beers, wines, spirits, and so on. In reality such bars may vary enormously in terms of their market and hence their product range, price and premises. The range includes the local pub or working man's club selling mainly beers in traditional surroundings; clubs and hotels with cocktail bars that specialize in mixed drinks for which a premium price may be charged; and all kinds of other bars in city centre, suburban and rural locations. In some cases these bars may also serve food. The distinction between a pub that serves food and a restaurant that serves drinks is nowadays a difficult one to make. One way that it is still possible to differentiate is in the type of licence held by the premises. In reality, the difference may be hard to see. TGIFridays is a restaurant chain in which a particular feature of their operation is the bar, while All Bar One is a bar chain that sells restaurant-style meals.

SYSTEM PROCESSES

There are four basic operational processes in bars:

- the stocking of the bar
- the dispensing and sale of drinks
- entertaining the customers
- the clearing and cleaning process.

The clearing and cleaning process has been discussed in detail in Chapter 12.

Stocking the bar

Bars are usually stocked to par, that is to say each item has a specified number of bottles (or cans) that should be in stock, and each day the stock is replenished to this level. To make things even easier, this is often related to the width and depth of the shelf space available, so that replenishment requires only a visual check of the shelf to identify when it is at par stock. It is important that stock is always in the same place, as this makes it easier and more efficient for the bar staff to locate items.

Dispensing drinks

Drink is dispensed in all kinds of measures and forms. In the UK, specific measures must be used and a notice stating these must be displayed in the bar area, where it can be read by customers. Many drinks, as well as being dispensed, also have to be garnished.

Beer and cider

Draught beer and cider may only be served in one-third pint (rarely if ever used in practice), half-pint or multiples of half-pint (typically one pint) measures. Measurement is 'certified' by ensuring that metered dispensers are used, or alternatively served free-flow and measured in a government-stamped glass. Such beers may also accomodate a 'head' of foam, so long as it is not more than 5 per cent of the total volume. Bottled beers and ciders are sold by the bottle and may or may not be in half-pint or pint sizes. Glassware for beer drinking is of four main types – the 'straight' glass, dimpled mug, lager/pilsner glass or 'Worthington' stemmed glass. A current trend, following American practice, is for customers to drink branded bottled beers directly from the bottle.

Wine

Wine by the glass may only be served in measures of 125 ml or 175 ml or multiples thereof. Bottles of wine are typically 75 cl and half bottles 37.5 cl. Some wines, notably champagne, come in larger sizes than these, for instance a magnum is 150 cl. Red wine is served at ambient temperature in a round-bodied, stemmed glass, typically a Paris goblet. This ensures a relatively large surface area, so that the aroma or 'nose' of the wine can be appreciated by the drinker. White wine is served chilled in narrow-bodied, stemmed glasses, with sparkling wine in even narrower glasses or 'flutes'. The latter ensure that the wine remains effervescent. Hence the popular image of champagne being served in a very wide, flat glass is incorrect.

Fortified wines

A fortified wine is a wine to which spirit has been added. Typical examples are sherry, port and vermouths. There is no legal requirement as to what measure these should be served in but typically they are dispensed in 50 ml measures (i.e. a double spirit measure). Sherry is served (in the UK at least) in sherry glasses, while other fortified wines are dispensed in Paris goblets if served straight, or in tall tumblers if served with a soft drink.

Spirits

Gin, whisky, vodka and rum may only be served in measures of 25 ml, either through a certified and sealed optic or in stamped thimble measures (except when making cocktails with three or more liquid ingredients). For control rather than legal reasons, all other spirits are also likely to be served in the same measure. The glassware for the service of spirits varies widely depending on the type of spirit (for instance, brandy may be served in a brandy balloon glass, liqueurs in liqueur glasses) or whether it is served straight, with a mixer, or in a cocktail.

Non-alcoholic drinks

Soft drinks, such as colas, bottled waters and fruit juices, may be served in a variety of measures. Today it is less common for soft drinks to be bottled, they may be in cans or served from a dispenser that mixes the syrup and carbonated water as it is dispensed. A wide range of glassware may be used for these types of drink.

Entertaining customers

Customers go to bars for a variety of reasons – drinking is only one of them. Most also go for social reasons, and expect some form of entertainment. At the simplest level such entertainment may be just the convivial company of friends who socialize together. Increasingly, however, bar operators are providing far more than space for people to meet. The range of alternatives is now quite extensive, and includes gaming machines, quiz nights, karaoke, games such as darts, pool or bar billiards, televised football and other sporting events, theme nights, recorded or live music, and live entertainers such as comedians or magicians.

The commercial value of such entertainment cannot be underestimated. A well-used pool table in a typical pub may generate a profit of £100 per week. Other revenue-generating equipment includes juke boxes, AWOP (amusement without prizes) video machines, quiz machines (SWPs – skills with prizes) and AWP (amusement with prizes) gaming machines. The last in particular, may generate between £5,000 and £20,000 of profit per year. To maximize this revenue, these machines must be carefully sited in the bar. They should also be replaced on a regular basis to maintain interest, which is why they are usually rented rather than purchased. Most AWPs maximize their revenue between three and ten weeks after installation. About 25 weeks after installation, usage flattens off to only 40 per cent of the peak usage. Painter (quoted Sargeant and Lyle, 1998 p. 153) argues that a machine should be replaced approximately every three months.

SYSTEM ADOPTION

The following two case studies illustrate bar operations practice.

CASE STUDY: ALL BAR ONE

All Bar One is a successful UK-based chain of over 50 fairly up-market bars belonging to Bass Leisure Retail. The All Bar One concept began in 1994 in response to a need for a new kind of bar that was refreshing, individual, welcoming and simple but sophisticated. The emphasis is on getting things right and upon good food and drink, prime locations, fast and efficient service, spacious design and value for money. The bars are stylish, lively and cosmopolitan, designed to appeal to a wide cross-section of customers. They are particularly appealing to women, who account for about 50 per cent of customers, with their light, bright and contemporary environment.

Bars are usually sited in busy commercial areas to attract the business community, office workers and professionals. Each bar has a typical capacity of between 200 and 300 and features a large glass 'shop-like' frontage enabling people to see in before they enter. They also have open, uncluttered and airy (air conditioning is present) interiors. The bars are designed to a single formula, having oak floor panelling and cream and fresh green walls with antique gilt mirrors, long wooden refectory like tables and chapel chairs. Any signs of the bar being a male preserve have been eradicated, so there are no traditional pub games, machines, bar stools, smoky corners or dark Victorian decor. Magazines and newspapers are provided, seating is flexible and food and drink service is either at the bar or at tables.

The chain focuses more on its food and wine than beer and is open throughout the day with food from breakfast onwards. The actual bar is a large wooden structure selling many fashionable drinks, a varied selection of wines ranging from £14 to £35 and its own labelled wine, costing about £10 a bottle. Beers are sold, with bottled beers being particularly popular. Soft and hot drinks are also on sale.

There is a blackboard menu that changes on a weekly basis. The food comes well presented on very large plates. Both light snacks and full meals are available. A typical menu includes five luxury sandwiches at about £3.50, half a dozen small dishes, eight large dishes (£5–£9) and four desserts. Offerings are varied and slightly up-market, such as scallop and fennel salad with lime and sorrel dressing or roasted red pepper and aubergine tartlet on salad. Most dishes are liberally sprinkled with parsley. Food constitutes a significant proportion of revenue, at around 20 per cent.

Staff are important to the chain and tend to be young, enthusiastic and friendly. Many hotel-trained, restaurant or retail people are recruited, looking for high standards. All Bar One managers and staff work as teams and expect close customer involvement.

CASE STUDY: BIGFOOT AND BARS

As you have already discovered, this paragon of restaurant management has a distinctive approach to running a hospitality business. He applies the same principles to bars. Bourdain (2001) writes:

> 'I can still walk into a West Village bar and tell immediately if the bar manager is a graduate of the Bigfoot University. The bottles are arranged in mirror image, radiating out from a central cash register, free (but spicy/salty) bar snacks are laid out, equidistant from one another, along a flawlessly clean, wiped and polished bar. Ashtrays are always empty. And more than likely, the juices are freshly squeezed.' Bigfoot also understood the importance of staff in this socio-technical system – 'bartenders were chosen for their personalities as well as their ability'.

CURRENT TRENDS AND ISSUES AFFECTING SYSTEM

A key trend in the UK is the decline in the number of pubs. Between 1995 and 2000 the number decreased from nearly 59,000 down to 51,663 (*Caterer & Hotelkeeper*, 27 July 2001). This is due partly to the way in which the industry has been restructured, the level of demand from customers and the closure of uneconomic premises. A related trend has been a shift away from selling alcoholic beverages to serving food. In the same time period the number of meals served in pubs increased, from 982.8 million to 1,094.8 million. On average, pubs were serving 16,714 meals a year in 1995, but by 2000 this average was 21,191, an increase in volume of 27 per cent. In 1995 the average pub's sales turnover from food was £51,215 per annum. By 2000 it was £61,152.

Another key trend has been branding. The emergence of national chains of pubs has led to the development of specific brands to appeal to specific markets. Allied Domecq developed the Firkin chain aimed at students and young people, features of which include wooden floors, a long bar counter, quirky humour and hard finishes. J. D. Wetherspoons are in a similar market, incorporating some similar decor features, but with the added appeal of a variety of beers. Bass's brand Fork and Pitcher is a pub and eating house targeted at mainly older people. It tends to develop the architectural and decor features of the existing premises in order to create an individual and traditional feel to each outlet. This means revealing flagstone floors, using rugs rather than carpets, exposing brick or stonework, and revealing old wooden beams. To this are added old photographs of the locality, second-hand 'local' furnishing and appropriate bric-a-brac. Scottish & Newcastle have developed the James H. Porter brand designed to be a 'community' pub located on a main road, while their Cooper's Kitchen brand is a destination rural pub with a high proportion of food sales. Likewise, Greenalls have Country Fayre, a destination family steak house, Finn M'Couls Irish bar and Clubhouse a sports bar with a dartboard and games machines.

One problem that bar operators face is criminal behaviour, usually violence fuelled by alcohol. This became a more serious problem during the 1990s, such that in 2000 the government launched an 'Alcohol in Action' campaign. This includes measures such as a national proof-of-age scheme, the use of toughened glass for glassware, a ban on street drinking and a register of door staff. Clearly, ensuring the safety and security of customers is likely to grow in importance as an operational process in the future.

This concern about alcohol is in stark contrast to other trends in the industry, the most talked about of which is a relaxation of licensing hours in line with other European countries. Such relaxation may allow licensed premises to open 24 hours a day and admit children into bars. Another major concern is the current rate of duty on alcohol, which makes it more expensive to have a drink in the UK, and leads to the extensive smuggling of alcohol from the Continent. The industry has called for a reduction in duty, which might increase consumption.

SUMMARY

A bar is a system designed for the purpose of dispensing and consuming alcoholic and non-alcoholic beverages. Bar operations in the UK have some characteristics in terms of ownership and management that derive from the growth of brewers and UK licensing law.

Bars have a relatively simple infrastructure comprising shelving for storing and displaying the products, a counter over which these are dispensed and a seating area for customers. They are typically linked to a cellar or storage system.

There are basically three types of bar – the dispense, the narrow product range specialist bar and the general bar (pub or club). In all three types the operator is concerned with the processes of stocking the bar and dispensing drinks. In specialist and general bars, the operator is also involved with providing entertainment to the customer.

The key issue in operating bars is the extent to which the bar is a self-contained system or operated in conjunction, or as part of, some other operation such as a restaurant or hotel. In some operations there may be more than one bar A large hotel, for instance, may have a cocktail bar, a lounge bar, a dispense bar and a bar on the executive floor for premium guests. A key trend is for bars to be combined with other operations. Along with this has come the development of branding, especially among those operations owned and managed by the large chains.

Further study

Go to the website of the magazine *Chain Leader* (www.chainleader.com), an American publication about hospitality chains. Click on 'Issue Archive' and conduct a search for the key words 'bar design'. This will take you to over 150 stories about restaurants and bars that usually include a description and photographs of the bar.

Bibliography

Bourdain, A. (2001) *Kitchen Confidential: Adventures in the Culinary Underbelly*. London: Bloomsbury.

Sargeant, M. and Lyle, T. (1998) *Successful Pubs and Inns*, second edition. Oxford: Butterworth-Heinemann.

Recommended further reading

Sargeant, M. and Lyle, T. (1998) *Successful Pubs and Inns*, second edition. Oxford: Butterworth-Heinemann

CASE STUDY INDEX

SUBJECT INDEX

NAME INDEX